THE GREAT UNHE

Silence always has something to say – it's never neutral and speaks volumes if people are willing to hear. Our response to silence is often to dismiss or end it, to block it out with noise. Instead, silence needs to be taken seriously. This book explores the importance of understanding silence and shows how we can move from merely listening to truly hearing those around us.

The interplay of voice and silence in organisational life is not straightforward. We can feel pressured to speak and compelled to keep our silence. Knowing how to read silence, to make sense of its generative and degenerative capacity, is a rarely developed skill among managers and leaders at all levels – who have been brought up to see silence as evidence of compliance or a weakness to be addressed. But it is a critical skill for managers and employees alike. Written by two experts in organisational development, this book explores different types of silence and their implications for organisational practice, digging into the theoretical roots and engaging with real stories and voices. It provides everyone at work with an understanding of the different meanings of silence and how to engage well with it. When to stay with it, when to join in with it, and when to be struck by what's not being said and do something about it.

The Great Unheard at Work is essential reading for corporate leaders, HR professionals in all sectors, business students, professionals, and anyone interested in leadership development.

Mark Cole has over 30 years' experience working on development in organisations. His book, *Radical Organisation Development*, was published by Routledge in 2020. More recently, he co-authored with John Higgins *Leadership Unravelled: The Faulty Thinking Behind Modern Management* (Routledge, 2022).

John Higgins is an independent researcher, tutor, and coach specialising in how people use and abuse power throughout the workplace and society. He is widely published and has written extensively alongside the faculty and students of the Ashridge Doctorate and Masters in Organisational Change.

THE GREAT UNHEARD AT WORK

Understanding Voice and Silence in Organisations

Mark Cole and John Higgins

Routledge
Taylor & Francis Group

LONDON AND NEW YORK

Cover image: © Getty Images/z_wei

First published 2023
by Routledge
4 Park Square, Milton Park, Abingdon, Oxon OX14 4RN

and by Routledge
605 Third Avenue, New York, NY 10158

Routledge is an imprint of the Taylor & Francis Group, an informa business

British Library Cataloguing-in-Publication Data
A catalogue record for this book is available from the British Library

Library of Congress Cataloging-in-Publication Data
Names: Cole, Mark, 1960- author. | Higgins, John, 1962 June 27– author. |
Higgins, John, author.
Title: The great unheard at work : understanding voice and silence in
organisations / Mark Cole and John Higgins.
Description: New York, NY : Routledge, 2023. | Includes bibliographical
references and index. |
Identifiers: LCCN 2022047418 (print) | LCCN 2022047419 (ebook) |
ISBN 9781032283975 (hardback) | ISBN 9781032284026 (paperback) |
ISBN 9781003296683 (ebook)
Subjects: LCSH: Leadership. | Silence—Psychological aspects. |
Communication in management.
Classification: LCC HD57.7 .C6438 2023 (print) | LCC HD57.7 (ebook) |
DDC 658.4/092—dc23/eng/20221128
LC record available at https://lccn.loc.gov/2022047418
LC ebook record available at https://lccn.loc.gov/2022047419

ISBN: 978-1-032-28397-5 (hbk)
ISBN: 978-1-032-28402-6 (pbk)
ISBN: 978-1-003-29668-3 (ebk)

DOI: 10.4324/9781003296683

Typeset in Joanna
by codeMantra

CONTENTS

Foreword   vii
MEGAN REITZ

Acknowledgements   x

Part I   Seven shades of workplace silence   1

1   **An introduction to the seven shades of silence**   3

2   **The seven shades of silence in action**   7

**Part II   Creating and sustaining climates
of silence and voice**   33

3   **On silence**   35

4   **The meaning of silence**   48

5   **Silence as ritual**   55

6   **Self-silencing**   61

7 Silence at work   69

8 Silence is a password   99

9 Lessons for corporate life (on sustaining climates of
   silence and voice)   119

10 Silence descends   135

Part III Thirty-five voices... and beyond   141

11 Thirty-five voices   143

12 Some notes on method and practical application   171

Part IV Dialogue retethered   193

13 Putting dialogue to work   195

    Postscript – notes from an authorial process   215
    Index   225

FOREWORD

MEGAN REITZ

How I show up, affects your voice.

Speaking up and staying silent happen in relation. However, particularly in workplace settings, they are so often regarded as the product of individual bravery or cowardice respectively.

The popular invitation (or is it a command?) to "Speak up" and "Bring your whole self to work" is often pointedly aimed by those higher up in the hierarchy to those lower down it, in a desperate attempt to secure innovation, compliance, agility, or "talent" retention. It is made as if there exists a simple decision toggle that's operated solely by the would-be speaker.

That fallacy is the reason why many "Speak Up" campaigns in organisations go precisely nowhere and leave in their wake an even more deeply cynical workforce.

A while back, interviewing "them" (the would-be speakers) at the behest of a leader who told me that "they" needed to show some courage and just speak up more, I was told in hushed tones, 'but last time someone spoke up round here, they disappeared!'

The speaker does not make decisions to speak or stay silent in a void. Speaker and listener are engaged in a constant dance of gesture and response, each impacting and being impacted by the other and both situated in a web of conditions that construct power and expectations which in turn mould perceptions of risk that coerce their conversation.

In a long running and ongoing survey examining speaking truth to power in the workplace, currently standing at 13,000 respondents, around one third expect to be ignored in their organisation if they speak up with a problem. So, silence pervades. This raises phenomenally important questions: "what is the experience of being listened to?" "What is happening that leads these respondents to feel ignored and what would lead them to feel heard?"

Most agree that listening is not a matter of the other managing to rein themselves in from interrupting until you finish the sentence – although this in itself would be a marked improvement. Being heard requires a certain quality of *attention* and a felt sense of *intention*.

Our attention and our intention are the most remarkable gifts we can give both to ourselves and the other. When we show up with deep curiosity, empathy, and the energy of someone who just knows there is something to be created, to be learnt in between those in dialogue, the other finds their voice.

Dialogue.

That's another term carelessly used in organisations.

'Let's have a dialogue'.

For many I work with, the word conjures up some sort of harmonious, pleasant, well-behaved conversation between smiling participants experiencing leisurely heart rates, having a cup of tea.

Dialogue is profound meeting where voices emerge through the quality of attention and intention of those present. In the moment of dialogue, power differences in the labels of those present do not disappear, but they are acknowledged and the unlabelled power of human creativity becomes central.

Dialogue can be messy, conflicted, vulnerable, unchartered territory at the limits of our knowledge and experience. To invite another 'into dialogue' is to put down our relentless need to control, to perform and to live up to socially constructed expectations.

So, it is rare.

A certain relief washed over me when I read this book that finally Pandora's box that is 'silence', 'listening', and 'dialogue' has been opened and opened with utter humility by the authors.

John and Mark guard against the simplification of silence and the blithe use of the word 'listen' and rather immerse themselves, and the reader, in the power-laden complexities of what gets said and who gets heard.

And rather than lecture this topic, they practise reflexively in this book's pages for all to observe. Through pausing to inquire in the moment of 'listening' to thirty-five voices recorded in their research, they give the reader an insight into just how much of our history, upbringing, world view and personal fears and hopes weave into how we interpret and 'listen' to the other.

The never-ending simplification of 'how-to's' and 'five easy steps' contained within numerous books on the topics addressed in this one can on occasion be helpful as first impulses towards change. But if our engagement stays at that level, our workplaces just get more and more inhospitable, if not downright diminishing for the human spirit.

To flourish and to lead requires us to acknowledge the complexities of power and inquire into the spaces we create between us where we choose to enact old, damaging scripts or develop new, uninhibited, unimagined ones. It requires us to find spaces where we can pause, reflect and safely admit that we simply don't know and things simply aren't simple.

This book creates one of those spaces and as such I recommend it wholeheartedly to you.

Megan Reitz
Professor of Leadership and Dialogue,
Hult International Business School
Author of *Dialogue in Organisations*,
Co-author of *Mind Time* and *Speak Up*, and
TEDx speaker
Ranked by Thinkers50 as one of the top 50 global business thinkers and
ranked in HR Magazine's Most Influential Thinkers listing

ACKNOWLEDGEMENTS

Mark is hugely grateful to all those people who – one way or another – shared their experiences from corporate life and spoke so candidly about what they had seen and felt over the two years of an intense crisis. Their willingness to speak up in this way meant that Mark was able to explore the vital difference between listening and actually hearing, which is the foundation of this book.

He is indebted to John, his friend and thinking partner, and their weekly calls. They gave Mark a subtle blend of solace and stimulation. Importantly, they were the spaces where the thoughts and ideas about the topic of voice and silence were explored – and where thinking could be interrogated and contested in a safe environment.

As ever, Mark wants to put on record here how his family are central to who he is and the work that he does. At a time of great turbulence, he recognised even more than before how blessed he is to have his wife Sarah and his son Thomas alongside him. They inspire him to do all that he does in so many ways.

John would like to say thank you to the hundreds, bordering on thousands, of people he has spoken to over the last ten years as he tries to make better sense of the nonsense that passes as common sense. They have been an object lesson in the co-constructed reality of knowledge creation.

Mark keeps him in touch with a world of work that seems to be remarkably adapt at staying the same however much hoopla is claimed for its transformed nature. Meanwhile Megan reminds him to stay positive about the world and remember to engage with the world as it is – not as he thinks it should be.

And then there's Rosie who keeps fighting the good fight on all things carbon, his daughters Livia and Isobel who anchor him into the vitality of the generation to come, and Donald and Tim – who are new(ish) to the family and give hope for what the modern masculine can be.

Part I

SEVEN SHADES OF
WORKPLACE SILENCE

1

AN INTRODUCTION TO THE SEVEN SHADES OF SILENCE

Silence speaks volumes and is full of meaning if we pay attention to it.

Silence always has something to say – it is not a neutral phenomenon. It shows up in any number of ways and is always an expression of relational power.

In this section, Part I, we'll explore seven types of silence, a synthesis of the extensive review carried out later on in Parts II, III, and IV. Our intention at this point is to provide an overview, without too much reference to the theoretical argument that lies behind this field of practice. Keep it accessible for those willing to take our working on trust and who want to "cut to the chase".

Part II digs into the theoretical roots, while also including some extensive stories we've come across or lived through. It also has some finer detailed conclusions which need to be explicitly anchored into the theory to give them due weight. In Part III we share how we engaged with unexpectedly rich responses to a survey we circulated and how we found novel ways of presenting and interpreting the voices and silences of others. Finally, Part IV represents a manifesto for people in corporate life, shining a light

DOI: 10.4324/9781003296683-2

(we intend) on what can be done so that voice and silence are better understood by employees and managers.

We argue that understanding silence is a critical management and employee skill, essential if you aspire to have the agency you want in your workplace whatever your position in its ecology of power. Without an understanding of its forms and meaning well-intentioned moves to encourage people to speak up will founder, simply encouraging more people to speak into a void and then becoming frustrated at the lack of impact their words and listening have. Action without understanding is part of what fuels the addiction to management tools and techniques and the swirl of unproductive busyness they foment in the workplace – and our own sustained inquiry into the headwaters of organisational and management thinking (Cole & Higgins, 2022).

An overview of the seven shades of silence (and the implications for organisational practice)

Of course, this is an arbitrary and partial categorisation. It is intended to be a way of allowing people to engage with a topic which can otherwise be treated too simplistically or turned into an overwhelming treatise on the human condition. Its value is in its use as a framework for reflection, not as a tool for labelling and fixing.

Our advice is that we all need to be suspicious of any offer of a convenient, "off-the-shelf" solution, be that in the form of a technique, model, template, or checklist. We adhere very strongly to the view that leaders in particular need to stop outsourcing their thinking and actively engage with the world both critically and reflexively (Cole & Higgins, 2021). The starting point we always recommend is an intense scrutiny of what is taken for granted in terms of aims, claims, purpose, and origins. And we actively invite you to apply that level of inquiry to the ideas that we are presenting here.

With that intention in mind, here are our seven (which could just as easily have been 70 or 700) shades of silence, which inevitably overlap – and may exist in support of each other or in tension – but provide what we intend to be useful lenses into a complex social phenomenon with implications for how we experience and engage with work and life more generally:

1. *Silence that looks to include* – this is silence with a spacious, generous quality with an intention of involving or recruiting others. Where "Any

Other Business" on the meeting agenda is taken seriously, maybe seen as the first rather than the last item on the order of business

2. *Silence that intends to exclude* – silence as a barrier, a sign that a topic or an individual's views and contribution are unwelcome. This can be generative, in order to maintain identity or focus, or degenerative (in the experience of the silenced), intended to keep a perspective, person, or group in a subaltern position – a power play

3. *Silence that is chosen* – silence as an agentic act, a deliberate step by someone or some group. This can be for reasons of rebellion, thoughtfulness, safety, or disinterest. But it is a conscious choice – even if it is not immediately obvious to those on the receiving end of the silence

4. *Silence that is imposed* – silence that is involuntary. This could be self-imposed, the playing out of some internal or relational psycho-drama, or it could be a piece of force majeure – an external authority and practice banning, intimidating, or undermining the voice of others

5. *Silence that invites* – this is the silence of the pause that invites the other in. It is a deliberate halt to advocacy or extraverted self-thinking. It is what the dialogic movement assumes as a potential in all exchanges – a desire to be curious about and hear from the other

6. *Silence that manipulates* – this is the pause that is there to generate tension in the other. That tricks people into saying more than they intended, or is there to remind people – be a felt expression – of the enormity of the act required for them to stop being silent

7. *Silence that punctuates* – all speech has silence as a constituent part. It is an integral part of the rhythm and meaning of language, it gives and takes away weight and emphasis to what is being said. The quality of our talk is as much to do with the quality of our spoken silences as our words

Organisational practice often sees silence as either an absence, something to be filled, or an affirmation, an agreement to a course of action. Our argument is that organisational practice (be that as individual employees, managers, or professionals tasked with working in this area) needs to learn to tune into the nuances of silence, get under its skin – acknowledge the importance and impact of silence. We need to show a willingness to step into it rather than step on it, give ourselves the space and time to make sense of it in a non-superficial way. And we all need to own the impact we have on everyone around us in terms of voice and silence.

This gets complicated because it takes us into the world of omission rather than commission, a focus on what is not there and not just what is there. It is impossible to carry out a comprehensive audit of silence because it has the potential to be all but infinite – which might be why it gets filed away in the "too difficult to deal with" pile. Silence, what is not said, what is not emphasised, covers everything that has not been spoken about. And there are steps that can be taken to engage with its reality, while always accepting that any step taken is partial.

On a day-to-day basis it means noticing, for instance, why so many people do or don't fill in the ubiquitous staff survey – and it means noticing it not to fix it by urging people to fill it in or linking HR's performance targets to the achieved completion rate, but by being curious about why it is people are choosing not to join in. Maybe they are happy to go along with the way things are? Maybe they see it as another management intrusion? Or they don't value the questions, or what it results in or trust its anonymity? And why is an anonymous survey seen as the right way to consult in the first place? Who knows? But we can fill up the void with any amount of conjecture and theory.

The ultimate circularity would be to survey people to find out why they don't want to play the corporate game and fill in the survey. Fortunately, this is simply beyond the pale, as far as our experience suggests (although we stand to be corrected in terms of what others might have seen). Instead, we have seen in many settings HR be set (or choose to set) a participation target and then deploy people and resource in ceaseless pursuit of the people who – in light of the invitation to "engage" – have chosen to remain silent.

In the remainder of Part I, we'll explore each of the seven shades of silence in more detail, while also reflecting on what it says about an organisational practice that takes noticing silence seriously.

References

Cole, M. & Higgins, J., 2021. *Stuck in the middle – and feeling the pinch.* [Online] Available at: https://radicalod.org/2021/10/12/stuck-in-the-middle-and-feeling-the-pinch/ [Accessed 13 January 2021].

Cole, M. & Higgins, J., 2022. *Leadership unravelled: The faulty thinking behind modern management.* Abingdon: Routledge.

2

THE SEVEN SHADES OF SILENCE IN ACTION

1. **Silence that looks to include** – this is silence with a spacious, generous quality with an intention of involving or recruiting others. Where "Any Other Business" on the meeting agenda is taken seriously, maybe seen as the first rather than the last item on the order of business

Inclusion takes time. It can't be rushed – and in most workplaces, most walks of life, time is seen as scarce resource and inclusion is approached as something that can happen without time, or can be achieved to order and at pace. This insincere, rushed, noisy approach to inclusion can be seen playing out in how much of the taken-for-granted consultation and engagement is done – there is the hoopla and presentational focus of virtual and physical roadshows and other grand events, a fixation with messaging and PR, and an overwhelming privileging of the roll-out of the pre-known messages or hypotheses.

Engagement and consultation are not active experiences of inclusion, but instead an extension of habits of pacification and the treatment of people

DOI: 10.4324/9781003296683-3

as consumers rather than creators. To include means to entertain or to patronise, where someone else knows best and the role of the person to be included is to be silent, except to applaud on cue.

The silence of generative inclusion is a world away from this. It comes from a place of heartfelt curiosity by those who are experienced as having more social and positional power, whether or not it fits with their own internal narrative about their identity and authority. It is not the faux curiosity of the tilted head and the ritual listening exercise, it is the silence of suspended judgement, of the little practised discipline of listening without prejudice with the intention of unique understanding, not labelling, categorising, or generalising. More than anything it is listening without trying to leap to a solution and fix the other. At root, it is listening not simply to be seen to be listening – a leadership performance of breath-taking condescension – but instead it is listening so as to hear and open the opportunity for real dialogue as opposed to a ritualised exchange, subtly underscored by the dynamics of power in all its forms.

At work, and in the culture particularly of the Anglo-Saxon Global North, we recruit and promote for ego and narcissism, qualities not to be found by those keen to listen to include. Despite all the good work of W E Deming and his compelling insight into the dominance of context over individual agency when it comes to performance (Deming, 1982/2018), organisations and news media fixate on individual contribution, reward and recognition.

People continue to tune in to the TV show *The Apprentice*, which is not merely a frivolous entertainment but is instead a crude ideological representation and reproduction of a flawed business world. The contestants are neoliberal caricatures of the sovereign individual. Additionally, the whole thing is presided over by someone who reminds us that, notwithstanding what people say about leadership in the contemporary setting, our culture continues to celebrate the rugged entrepreneurial individual. They/he play their role in the power game, barely keeping a lid on their simmering anger and disdain, jabbing their fingers in people's faces, and acting in what looks like an employment context but where every vestige of employment protection has been evaporated by the sheer power of the performance of "charisma".

In the face of a recent leadership competency model John was invited to review, he concluded that only Saints or Narcissists would either apply for or occupy the senior posts in the world this model described, so ludicrous was the focus on page after page of perfect, ideal individualism. Self-referencing egoism would be the inevitable order of the day – and inclusion is a low-ego activity.

Inclusion is an act of exquisite attention towards the other; it is a relational act which looks to focus on making it easy/easier for the other to step into an encounter with you. In the too-often trivialised insight of Martin Buber, it is an I-Thou moment, a quiet place where people can show up and meet with each other not to debate, win, or refute what the other is but to discover more, to deepen connection – an encounter that can be just as much be about an inward encounter with other senses of self as it is an outward encounter with the external other (Buber, 1937).

This is so much more than water-cooler or coffee-break moments, although these can be an important part of the necessary social process for including, it is an orientation towards wanting to see more of the others and their experience – it is about inviting others to speak both to their scripted and unscripted identity, their historic and emerging self.

Invitational silence is a dance in which the deliberately less vocal, historically more powerful, partner allows themselves to be moved by what they hear. Too much faux inclusivity involves formulaic, pre-considered, procedurally and legally approved gestures by the more powerful party. Inclusivity in the raw is an emotional encounter, a flow of feeling as much as it is of thought. It frequently prompts defensiveness when it's encountered, with a Chief Executive or senior other immediately on the phone after such an experience, anxiously getting the internal communications team to rustle up a quick summary of "you said, we did", to put a lid on the messiness. Rather than staying with the discomfort of inclusivity in the raw, the retreat into familiar patterns results in an exercise in the propaganda of immediate action which can be crudely summarised as: 'Here's some stuff that we did – and, to make it look responsive to you as a person, we have contained and bent what you said for our own corporate purposes'.

In workplaces which privilege efficiency, speed, intellectualism, and predictability it is unsurprising that silence that looks to include is a rarity. Inclusive silence and what it engenders is all but certain to be inefficient, in the sense of delivering a pre-determined outcome with minimum effort. Most human connections grow like weeds, not hot-house flowers – to repurpose Henry Mintzberg's observations about strategy (Mintzberg, 2016).

It takes time to be inclusive, the human heart can be rushed, but is at its best when given time to reach out into connection – inclusivity demanded is often regretted or resented when not allowed to grow at its own pace, a negotiation between what is said and not said, experiencing an invitation to be included as a gift not an instruction. Inclusivity is emotional, which means it can get hot as well as cold, ungovernable by the pre-thought precepts of institutional process.

And it will therefore be unpredictable and not made readily measurable – how do you measure silence in a way that doesn't become absurd? Much as so much training and development has collapsed into an exercise of maximising bums on seats (or eyeballs on screen) because volume is so much easier to measure than quality, so inclusive silence too often becomes a numbers game, how many people have been talked at in silence (without audible complaint). Inclusive silence can happen at any time, in any encounter between people in any setting. What is needed is the desire to step into what it makes possible.

Top tips – how to be silent to include others

- Mean it
- Park your ego… and seek to find your ethical self
- Don't rush
- Expect to be moved

2. **Silence that intends to exclude** – silence as a barrier, a sign that a topic or an individual's views and contribution are unwelcome. This can be generative, in order to maintain identity or focus, or degenerative (in the experience of the silenced), intended to keep a perspective, person, or group in a subaltern position – a power play.

Silence can and does establish and police boundaries between individuals and groups – it also helps people split off parts of themselves they feel will be more or less attractive given the situation they're in. At the group or team level, be that as a formal or informal identity, it is part of the process of defining who is part of an in-group and who is in the out-group – which can result in exclusion from the goings-on of the in-group. Clearly, this relates to human interactions that stand outside of a monolithic hierarchy where, for instance, we divide the world up into the crude binary of "somebodies" and "nobodies" (Fuller, 2004). Such a simple divide can of course be found inhabiting the rungs of the corporate ladder but the hierarchical ladder doesn't tell the whole story, the core group in any given organisational structure may not necessarily be the people at the top (Kleiner, 2003).

We argue that this is a basic feature of human organising and recommend accepting this, rather than wishing it away as a primitive social legacy that we can ignore in our so-developed, so-called, modern era. To us wishing away this social need is a form of magical thinking and instead we strongly urge people in workplaces to embrace it, so allowing the focus of attention to shift to the potential for silence to be used both generatively and de-generatively in excluding people.

This is instead of solely addressing the role of exclusionary silence through a lens of radical transparency, which becomes a hymn to a somewhat naïve understanding of how people thrive and survive in group settings – and is an ideology that dominates much of the managerial orthodoxy. This has led one Group Analyst colleague of John's to give up completely on trying to get anything useful done in workplaces, addicted as they are to what he sees as instrumental and psychologically damaging rationalism which shows up in a basic illiteracy about the dynamics of people in groups.

The shorthand thinking so beloved these days throws the snappily titled idea of radical candour into this mix (Scott, 2017). This is a rehashed melange of notionally "kindly" management practices – such as using stories in your communications (a painfully condescending notion, to our minds), inviting feedback, and manipulating your conversational skills – that has a tenuous link to the idea of candour as an undergirding of genuine dialogue, misapplying the notion of radical as meaning rarely found (Radical Candor, 2022). Inadvertently, the manipulative nature of this so-called model is laid bare in its own promotional material (emphasis added):

> It turns out that when people trust you and **feel like you care about them**, they are much more likely to accept and act on your praise and criticism; tell you what they really think about what you are doing well and, more importantly, not doing so well; engage in this same behavior with one another, which means less pushing the rock up the hill again and again; embrace their role on the team; and focus on getting results.
> (Radical Candor, 2022, p. 3)

Generative exclusionary silence is not a fixed state but an ongoing negotiation, a permanent exploration of what belongs to who and where the limits to communality lie – within the visible and invisible needs of group life. It recognises that some things are off-limits to some groups and others sit within the legitimate fiefdom of others, although the assumptions behind this need to be made as explicit as possible.

Degenerative exclusionary silence is the secretive establishment of boundaries, invisible and undiscussable except to those who set the boundaries – this is the territory of secret societies and the tribal hand-shakes of groups such as the Freemasons. At its worst, and most common, are the existence of workplace fiefdoms which look to capture and lock-up knowledge for their own aggrandisement, a living and negative example of the habit that makes information power, where power is solely in the inter-est of the group without reference to the wider community within which the group lives.

In one takeover John had reported to him, the acquired company had an established practice where everyone had access to the data about its finan-cial performance, and was equipped to make sense of it for themselves. It is worth pointing out that this was not a professional services firm, filled with people armed with formal accreditation in financial numeracy, but a perfectly ordinary manufacturing and kit service operation. The acquir-ing company quickly disappeared this data from the workforce, privileging it for the Finance Department and for "management eyes only" reports. Widespread conversations about the financial health of the company were silenced. Much as the esoterics of option pricing and the inner working of the Black–Scholes model (Hayes, 2022) is beyond most of us, most firms' financial reporting can be made readily accessible, if those who generate the data have the mind to make it so.

The orthodox leadership reaction to this challenge is to assume that the poor benighted workforce couldn't possibly understand this material, so leaders need to infantilise them by telling them soothing personalised sto-ries rather than allow them to engage in a dialogue about what the numbers mean (Salmon, 2010). Importantly this enables the in-group to maintain its centrality by its supposed access to, and understanding of, material that oth-ers cannot possibly appreciate. And it allows a shift in the modality of power, whilst leaving power intact and unquestioned, as the following suggests:

> Plato stated that the one who tells the story governs. In other words, the owner of the story – the narrator – resorts to discursive exercise

of power. Unlike during the exercise of force and coercion, the source of such power lies in discursive reality and the mental: the storyteller aspires to influence the social reality with a view to shaping it in a desirable direction.   (Takala & Auvinen, 2016, p. 22)

There are any number of contradictions in play once you pay attention to exclusionary habits of silence. This includes, for instance, a belief in the value of workforce engagement butting up against a distrust in the capacity, or value of, the workforce to engage with contentious topics, be that around matters environmental and social, executive pay or organisational restructuring. Or a belief in the value of empowerment and distributed leadership co-existing with an executive desire, or external requirement for, senior management to demonstrate visible control and grip.

In response to this muddled thinking, which in turn serves an ideological purpose of maintaining the status quo, a powerful manifesto has appeared that convincingly makes the case for the democratisation of the workplace, which argues that 'Human beings are not one resource amongst many. Without **labor investors** [emphasis added], there would be no production, no services no businesses at all' (Ferreras et al., 2022, p. 19). These authors go on to conclude:

Issues such as the choice of a CEO, setting major strategies, and profit distribution are just too important to be left to shareholders alone. A personal investment of labor, that is, of one's mind and body, one's health – one's very life – ought to come with the collective right to validate or veto these decisions.   (Ferreras et al., 2022, p. 20)

Then alongside all of the above, of course, there's the belief in the importance of fostering a speak-up culture, be that around innovation or malpractice, while at the same time instituting policies and processes which put most of the responsibility for rocking the boat on the most marginal and precarious.

At its worst what all this sustains is a silence around power and hierarchy – excluding everyone from being able to name and talk about the day-to-day reality of who silences who, and how. This is what makes a generative discussion about exclusionary patterns of silence so difficult. How can you name something when everyone has bought into the habit of saying it's not there?

In a recent HBR piece John co-authored with Megan Reitz, he recalls arguing long and hard with the editor who wanted to denude the thrust of their argument, which was that power and hierarchy are an essential part of human organising, by asking them to take this part of their article out. After all, they put it to John and Megan, hasn't the world moved on from hierarchy now? Hasn't the world become flatter? That's certainly what the orthodoxy of management thinking increasingly takes for granted.

Breaking this modern omerta around exclusionary silence is also at the heart of the complexities of whistleblowing. As a provocative title for the Journal of the Royal Society of Medicine, John wrote: 'If whistleblowing's the answer, ask a better question' (Higgins & Reitz, 2019). That better question is core to the habits of exclusionary silence and starts by acknowledging our assertion at the beginning of this section, namely that people like to (need to even) belong to a group they can relate to, and part of that group identity is in opposition to, or contra-distinction to, other groups.

When management gurus and jobbing advisers go around casually advocating the dismantling of organisational silos and long-established teams in the service of organisational transparency and a sense of the whole, they reveal a profound ignorance about people as social beings. We need groups. We need boundaries. We need something that is ours (and not yours or theirs). We need your silence around what is ours because it is an essential feature of a satisfying group (and individual) identity. As was observed in the movie Fight Club, the first rule of the club is not to talk about the club.

Top tips – how to be silent to exclude others

- Acknowledge that exclusionary silence can be generative or degenerative
- To be generative, start by naming the realities of power and hierarchy
- Work with the reality that people need boundaries and groups – and silence is one of the currencies in their definition and management

3. **Silence that is chosen** – silence as an agentic act, a deliberate step by someone or some group. This can be for reasons of rebellion, thoughtfulness, safety, or disinterest. But it is a conscious choice – even if it is not immediately obvious to those on the receiving end of the silence

As a long-term researcher and confidante, John has been privy to thousands of stories, nearly all of them off the record. People often tell him about what they have chosen to be silent about in the public domain or have spoken about in such a way that large swathes of meaning are deliberately lost. They also speak to him with the promise that what they say will be anonymised and made non-attributable. His job, therefore, becomes a safe way to bring things into the public domain, give voice to the silence, that individuals and groups perceive to be too dangerous, risky, or disadvantageous to have attributed to them.

There was a Scandinavian manager who wanted to challenge the public orthodoxy of collective niceness that permeated her company. 'We're all in it together', she told John, parroting the company line, 'until there's a shitstorm', she continued, moving off script, 'then you're on your own'. Up until that point she'd been silent about the experience of being hung out to dry whenever something difficult happened, but because of what John had been tasked to do she felt able to give him the words to use that she felt unable to say.

In his interview process, John is not infrequently asked to stop taking notes or recording, to signify that a particular part of the conversation will no longer have any permanent record outside of the air between them. Silence and the breaking of silence are wrapped up in the social and relational context in which it happens – and the silence that comes with impermanence can be reassuring. Silence reasserts itself unless active steps are made to keep it at bay. The need to reassert silence has only played out once in the many encounters John has had when an interviewee instructed him to erase all record of their meeting, appalled by the record John had submitted to him for approval – 'I do not recognise the egoist you have made me', is John's suitably disguised memory of their exchange.

In their encounters with "John the Researcher", his interviewees act as if they feel they have greater agency than in their usual encounters with the world. They have control over what words will be used and the degree to which their situation will be identifiable. They are freer to speak their secrets, play with their words, shape how they will appear – an experience often lacking in their workplaces, where silence is often easier and safer than words, be they spoken or written. There is something in play about the relative insignificance of John in their lives, the liberty of talking to the stranger they'll never meet again, the seeming powerlessness of a visiting researcher in the context of the power-webs they live in.

Choosing not to speak in the formal domains of organisational life, or only to speak in keeping with the approved and mandated form, is an understandable response by people who are invested in their membership of a community – and the nature of that investment and the reasons for it mattering to people will be legion, from the brute need to get paid so they can get through the next week through to the meeting of some form of self-actualisation that requires the structured company of others.

In John and Megan's research into "Speaking truth to power", two very simple and obvious reasons stood out for why people choose to stay silent; firstly, because they don't want to challenge and so shame someone, especially someone they experience as a more powerful someone. Secondly, they don't want to shame themselves by having others think of them as a fool (Reitz & Higgins, 2017, 2019).

Wrapped around these two seemingly obvious statements are, however, a myriad of social habits that amplify a sense of inter-personal and individual shame. Considerations of class, gender, and ethnicity come to the fore – John and Mark, for instance, play with their different class backgrounds in their work together and how it plays out in their experience of silence and voice. While John has been deeply and persistently schooled in the belief that he should speak up and not be silent, Mark lives with the persistent voice of his shop window dresser Dad instructing him to 'keep your head down'. John has to take active steps to keep his mouth shut and choose silence, whereas Mark has to consciously quieten the sound of his father and park his physical anxiety if he is to choose not to be silent. And for the two of them as white, straight, degree-laden cis-men this challenge to choosing and not choosing silence is a walk in the park compared to the complications that so many people face, living with labels that give them a lived subaltern experience.

Chosen silence can be seen to be somewhere along a sliding scale of defensively and offensively chosen silence. We are using a sliding scale here to avoid getting hooked into an unhelpfully binary frame. Human choices are rarely clearly one thing or another, especially when one begins to pay attention to those choices which are a mix of the conscious, considered, spontaneous, and unconscious.

At the defensive, conscious end of the scale is silence chosen to mitigate risk to yourself or to a group whose association has significance for you. At the offensive end is silence practised for such reasons as undermining a competitor or enemy – or simply because of some inchoate personal animosity. If you don't like someone, why actively help them out? The silence that withholds information so that someone will appear ill-informed or fail.

Often in workplaces there is silence about the day-to-day consequences of some grand scheme announced from the mountain tops and approved by the high priests of the consulting industry. This silence often being evidence of personal and collective resignation in the face of an overwhelming rightness endorsed by those with positional authority – silence is chosen as an act of powerlessness in the face of an unquestionable ideology. Why speak up when historically it has had so little impact beyond a superficial and often trivialising "You said, we did" response? Why speak up when you've been on the receiving end of so much corporate bullshit that the best you can do is suck it up?

Top tips – the reasons for choosing silence

- It keeps people safe – it keeps them out of the firing line
- It can be a political tool, to keep some people in the dark
- It is a way of negotiating between what can be said formally and what is known informally
- It can be an active or passive choice, a default or something that has to be stepped into, depending on personal and group history
- Because choosing to speak is pointless

4. **Silence that is imposed** – silence that is involuntary. This could be self-imposed, the playing out of some internal or relational psychodrama, or it could be a piece of force majeure – an external authority and practice banning, intimidating, or undermining the voice of others

We are all at risk of being prisoners to our unexamined habits of mind and also how we pay attention to these habits. It is in our taken-for-granted assumptions about the world where the seat of imposed silence lies, those things that are so obvious, so usual, so normal, that there is no need to talk about them.

It is in these unspoken assumptions where the boundaries to how and what we know about the world get set – and what therefore is discussable and what is cast into outer darkness, banished and so silenced. Rather than rehash our last book (Cole & Higgins, 2022) that explored these assumptions through the lenses of myths and paradoxes, here we're going to touch on two particular realms of silence that are imposed by our habits of organisational mind.

The first realm we want to foreground is the "Silence of the Intangible", and what gets lost because of our obsession with material artefacts and countable things. Within the largely silenced realm of the intangible lives the world of the qualitative, the imaginative, and the relational. The managerial discourse in practice outlaw's serious attention to these matters because the only truths that count are the ones Charles Dickens attributed to and created for his schoolmaster Thomas Gradgrind in Hard Times. Gradgrind was of the view that the only truths about a horse, for an instance, were the ones that were as solid and objective as the fact that a horse is a quadruped – other considerations being frippery. A positivist orientation is increasingly dominant in wider education, so supporting the managerial tradition, reinforcing the regime of silence around the intangible.

The second realm to touch on here is the "Silence of the Impractical". When unpacked, the managerial and organisational hymn to practicality is actually an assertion that for anything to have value it must fit within the current world order – to do otherwise is by definition, impractical. It denies the reality of social and technological progress that doesn't fit within its current paradigm – so ensuring that stuck-ness of thinking delivers stuck-ness of practice. It silences the novel and the innovative – and then is surprised by how little all this organisational investment in change ever achieves. Here we are relying on the excellent work that exists around the notion of change in organisational settings, especially the difference between first- and second-order change (Watzlawick et al., 2011), with first order being change that fits within the existing way of seeing the world, while second order does not.

Imposed silence is of course not just a result of a particular intellectual construct, or rather a consequence of what it shines a light on and what it obscures; silence is also brought about through the brute force of the status quo, or the way things are and which in quick time can get to be seen as a natural, all but eternal, phenomenon. The status quo is a force to be reckoned with, which both explicitly and implicitly polices what is discussable in the context of the current configuration of power. It sustains reporting structures and meeting agendas, it sets budgets and interprets the performance data, it also allocates favour and determines who and what is of merit – merit being an expression of the current power-system and the rules it lives by, not some Platonic ideal form floating outside of existing custom and practice.

The status quo hires and fires – and promotes those who do and don't fit, so ensuring that voices that don't fit are silenced. It determines what words mean and whose meaning wins through – so every passing fad and long-standing orthodoxy, from "agility" to entrepreneurialism and on, gets translated into something that pleases the status quo – and alternative meanings that don't fit get cut off at the knees. We can assure you that the word "entrepreneur" for instance, so popular in competency models the world over, means something very different to a Civil Servant, or a Rocket Scientist or a bedroom technology tinkerer. Whatever is the current word of the moment, its meaning will be taken and made to fit – and alternatives silenced.

As well as this external imposition of silence, there is also the self-told imposition. We've already told the story of the different class-inspired narratives that John and Mark carry within them. All of us carry scripts about what we should and shouldn't talk about at work, especially when it comes to what we disclose about ourselves, our histories, and our motivations. A Swedish interviewee John spoke with recently, revealed that for many years he'd refused to discuss his HIV status at work, although it was at the heart of his drive and desire to work in a pharmaceutical company.

In John's work with Megan Reitz and Emma Day-Duro on workplace activism (Reitz et al., 2021), they have come across numerous instances where people have struggled to have their wider social concerns taken seriously at work – and even those who work in contexts where Unions still have the power to shape the management agenda, the Unions often struggle to champion concerns that don't fit with their historic remit and a focus on pay and conditions (important though that focus is).

This divide between workplace and wider society is one of the emerging areas of contention when it comes to imposed silence. Workplaces have, in the main, been comfortable not seeing social issues (beyond legal compliance) as being part of their brief and silence has been effectively imposed. It has even extended to some firms insisting that employees sign away their rights as citizens by committing to not doing anything that might besmirch the reputation of the employer (as the employer sees it). This may now be ending, as social unrest and concerns play out in workplaces, whether they are invited or not. Impositions of silence are rarely permanent and are always subject to change – subject, if you're in China, to the rulings of the Chinese Communist Party, which imposes silence in a definitive way.

Top tips – the reasons for imposing silence

- To sustain a particular world view and way of knowing the world
- To maintain the status quo and the hierarchy of who gets to speak up about what
- To create a common language, an organisational truth for talking about the world
- To stay in tune with external social and political norms

5. **Silence that invites** – this is the silence of the pause that invites the other in. It is a deliberate halt to advocacy or extraverted self-thinking. It is what the dialogic movement assumes as a potential in all exchanges – a desire to be curious about and hear from the other

A colleague of John used to work at one of the big technology firms. Part of the tradition on joining was to be invited to meet with one of the founders in their office. John's colleague arrived at the meeting expecting to wait, the founder must be a busy person, and with a series of prepared notes demonstrating the impact he was already having on the company – and generally showing what a high-flying, fast-moving, lip-smacking, Pepsi sort of guy he was.

When he arrived at the plush lobby to the executive suite where the founder's office was, he found he was expected and that he was to go straight through into the office. Once through the door he was met by the sight of an empty desk and the founder getting up to greet him. When they sat down the colleague went into his performative piece, rolling his CV out in that practised way that everyone has when we're all our own brand and want to present the best possible shop window to the world. The founder held up his hand and stopped the flow of self-importance: 'But I want to know about you', he said. And he meant it. He was inviting the new joiner to show up, to give voice to aspects of his identity the corporate world too often forces people to hide.

Of course, this story even in this anecdotal form is deeply problematic. There are lots of the trappings of power in play, and if the founder wanted to be truly invitational why didn't he meet with the new joiner somewhere else, where the status gap would have been less figural and the new joiner might be more at their ease? The story serves to remind those in leadership positions of the power mesh that lives in the moment and directly affects what gets said and may or may not be heard. Regrettably it should also be borne in mind that much of what passes for leadership at work is inauthentic, a performance of human connection. So, if you're a senior person asking to know about someone, you had better make damn sure that you mean it at a deeply human level – rather than just saying it because that's what you've been told "leaders" do.

We can argue the toss, but two things stand out about the invitational nature of the listening silence here. Firstly, as the founder was someone who in this context had considerable rank and authority, his silence was a gift he could give to others, especially others who were more used to him and others like him filling the silence. Secondly, where people of rank choose to be silent matters; invitational silence by a powerful other is an exercise in working with and dialling down power differentials and power shadows. This is why location matters – particularly a location that will help the less powerful feel more secure.

In John's work as a researcher, coach, and action learning facilitator he often has to do little in terms of speaking, his contribution is his silence – the old cliché still works for action learning, that it gives people the experience of being given "a damn good listening to". He knows when his silence is more invitational than at other times, when it is a better quality of quiet and he's really paying attention to what is being said and not said by the other. When he's not trying to "add value" by reframing their experience through one of the myriad models and frameworks that knock around his head.

In his research he often starts by telling people, warning them even, that he will probably say very little – and that whatever they say is what he wants to hear. People are very rarely in the company of a silent partner and it can be unnerving; when it comes to work settings people are also wired to being listened to through the lens of appraisal. John used to agonise over framing questions when he met to interview people, to ensure that the silence he was inviting people into was properly bounded and purposeful. He's less concerned about this these days, more like the shambling 1970s detective Columbo and given to vague gestures and open mumblings rather than open questions. In the face of what they feel as invitational silence he finds that people say what they need and want to say, whatever question they're asked – and what they say nearly always turns out to be pertinent to a research agenda at some point in time.

The difference between the invitational silence of John the Researcher and that of the invitational silence of a boss or manager is that it is all but without jeopardy. He brings the silence of the witness, someone who sees what you want him to see, without an agenda which makes it qualitatively different to encounters with Therapists or Priests – both of whom can bring their largely silent presence into a relationship. The work of the Samaritans helpline in the UK also privileges and understands the profound and life-affirming potential that exists when people feel heard – and if no one's listening, if no one's being silently present with you, how can you feel heard?

Silence is at the heart of bearing witness to the other – and doing invitational silence well is a hard-won discipline for most of us, certainly for John whose self-worth was for so many years wrapped up in his ability to articulate and represent the world, tell people what it was they meant to say, escape from their subjective false-consciousness.

At its best, practices such as mindfulness and related techniques can be a useful gateway into invitational silence, by stilling the internal self-chatter so many of us are full of and allowing us to be more attentive to the world around us, bringing the gift of personal quietness into relationships with others.

Invitational silence is a difficult practice in a world addicted to busyness and outcomes, especially predictable and pre-known ones. It does not sit well with the performative nature of organisational life, where silence is largely an embarrassing pause waiting to be filled with noisy action and charismatic management. Invitational silence requires an orientation to the other and attention to the relationship silence lives in; not a popular framing in a world of agentic egos and sovereign individualism.

Top tips – the needs for and practice of invitational silence

- It enlivens and deepens relationships
- It helps others know themselves
- It creates opportunities to know the world differently
- It can't happen without positive intent
- It always happens in a context that shapes expectations
- It's a skill and a discipline that can be developed

6. **Silence that manipulates** – this is the pause that is there to generate tension in the other. That tricks people into saying more than they intended or is there to remind people – be a felt expression – of the enormity of the act required for them to stop being silent

There's nothing quite like the Q&A session at a Town Hall meeting to bring to light how easy it is to manipulate the public agenda of an organisation. The wise learn to keep their heads down when someone asks a contentious question, while most such events are dominated by pre-prepared questions and stock answers. When John speaks at such events he is rarely presented with an unscripted question. Emollient titles are accorded to the censors at such meetings: they might be described as **moderators** (a lovely intimation that they sit somewhere in the middle to offer some balance); as a **curator** (which conjures up notions of someone scrutinising and arranging the valuable artefacts so as to showcase them best); or – heaven forfend – as a **facilitator**, which seems to have sown into it a deep layer of condescension in respect to the person fulfilling this role offering others the encouragement to articulate their thoughts… when, in actual fact, the role constrains when, where, and how people might express themselves by managing the timetable and defining the agenda.

Even in the seeming democracy of the Zoom meeting, questions are tightly selected and these days anonymity is frequently denied. Collective silence dominates and time is kept short – so people are given little time to make sense of what they hear, either individually or collectively. Atomised sense-making gives little chance for people to test the waters as to whether they are alone in what strikes them. There is lots of good practice out there to address this, but what stands out is the persistence of agenda management through broadcast advocacy rather than dialogic inquiry.

Then there is the manipulative potential for silence within inter-personal contexts. In the early stages of John and Megan Reitz's research into speaking truth to power they came across a manager who said he used silence to get people to tell him more than they meant to. He found this worked particularly well with more junior staff. We suspect he is not alone. Nothing like a bit of silence to up the tension in most workplace conversations between manager and staff member. This is not a conversational tactic; it is – quite simply – an interrogation technique.

How silence is experienced is of course highly culturally and contextually specific. Within the world of group psycho-dynamics it is not unusual for a group to come together and stay in silence for many minutes, treating the silence as experience and data for them as a group. While people from a Quaker background, with their tradition of silent meetings when people speak as and when the spirit moves them, are also used to being in silence in the company of others – the manager in the anecdote above was from a Quaker background so even if others were new to silence, it was normal for him.

In most workplaces we encounter, however, silence is an unfamiliar group experience. When people come together the point is to talk, to share – and to inject unexpected silence can feel disturbing. The highly extraverted in particular can find it oppressive.

The use of silence in group and inter-personal settings to provoke discomfort and get people to speak from their anxious, unguarded self is only one form of the manipulative potential of silence – silence as micro-aggression, crowd control, and group norming. In John's research he has come across the overt use of silence to attack colleagues – it may be straight out of the playground, but ganging up on someone and ensuring that no one will talk with them (sending them to Coventry) still happens… people in groups can be pretty cruel.

At one health sector Whistleblowing conference John attended, one whistleblower reported how his colleagues turned their back on him whenever he walked into a communal space. Silence is used to create an intolerable environment and so induce someone to leave – in one case John followed this type of treatment pushed the individual to the brink of suicide. Voice and silence are not merely verbal or non-verbal actions – and we can silence people without resorting to the theatrical "Shusssh!" of the caricature of a librarian. We can give someone "the cold shoulder", for example, an active gesture that occurs in silence – and commands silence, as well.

At the organisational level silence shows up in avoided topics and the glossy spin put on corporate activities, while the embedded assumptions in AI systems remain largely hidden from view. Of course, we are now all bombarded by all sorts of manipulative advertising and information feeds, which lead us in one direction rather than another. Manipulation by the ease of use and habit is a sly old beast which can wind up shielding us from data or perspectives that might upset us. Given Mark and John's long-running critique of the intellectual habits of workplaces, it is no surprise that we see silence around what is taken for granted as deeply manipulative – normalising what we frequently don't think should be taken as normal. A collective silence invariably exists around the commonplace – when our contrary view is that the commonplace needs to be explored and challenged.

One of the great normalisations of the workplace is the idea of a collective common purpose, of alignment which encompasses all. Difference, contention, and conflict get silenced; or rather hide in plain sight, often behind the glib litany of statements that are declared to be the values of an organisation. In the case of gross differences in pay it is striking how it is and isn't talked about – so senior leaders need to have generous incentive programmes if they are to do their jobs well, while everyone else has to scrabble around for inflation-linked increases if they're lucky and aren't being benchmarked against a no-frills outsourcer.

To challenge this "natural" order and the paradoxical conception of the role that pay and reward play depending on where you are in the pecking order, is to be seen as a troublemaker or something from a bygone era. Meaningful inquiry into the role of performance measures and reward systems very rarely happens – with all sorts of questionable and frequently self-serving assertions going unchallenged because they are in practice undiscussable. And in time silence around this and similar serious topics grows and the opportunity for inquiry and questioning gets squeezed out.

Like any ideology, management orthodoxy creates its axioms, its unquestionable truths, and so shapes what is discussable, condemning awkward insights to the outer Badlands of silence. In the growing absence of alternative centres of workplace power, Unions being so increasingly powerless and Staff Networks operating with licence granted to them by management, so the corporate agenda is manipulated into a shape which serves the status quo nicely.

Even in organisations that are notionally committed to supporting Union membership and have arrangements for representation and consultation, elected representatives are under attack from management, in terms of compelling their silence. In a recent article, it was reported that:

> RMT transport union general secretary Mick Lynch [said that] his union has seen an increase in the victimisation of union reps over the course of the Coronavirus epidemic, with reps under pressure to "keep the show on the road and not to question management". Several RMT reps who have taken up safety cases, or who have a history representing members, have been dismissed on the basis of their activities as reps, he added. For example, the union has been campaigning for the reinstatement of Southampton bus branch chair Declan Clune. He was dismissed in February 2021 for bringing bus operator Bluestar into disrepute after he reported concerns to Network Rail about a bridge being struck by vehicles. (Labour Research, 2021, p. 9)

To see how silence manipulates an organisation's agenda all that is needed is a close examination of all those things which are not seen as worthy of meaningful executive attention.

Top tips – How silence manipulates

- It invites unguarded disclosure by the less powerful
- It advertises the risks of speaking up in public
- It polices what is and isn't part of the management agenda
- It creates a hostile environment for people who break with established custom and practice

7. **Silence that punctuates** – all speech has silence as a constituent part. It is an integral part of the rhythm and meaning of language, it gives and takes away weight and emphasis to what is being said. The quality of our talk is as much to do with the quality of our spoken silences as our words

In any sentence we speak there are pauses, words don't just run into each other. We pause when we want to give weight to what is to come, or what has just been said. Sometimes we pause because we are nervous about what we are about to say, because words once said cannot be unsaid. The pauses in speech are like the gaps between the notes in music, they give it pace and rhythm, without the silence speech and music don't work.

In people's lives, however extraverted they are, silence is needed in order to catch breath, to digest experience. This is a part of working life that is too easily squeezed out and relegated to being a luxury. Too much working life sees people at all levels, either because of the nature of the role or how people have been encouraged to see themselves, as ceaseless "Duracell Bunnies". In the advert a toy rabbit branded as the Duracell battery has a drum fixed to its front, which it relentlessly hits with a stick. The voice-over and the accompanying strapline is proud to tell the world that this Duracell-powered bunny will go on bashing its drum "for up to six times longer", compared to some lesser-powered herbivorous mammals.

The Bunny doesn't stop, it never has the chance to pause and make sense of what it is doing and why – it is, as the unwilling Psychoanalyst in the film *Grosse Pointe Blank* (1997) points out, a deeply depressing image. The taken-for-granted fixation with novelty and action at work often strips out the times and places where people can stop being the relentless rabbit and can actually learn something. Without punctuating silence, from within ourselves and from the world around us, all people can do is career on from one thing to another, until we get fired, retire, get ill or die.

Silence gives us the chance to catch our breath, it is the bedrock of self and collective reflection. One of the ways we keep ourselves stuck in the status quo of our lives, including the status quo of our assumptions and beliefs, is to always be too busy to stop and think. Everything at work has to be done at pace, with energy – when sometimes what is most needed is to travel slowly and calmly. Unless, that is, you want to keep people tied up on the treadmill of busyness for reasons of control – which is how the two of us made sense of the working practices in the Amazon warehouse we visited back in January 2020.

As purveyors of workshops to numerous organisations, John and Mark are always having to play a subtle game when it comes to meeting the world where it is while trying to nudge it towards somewhere else. People who come to these events usually expect to get something of immediate use, that adds to the arsenal of their professional knowledge – the expectation is that they are going to have their knowing filled up some more, in line with pre-specified takeaways that they can easily share with others. We have to play this game enough so that they can demonstrate some traditional value when they go back to their day jobs – and have a ready answer to the question: "What did you get from the latest Mark and John show?" And much as we play that game, we know as surely as we can know anything, that the greatest value we can add is not to fill people up with yet more stuff, but to help them pause and notice what they already have and already are. Bring some punctuation into their lives.

Punctuation comes in many forms. Sometimes what's needed is a full stop, the opportunity to notice that a particular way of talking or being in the world has run its course. Time to mark it as finished, full stop. As someone invested in the Jungian tradition, John always pays attention to what phase of life people are at – are they still in the morning, still at the collecting experiences phase? Or are they now in their afternoon, able to exercise informed choices about the life they're best suited to lead?

A comma speaks to the need to simply catch breath, stay with the basic logic of current ways, but maybe fine-tune things. A question mark is an inflexion point, a time obviously for questioning and not just accepting what has been taken for granted – while an exclamation mark highlights something worthy of attention, a heightened experience to be looked at closely. Or, sometimes, it is an expression of power, when the voice moves from a whisper to a scream – and where the speaker is trying to command attention, which can be achieved through an aggressive hiss or a dominant shout.

As with so many applications of silence, there is no one size fits all. The temptation will be, almost inevitably in a world that likes to package and standardise, to try and over-formulate the application of silence. Nothing makes our skin crawl more than the idea that companies will try and roll out a compulsory two-minute silence at the end of every meeting. The challenge is for people to notice what type of punctuation point an individual, pairing or group needs in the moment – and our experience is that whatever the type of pause most needed, most workplaces will cut it too short, always wanting to rush on to the next task, desperate to fill every minute with sixty seconds worth of distance run (as that hyper-active friend of empire Rudyard Kipling would put it).

Legitimising time to think is no easy matter for people at all points of the workplace system. An example of the bizarre steps people go to comes from the experience of "Kim", a colleague of John's, who was the coach to a very senior leader in a world-famous institution. Kim's coaching clients would arrive at the offices of the business school where she worked and Kim would usher them in and sit them down in a quiet study come sitting room, with a cup of tea and a biscuit. Kim would then leave the room and come back in an hour to see if there was anything her client wanted to talk about, usually there wasn't. The purpose of the coaching contract was to legitimise the client taking time out from their otherwise packed diary

Everybody needs protected time like this, to step back, pause and still the clamouring voices. The challenge is how to prioritise it when everyone is so busy, or at least is having to go through the motions of looking busy.

Top tips – The silence that punctuates meaning

- Without silence there is no digestion, no learning, simply repetitive busyness

- Punctuating silences come in all types – they can be short or long, indicate endings or new beginnings
- Please, please don't mandate a corporate-wide silence policy

Shades of silence and their implications for organisational practice

We can see the bandwagon rolling already, with headlines like: "Embracing the power of silence" and someone, somewhere will be working on the metrics and missing the point entirely. To take silence seriously is to pay attention to what gets missed by the gross over-simplifications that pass as good management practice.

It means paying attention to the qualitative dimensions of life – and not substituting them with crude attempts at objectification. It means putting what is going on now in context and history rather than imagining that life can exist in some permanent, future-focused present. It means realising how impoverished and misleading the current organisational discourse is, with its "views from the top" and "management by objective" (although "management by fantasy" would be a more honest description). Above all else it means paying attention to power and truth, and how these two ever-present and conjoined terms shape what is and isn't allowed to be discussed and what must remain wordless.

This plays out in the everyday of the workplace and with that in mind let us finish this overview with an ordinary story. John was recently talking to Martin, a friend of his, who was filling in his annual appraisal. Martin was playing the game, identifying things he didn't give a damn about but would get him a tick in the corporate box when it came to his proudest achievements for last year and ambitions for the next. There was nowhere for him to talk about what really fired him up and pissed him off – how what kept him at the company was a younger colleague, who burst with energy, had a wicked sense of humour and just got things done without making a song and dance about them. While what was going to drive him away was the mealy-mouthed company President who talked the language of collegiality, which meant a self-regarding "boys club" could go on lauding it over everybody else.

To take silence seriously is often more about noticing what's going on in the playground of life, rather than what gets reported in the classroom.

Concluding "hot tips" – the hopelessly digested read

The things to pay attention to when noticing silence:

- Group and self-identity cannot be ignored
- Power and hierarchy show up in how silence is interpreted and manifested
- Silence is data and never neutral

References

Buber, M., 1937. *I and Thou*. Edinburgh: T & T Clark.

Cole, M. & Higgins, J., 2022. *Leadership unravelled: The faulty thinking behind modern management*. Abingdon: Routledge.

Deming, W. E., 1982/2018. *Out of the crisis*. Cambridge: MIT Press.

Ferreras, I., Battilana, J. & Meda, D., 2022. *Democratize work: The case for reorganizing the economy*. Chicago, IL: University of Chicago Press.

Fuller, R. W., 2004. *Somebodies and nobodies: Overcoming the abuse of rank*. Gabriola Island: New Society Publishers.

Hayes, A., 2022. *Black-Scholes Model*. [Online] Available at: https://www.investopedia.com/terms/b/blackscholes.asp#:~:text=The%20Black%2DScholes%20model%2C%20aka, free%20rate%2C%20and%20the%20volatility. [Accessed 5 August 2022].

Higgins, J. & Reitz, M., 2019. If whistleblowing is the answer, ask a better question. *Journal of the Royal Society of Medicine*, 112(11), pp. 453–455.

Kleiner, A., 2003. *Who really matters: The core group theory of power, privilege and success*. New York: Currency Doubleday.

Labour Research, 2021. Attacked for standing up for their members. *Labour Research*, November, 110(11), pp. 9–11.

Mintzberg, H., 2016. *Need a strategy? Let it grow like a weed in the garden*. [Online] Available at: https://mintzberg.org/blog/growing-strategies [Accessed 13 January 2022].

Radical Candor, 2022. *Six steps for rolling out radical candor*. [Online] Available at: https://www.radicalcandor.com/wp-content/uploads/2021/06/6_Steps_Radical-Candor-1.pdf [Accessed 17 January 2022].

Reitz, M. & Higgins, J., 2017. *Being silenced and silencing others: Developing the capacity to speak truth to power*. Berkhamstead: Hult Research.

Reitz, M. & Higgins, J., 2019. *Speak up: Say what needs to be said and hear what needs to be heard.* Harlow: Pearson Education.

Reitz, M., Higgins, J. & Day-Duro, E., 2021. *The do's and don'ts of employee activism: How organizations respond to voices of difference.* Berkhamsted: Hult International Business School.

Salmon, C., 2010. *Storytelling: Bewitching the modern mind.* London: Verso.

Scott, K. M., 2017. *Radical candor: How to be a kick-ass boss without losing your humanity.* New York: St Martin's Press.

Takala, T. & Auvinen, T., 2016. The power of leadership storytelling: Case of Adolf Hitler. *Tamara: Journal for Critical Organization Inquiry,* 14(1), pp. 21–34.

Watzlawick, P., Weakland, J. & Fisch, R., 2011. *Change: Principles of problem formation and problem resolution.* New York: W W Norton & Company, Inc.

Part II

CREATING AND SUSTAINING CLIMATES OF SILENCE AND VOICE

3

ON SILENCE

Mark recalls a story told to him by a friend with whom he has sadly lost contact. She was committed to doing a great deal of therapeutic work to make sense of her life and how she wanted to live it. The process led to her abruptly abandoning her husband, leaving him smarting from the finality and impotence of her closing statement: 'It's not you, it's me', even though that was precisely the case in this instance.

One time, she spoke to Mark about a therapy session where she had sat in utter silence throughout. The counsellor, of course, said nothing and merely allowed the session to progress on this basis. At the end of the 50 minutes, the therapist calmly said: 'That's all we have time for this week. I will see you the same time next week'. And the session finished. Two people had sat together in a room and – other than introductory and concluding pleasantries – they had seemingly said nothing to one another.

Mark was transfixed by this story and it has powerfully remained with him since. He struggles to imagine how it would feel to sit with another human being in such close quarter and for nothing to be said, given their

DOI: 10.4324/9781003296683-5

mutual capacity for language. When Mark has run workshops, even though allowing participants the option to be silent is deemed integral to a wider developmental process, the oppressiveness of silence feels overwhelming to him and he will intercede sooner rather than later.

There may be something in his childhood that nudges him in this direction. He and his younger brother shared a bedroom in the small family home for many years. At night-time, when the two were meant to be settling to sleep, they would relish the chance to chatter away in the darkness about everything and nothing, just enjoying the cosy comfort of talking together. Their conversation would begin as a whisper but the joy of the exchange would gradually nudge up the volume until their father would rush to the foot of the stairs and bellow up to tell them to be quiet.

The conversation would drop back to a whisper again but then they would forget themselves and begin speaking louder and louder. This ritual would run a couple of cycles until such time as their father's patience finally ran out and he would rush upstairs to "have the last word", which was inevitably in the form of a stinging rebuke.

Mark has noticed that when he is running a session where he's encouraging collective conversations, the sound of people talking – the rumbling music of people talking animatedly, especially in a confined space – fills him with joy and he feels deeply unhappy when he calls a halt to those conversations, so as to stay on track with some overall and usually artificial plan that he has confected in order to justify bringing people together.

Silence becomes for him a negation of vitality, of the vivid and connective to and fro of spoken ideas. And a 50-minute silence seems like a denial of human connection, whereas Mark's friend had found that session useful (although she was never able to explain what it was she got from it).

The psychotherapeutic relationship is fraught with power, as Michel Foucault declares in his incisive study of madness. As he notes in regard to the discursive transition of madness from ostracism to "treatment" and thence to psychology:

> Freud demystified all the other asylum structures: he abolished silence and the gaze, and removed the recognition of madness by itself in the mirror of its own spectacle, and he silenced the instances of condemnation. But, on the other hand, he exploited the structure that enveloped the medical character: he amplified his virtues as a worker of miracles,

preparing an almost divine status for his omnipotence. He brought back to him, and his simple presence, hidden behind the patient and above him, in an absence that was also a total presence, all the powers that had been shared out in the collective existence of the asylum: he made him the absolute Gaze, the pure, indefinitely held Silence, the Judge who punishes and rewards in a judgement that does not condescend to language; and he made him the mirror in which madness, in an almost immobile movement, falls in and out of love with itself.   (Foucault, 1972/2009, p. 510)

From this departure point Foucault declared his ongoing commitment to study '…the emergence of the power of normalization' (Foucault, 2004, p. 26). It is possible to trace the range of points across the social fabric where this new modality of power appears, including the observations about the arrival of psychology and psychotherapy as different ways of incorporating and making sense of madness. It also reminds us of the power embedded in the relationship between the analyst and the analysand, where the gaze resides with the former and silence is their default position, particularly amongst Freudian practitioners.

Was then Mark's friend's embrace of a session of silence an assertion of power? There may have been some element of that, although we cannot know. Only psychoanalysts, and practitioners in that vein, presume to understand the speech and non-speech acts of their patients to a better and more honest extent than those clients themselves. To this end, the idea of the unconscious − wherein resides the keys that unlock the riddle of the patient's behaviours − is akin to the condescension associated with the Marxian notion of "false consciousness", which in turn is intimately connected with the companion idea of ideology and generates the following conundrum:

On the one hand, if ideology is a form of false consciousness, then historical materialism must represent some "true" consciousness. On this view, Lenin's use of the term "socialist ideology" cannot be compatible with Marx and Engels's understanding of ideology as implying a defect in perception, and historical materialism should rather be understood as a "science." On the other hand, if all systems of thought are materially and socially determined, how does historical materialism claim the validity and superiority of its worldview without falling into a form of ideology of the kind Marx and Engels originally critiqued? (Hamati-Ataya, 2015, p. 1227)

In both instances, it is declared that we do not know ourselves or have a partial or obscured view of the world. However, the analyst or the social activist is deemed to be able to see our reality better than we ourselves can see it. This makes interpretation of the client inescapable, makes it the preserve of analyst/activist rather than something available to either person in the dyad. The silence could have been a resistance, in terms of refusing to fill a space and time ordinarily filled with the articulation of the experiences and thoughts of the client. But it is, in turn, accepted by the therapist as part of the process – and prone to interpretation, wherein the client's understanding of what they are doing is subsumed by the superior reading of their counsellor.

That in this instance the analyst allowed the silence to prevail intimates that it was seen to hold some value. Perhaps more accurately, it was invested with value in that moment and at that particular time by both the client and the therapist. There was a silent collusion that meant they both valorised that silence, although it is unknowable as to what motivated each of them in this context and they may well have had entirely different reasons. Not knowing what brings each of the agents in this relationship to embrace silence leads us to two observations: first, voice and silence can occasionally be seen to have comparable value, depending on the circumstance; and, second, power is inscribed both in someone's silence and also in their interlocutor's welcoming of that silence.

What matters is the way in which those dynamics play out within a specific context. A colleague of John's described a recent online meeting of staff and managers that lighted on a discussion about the shape and direction of another meeting that this group were expected to attend. (The irony of a meeting to talk about a meeting should at least be acknowledged at this point, a reminder that organisational communication fills up with epiphenomenal topics rather than with what matters to those who work there. In the realm of leadership – particularly among those at senior levels of organisations – the signal-to-noise ratio can be difficult for listeners to process – and it can lead people very quickly to switch off.)

The "leader" of the meeting invited people to contribute individually to this largely unwelcome exchange. There was silence in the online space as people chose not to speak and to keep their peace. Taken at face value it was a group of adults in a corporate context being invited to speak and actively choosing not to, for whatever reasons.

Leaders in organisations, however, often seem to become distressed when this happens. Perhaps they have swallowed the leader–follower ideology (Learmonth & Morrell, 2019) and feel destabilised when those they consider "followers" fail to follow, cutting them off from the persona of leader on which their corporate identity depends. Perhaps there is something parental at play, where the obstreperous child sullenly refuses to respond. More generously, perhaps it is something teacherly, where there is a tacit assumption that everyone wants to or needs to respond in the world of the "corporate classroom" and so should be encouraged or compelled to contribute.

In this instance, the meeting "leader" could not accept the silence. They pushed again, acknowledging that while everyone was going to have the chance to speak about it one-to-one at another time, here was an opportunity to offer some opinions NOW... and someone should take the chance to speak up. Here, woven into the power fabric of that particular gathering, there was zero tolerance for silence and the leader was not going to accept the silence as a legitimate discursive response.

A voice finally and seemingly with reluctance piped up with an opinion. Maybe they had been guilted into finding something to articulate solely for the purpose of breaking the silence the leader did not seem able to bare? However, the response to their speaking up is of note. The leader listened to the remark that had been forced into the open but, instead of taking it at face value, accepting it as a datum of the feeling across the staff group with respect to this matter, they decided to assume a new conversational role for themselves. They smilingly declared: 'Ah, OK. Thanks. But let me play devil's advocate here...'

Some might think this akin to an innocuous parlour game. More philosophical minds might ascribe to it a positive Socratic intent. Regardless it serves to bring the issue of power firmly to the foreground. Leaders would do well to look at this phased analysis of this story and reflect on its implications for their practice:

Your silence is refused, your right to silence is denied;
Your voice is demanded, you are commanded to comment;
Yet your contribution has no value other than to serve as a means by which I might promote my opinion.

Just recently, Mark's eight-year-old son was reading his school book aloud at bedtime. It was called *King Flashypants and the Toys of Terror*. The eponymous hero is actually a young boy called Edwin, attended by a minister called Jill. In an adjoining realm, there is an evil emperor called Nurbison. There was one passage that leapt out at Mark and chimed with his corporate experiences. In it, Edwin and Nurbison – and those around them – have made common cause to defeat a shared enemy. Jill steps forward to a chalkboard and invites people to share their ideas, introducing the exercise with the invitation, 'We need some ideas. Let's get creative' (Riley, 2017, p. 130).

Edwin begins to share an idea but before he can get to the point, Nurbison speaks across him with a resounding 'NO!'. This happens six times until Jill asks Nurbison how he knows whether they are good or bad ideas when he's not even hearing them. 'How can they be good ideas if it wasn't me who thought them up?', replies the Emperor, prompting Jill to state that they are going to capture all the ideas that come forward, '…no matter how daft they might seem' (Riley, 2017, p. 131). At this point, someone suggests what seems to be a silly idea and the following occurs:

> It really was the worst idea Jill had ever heard. But she had to play by her own rules, so she wrote it on the chalkboard. Hours passed. The board filled up with ideas, ideas and more ideas. But deep down Jill knew none of them would work.
> (Riley, 2017, p. 132)

Welcome to the interplay of voice and silence at your team awaydays...

Away from the prescient world of children's literature, Mark recalls completing a leadership 360 feedback tool and receiving feedback that he was seen not to contribute to meetings as much as he might, which led one Executive Director respondent to suggest that Mark was therefore seen as lacking in confidence. Perplexed by and anxious about this observation, Mark found a way to have a conversation with the respondent, despite the fact that these instruments are invariably anonymised. As a sidebar here, it is worth observing that, if we found ways in which to have honest conversations with one another that did not have to shuttle up and down the hierarchy and were founded on a human rather than an organisational relationship, the need for such instruments would largely disappear.

The Director was fulsome with advice: 'You should be like me', they advised, an opening gambit that instantly set off the alarm bells in Mark.

'Whenever I go into a meeting, I always make sure that I say something within the first six minutes'. The sheer artifice of this tactic momentarily stopped Mark in his tracks. More importantly he reflected that if everyone were to assume this approach – alongside other similar techniques to make it appear as though one were engaged in a meeting and moved to make a contribution – the chance of anything like an honest human exchange in an organisational setting seemed to be lost.

Hierarchy offers those nearer the top of the structure the opportunity to set permissions around voice and silence for those around them. In the realm that they create for themselves, their advice – however misjudged – is mostly unquestioningly accepted. They compel silence and invite speech, occasionally lapsing into gaming those around them in order to force people to contribute.

*

Silence is said to be golden, which underscores for us the value that is placed on soundlessness. It is perhaps possible to extrapolate from this to embrace the notion that our individual silence is taken to be an inherently good thing. We are better when silent than when speaking. As an indication of a parity of esteem between these two states and their interrelatedness, it has been suggested that:

> Silence is not simply what happens when we stop talking. It is more than the mere negative renunciation of language; it is more than simply a condition that we can produce at will. When language ceases, silence begins. But it does not begin because language ceases. The absence of language simply makes the presence of Silence more apparent. Silence is an autonomous phenomenon. It is therefore not identical with the suspension of language. It is not merely the negative condition that sets in when the positive is removed; it is rather an independent whole, subsisting in and through itself. It is creative, as language is creative; and it is formative of human beings as language is formative, but not in the same degree.   (Picard, 1964, p. xix)

Perhaps all of this builds on the old saw that 'children should be seen and not heard', by which it meant not that their exchanges should be conducted in whispers but rather that they are best when they do not speak. In this formulation, it is not merely that they should not converse or engage with the adult world but also that their own exchanges should not be audible. The shift in the modality of power here seems brazenly apparent: it is possible to intervene with another human being on a corporal level to render them speechless, even soundless, by applying a gag to their mouth. Such practice would now be seen as barbaric but in this broadly Victorian development, the parent assumes the role of admonishing the child so as to train them to keep silent when otherwise visible.

Even in our supposedly enlightened age, the classroom remains a place where silence and power are intimately entwined. There is a recognition that '…silencing is an indispensable disciplinary act that aims at establishing an ordered milieu for effective teaching and learning' (Li, 2004, p. 69). This both reveals and sustains the dynamics of power at school, from our very earliest exposure to (and immersion in) it as an institution. On a more positive note, however, silence can be a pedagogical device, designed to support reflection and open up space for voice (Li, 2004, p. 70). It is noteworthy that traditional pedagogy, wherein a teacher runs the class in order to manage the learning of their students, cannot be abstracted from power in the way in which this observation seems to suggest, insofar as power is an intrinsic quality of human relations and the roles of "teacher" and "pupil" arise out of that and reinforce it.

It nudges us to see how silence might quite reasonably be seen to be a key element of what is often described as the "hidden curriculum". Theorists from Durkheim onwards have acknowledged this tacit instruction and sought to articulate it, not least Phillip Jackson who first published his study on Life in Classrooms back in 1968. In this work he underscores the fact that our experience of school, which can be positive in many instances, is undergirded by what he describes in his first chapter as the "daily grind" of sitting, waiting in line, handing things out, and so on – practices that are drilled into the students so that much teaching can be seen as a call and response between the educator and their charges (Jackson, 1990). Hence, Jackson's notion of "hidden curriculum" is summarised thus: '…learning to wait quietly, exercising restraint, trying, completing work, keeping busy, cooperating, showing allegiance to both teachers and peers, being neat and punctual, and conducting oneself courteously' (Kentli, 2009, p. 86).

Let's leave behind the way in which formal education might offer early insight into social expectations of silence to return to the intimate connection between the expression of words and silence. This is especially important when considering how this interplay is defined and gives shape to our day-to-day experience of power in a range of social contexts. In considering the work of Georges Bataille in this regard, the following observation is made:

> What we need to do, [Bataille] writes, is to block *"discours"*—the organized, structured thinking, speaking, writing, encoding. In so doing, we notice that the most important part of silence is precisely this loss of words, the imposition of order from conscious human interaction with the world.   (Hegarty, 2015, p. 99)

From this, it is possible to recognise silence as something potentially seditious, a refutation of the ordering of the world through language.

Perhaps it is this challenge to order that leaders in corporate life find so challenging. Through all the corporatised initiatives to involve us, engage us, and empower us as employees, we are actively encouraged to use our voices, to speak into the organisational void. It might be argued that this simply reinforces our experiences to date in these contexts and reproduces the way in which they are constructed through language. There is a significant literature in support of the notion of the "communicative constitution of organisation" (Schoeneborn & Blaschke, 2014), so – through this lens – it is possible to see how silence might be seen to be disruptive.

To continue this inquiry into the currency of silence don't forget that a person's silence can be bought. The non-disclosure agreement (NDA) was traditionally a legal instrument to protect intellectual property. It has now been added to the HR armoury of ways to exercise control of people in the workplace, often trading a sum of money for the individual's legal commitment not to speak about a workplace issue of importance to them.

The Advisory, Conciliation and Arbitration Service (ACAS) in the UK offers advice to organisations via its website as to how to create NDAs. There we find this statement, outlining a key instance where an NDA might be used:

> When an employer and employee or worker make an agreement to resolve a dispute in the workplace, they might use an NDA to keep either of the following confidential: the details of an agreement; the fact that an agreement has been made.   (ACAS, 2021)

In a good many instances, this reflects a business silencing a member of staff in return for a sum of money. And in so doing that company creates a silence across the organisation, where others who might make common cause with the person whose silence has been purchased are denied knowledge of both the event and the existence of an agreement to hush the matter up. So much for the myth of staff involvement and engagement.

While these instruments appear under the liberal democratic conceit of the "contract", which is assumed in juridical terms to be an equal agreement between a number of parties in parity, power flushes through these negotiations and distorts the process. The example of the 45th President of the United States offers breath-taking insight into the use and abuse of this practice:

> In August 2018, the American public became privy to the President's use of an extensive system of nondisclosure agreements (NDAs) and nondisparagement clauses to prevent campaign staff and White House employees from betraying his confidence, leaking information to the press, or besmirching—in any way—his administration or family. These contracts for silence were particularly restrictive, even for a man with a fondness for management-friendly employment agreements and a penchant for "information mischief." For instance, not only did his campaign NDA apply to *any* piece of information then-candidate Trump deemed covered, it also stated that campaign employees' obligation existed in perpetuity. A draft of the NDA he imposed on White House staff, meanwhile, stipulated a $10 million penalty for each breach.   (Lampmann, 2020, p. 124)

These NDAs are less about silence being golden as establishing the threat that if they were to speak out, they would face being legally fined. For a man seemingly lacking the most basic level of self-awareness, it would seem as though his unbridled ego did acknowledge that some of what he would be doing in office – and outside of it – would be of considerable public concern.

Most of us can think of an instance where an NDA has been used to silence someone. The expansion of this practice takes place at a time when there has been even more intense public scrutiny of abuse in society at large, in businesses and institutions, most notably finding its voice via the #MeToo movement. Legalistically, the point has been well made that the NDAs with respect to the sorts of things raised by this movement may have resolved particular cases but left the perpetrator at liberty to persist with their behaviours wholly unchecked (Weston, 2021). Elsewhere, in the realm of organised religion, for example, a legal commentator in the US back in 2003 offered the following estimate:

> Because most victims signed confidentiality agreements, the [Catholic] Church has never had to disclose either the number of settlements or their cost. Financial experts, however, estimate that settlements have cost the Church between four hundred million to one billion dollars over the past two decades.   (Philp, 2003, p. 846)

The NDA is not an agreement between equals: it is a means by which power buys silence, not merely the silence of the signatories to that contract but throughout society. Many will be aware of the light entertainment format called *The Voice*, a game show for those with a modicum of singing talent. It is a popular programme in the US where the contestants are all expected to sign an NDA in advance of their participation in the show that stipulates they will pay $500,000 for each occasion where they might publicly share details of the business practices of the programme (Arditi, 2020).

*

To conclude this introductory section, building on the sentiment of Simon and Garfunkel, there is a sound to silence; perhaps the suggestion is that the world can never be fully silent and that, in quietness, we hear things normally buried in the blaring sound-bed of our daily real and online lives. Many of us will have been part of training on active listening, where we have been told to sit in silence and take time to listen to the sound-bed that surrounds us. Here, of course, silence is not soundlessness, it is the absence of speech. And, broadly, it is about opting to mute one's own speech, notionally to pay better attention to an interlocutor.

It is our view that this superficial training has led us to a situation in corporate life where leaders know that they are meant to listen and have acquired techniques that simulate that human act (a tilt of the head, an open body language, an occasional nod or "hmm-hmm" to support the speaker, a studied effort to avoid offering their opinion, regardless of the fact that it is whirling around in their heads). They appear to listen to the content that people share with them superficially and without an ongoing commitment to true dialogue because creating the pretence of listening can be coached; however, they are not really hearing what is being said – the words, the ideas and experiences being conveyed, the emotion and feelings, the frustration and desire – because they are too busy pretending to listen.

Returning to the idea of the "sound of silence", it is this notion that seems to underpin the packaged practices that sit under the rubric of "mindfulness" in corporate settings. We are encouraged to listen to our breathing and the gurgling of our stomachs, our physical interiority and this attention to those physical sounds invites us to turn into ourselves mentally. Such an orientation underscores the crude individualism that undergirds neo-liberalism.

Similarly, a crashing noise will crowd out quieter sounds. In regard to the central issue for us of the interplay in corporate life between voice and silence, the old adage "Empty vessels make most noise" will be perhaps familiar to the reader.

References

ACAS, 2021. *Non disclosure agreements.* [Online] Available at: https://www.acas.org.uk/non-disclosure-agreements [Accessed 17 September 2021].

Arditi, D., 2020. The Voice: Non-disclosure agreements and the hidden political economy of reality TV. *Popular Communication,* 18(2), pp. 138–151.

Foucault, M., 1972/2009. *History of madness.* Abingdon: Routledge.

Foucault, M., 2004. *Abnormal: Lectures at the College de France 1974–1975.* New York: Picador.

Hamati-Ataya, I., 2015. False consciousness. In: M. T. Gibbons, ed. *The encyclopedia of political thought.* Chichester: Wiley, pp. 1225–1228.

Hegarty, P., 2015. Violent silence: Noise and Bataille's "Method of Meditation". In: J. Biles & K. L. Brintnall, eds. *Negative ecstasies: Georges Bataille and the study of religion.* New York: Fordham University Press, pp. 95–105.

Jackson, P. W., 1990. *Life in classrooms.* New York: Teachers College Press.

Kentli, F. D., 2009. Comparison of hidden curriculum theories. *European Journal of Educational Studies,* 1(2), pp. 83–88.

Lampmann, E., 2020. President Trump's contracts for silence. *University of Pennsylvania Journal of Law and Public Affairs,* 5(3), pp. 123–156.

Learmonth, M. & Morrell, K., 2019. *Critical perspectives on leadership: The language of corporate power*. New York: Routledge.

Li, H. L., 2004. Rethinking silencing silences. *Counterpoints*, 240, pp. 69–86.

Philp, R. M., 2003. Silence at our expense: Balancing safety and secrecy in non-disclosure agreements. *Seton Hall Law Review*, 33(845), pp. 845–880.

Picard, M., 1964. *The world of silence*. Chicago, IL: A Gateway Edition/Henry Regnery Company.

Riley, A., 2017. *King Flashypants and the toys of terror*. London: Hodder & Stoughton.

Schoeneborn, D. & Blaschke, S., 2014. The three schools of CCO thinking: Interactive dialogue and systematic comparison. *Management Communication Quarterly*, 28(2), pp. 285–316.

Weston, M. A., 2021. Buying secrecy: Non-disclosure agreements, arbitration, and professional ethics in the #MeToo era. *University of Illinois Law Review*, 2021(2), pp. 507–544.

4

THE MEANING OF SILENCE

Whereof one cannot speak, thereof one must be silent.
(Wittgenstein, 1922, p. 90)

Much is made of silence as an absence of sound. Of course, this is one way in which we understand the term, although the notion that we can create a circumstance in our everyday lives where no noise can be heard is surely illusory. Back in 1952, the minimalist composer John Cage premiered the piece **4′33″**. In the score for this piece the instrumentation is suggested to be as follows: 'Tacet, for any instrument or combination of instruments' (https://johncage.org/pp/John-Cage-Work-Detail.cfm?work_ID=17; accessed 20 September 2021). It consists of four minutes and 33 seconds of silence, although this takes place in a musical context with an instrument in place. In a commentary that forms part of this **4′33″** web page, a number of ideas are mooted as to what Cage was seeking to do.

It is suggested that it is a simple attempt to draw people's attention to the impossibility of soundlessness. This quote appears in a number of sources: '"There's no such thing as silence", Cage said, recalling the première.

DOI: 10.4324/9781003296683-6

"You could hear the wind stirring outside during the first movement. During the second, raindrops began pattering the roof, and during the third people themselves made all kinds of interesting sounds as they talked or walked out"' (Ross, 2017).

The year before this premiere at the Maverick Concert Hall, near Woodstock, NY, Cage had sought out the opportunity to immerse himself in an anechoic chamber at Harvard University, a space designed to shut out all sounds and create the conditions of silence. Cage's experience was contrary to this ambition:

> Constructed at the behest of the US army air forces during the second world war, the chamber's designers originally used it to find ways of combating the fatigue inflicted on bomber pilots by the immense noise of the piston engines then in use. Insulated against external noise by thick concrete on the outside, and lined on the inside with 20,000 fibreglass wedges to suppress echoes, the Harvard chamber was supposed to be one of the quietest places on Earth. Yet Cage claimed that he could still hear two distinct sounds, one high and one low, asserting that the former came from his nervous system and the latter from the circulation of his blood.   (Wragge-Morley, 2018)

An alternative perspective on the thinking behind **4′33″** is that it is a radical challenge to bourgeois notions of music and how audiences relate to it. Firstly, it reminds us of the way in which sound can only be understood in relation to silence; the tiny noteless gaps that exist within a musical composition are as much part of our experience of the piece as the melody or beat. Indeed, the melody is made up of both notes and silences in rich interaction – whilst the definition of a beat is that each tick of the metronome or snap of the snare drum is separated by that which both proceeds and follows it by silence. Hence, silence is not the absence of a beat, it is that which is integral to the formation of beat itself.

Secondly, it is possible to view **4′33″** as an open critique of the acculturated practice of listening to music in specific contexts. The audience attends in silence. In classical music, there are points at which it is permitted to applaud and many where it would be seen to be utterly infra dig were one so to do. A great deal of what passes under the rubric of classical music is solidly unidirectional, where the player plays and the listener listens. This is not an interactive cultural experience: it is an activity that hinges on one active partner and one passive. This stands in sharp contrast to the experience of "sing-songs" at family parties or in karaoke. At the risk of stretching the point this active–passive dynamic mirrors that which we see between leaders and followers, as we will explore in the next section of this chapter, where silence is also critical.

This draws us in a direction that raises two elements, both of which are crucial in moving towards an understanding of voice, silence, and power. Silence is not soundlessness, as **4′33″** makes it possible for us to appreciate. As Wittgenstein suggests in that final axiom from the *Tractatus* with which this section opened, it may make more sense to understand silence in terms of the specific aspect of speech, although not being equipped to speak about something does not automatically mean that we are silent. Wittgenstein is said to be arguing that language is ill-equipped to enable us to have knowledge of a vast array of things in our everyday… so, in light of this deficit, there are things about which we cannot know anything, and we would do well not to expend time trying to circumvent this logical conundrum.

What's important for us is the intimacy between speech and silence. Hence, we are talking about silence not as mere soundlessness but as something that has a rich interrelatedness with what we say, how we say it, and when we choose to say it. Hence, to return momentarily to what we hear when we hear music, it is possible to see it as an intimate and virtually seamless weaving of sound and silence, with each of those intertwined, the one generating and defining the other in a systemic fashion and vice versa. Silence is part of speech and speech is shaped (and gives shape to) silence.

Writing of their experience of arriving in an initially deserted mountain village, bereft at that moment of the tourists who frequent it, Voegelin (2010) describes the phenomenological shift that occurs as the soundscape changes from silence to the noise generated by holidaymakers arriving:

> Back in the snowy mountains the tourists start to arrive. The village fills up. One by one the chalet lights are turned on and gradually the noise levels rise. Now I can hear real people, rather than hyper-real monsters, walking about above my head. Their presence, their real noises, divorces me from my own sound making and listening. The tiny sounds hush away, underneath the carpet, back into the radiator, out through the chimney and down the icy drainpipes away into the snowy landscape.

> Now I do not bond with these tiny sounds anymore. They no longer combine with my own sonic presence in the bed of silence that covers and reflects us both.   (Voegelin, 2010, pp. 116–117)

This leads us to think of silence as an active element of our interlocution in social settings. Such silence can be said then to carry meaning, which somewhat inverts Wittgenstein's obtuse observation of silence deriving from a paucity at the heart of language to engage with the richness of the world. In this regard, Risser (2019) posits a three-fold schema. To begin with, he argues the following:

> The idea of a voiceless voice suggests that there can be a form of silence that is not simply the absence of sound. There is also the silence of keeping silent. This act of speech that keeps silent is silence as withdrawal of the word.   (p. 3)

Risser's second element speaks about silence giving voice to words. To do this, he argues,

> ...it must be able to intervene within speech, but do so not in the manner of a simple break as if it were simply a pause between words that amounts to nothing, as if silence were nothing. Rather, it has to intervene by being involved in the work of language as discourse, so as to aid the generation of meaning in language.   (Risser, 2019, p. 4)

To this end, he draws attention to the observations made previously in this chapter about the intimacy between silence and sound in music. Finally, and perhaps most contentiously, he discusses silence as preceding the word as in referring to a silent pause as a pregnant one.

This thinking is helpful to our work because it lifts silence from its relegated position as that which occurs when speaking is not taking place. Instead, it can be the active withdrawal of the word, which gives silence in the conversational context a deep linguistic meaning. Equally, we can also see that sound and silence interplay, not merely as the negation of one another but as an intimate connection that serves to generate capacity for meaning in dialogue. Hence, human silence is not merely the condition of being without sound; it is instead an implicit part of the complex to and fro between people as they use language to connect with one another and to make sense of the world.

To give some texture to this, John recalls the story of a professional acquaint-ance from many years back who worked in Human Resources, who we will refer to as Sue. Sue worked with an HR Director who was possessed of a par-ticularly mean streak and who – notwithstanding the various policy positions that they prescribed for and promoted in their organisation in terms of how staff should be respected and treated – was perfectly content to abuse their power as and when they took exception to someone. John was told by Sue that the HRD – let's call her Rita – had suddenly and for no apparent reason taken against a member of staff in their department, hereinafter referred to as Bob. Rather than manage this irrational dislike reflexively and bracket it off as a per-sonal glitch that should not enjoy a professional presence, Rita opted to indulge it openly, which was particularly difficult because Sue directly managed Bob.

In conversations with Rita, it was apparent that Sue was expected to find a way to get Bob out of the department, despite the fact that Sue had no concerns about Bob or his work. Soon, the dynamics of this vicious triangle became dramatically problematic: Rita pressured Sue to find ways to make Bob so miserable and uncomfortable that they would leave; at the same time, Rita was directly pursuing their vendetta against Bob, leaving the lat-ter feeling bullied and battered; and finally, Sue was meeting with Bob for management supervision and trying to manage the discomfiture that the latter faced pretty much on a daily basis.

In the course of this, Sue was obviously speaking with both Rita and Bob – and those exchanges involved both speech and silence, each freighted with meaning. In the latter regard, it was not an absolute soundlessness: it was instead a failure to say to Rita what ethically needed to be said. Hence, it was a silence that undergirded the superficial conversations between Sue and Rita. In that silence, though, Sue's voice was actually being heard. Not to say something is to be heard to be saying something, as was the case here. Sue's choice not expressly to say to Rita that they should cease and desist with the persecution of Bob meant that it wasn't a silence that was being heard, but an absence of what should have been said which actually "said" the contrary.

Meanwhile, Bob was exasperated by Rita's bullying pursuit – and deeply perplexed by Sue's silence in the face of something so unacceptable. Sue spoke to John about pleading with Bob to acquiesce to the absurd and unreasonable demands that Rita was making, even as she knew that this accommodation would not stop the harassment and its ultimate target, namely to force Bob to leave the department. But never once did Sue openly acknowledge that she felt sympathy for Bob; this was the second silence that went beyond a mere absence of words and instead spoke voiceless volumes in the middle of this grotesque muddle.

Sue, Rita, and Bob were all in communication with one another, of course, with varying degrees of hostility with respect to each of those three connective lines (S to B; B to R; R to S). But, amidst all of the words, we can see the withdrawal of words, silences that carried deep meaning in the flow of the dynamics between these three people. Importantly, it positions silence not as a personal withdrawal into silence but instead as the withdrawal of words that by their absence tacitly contribute to the conversational exchange. To underscore this notion, we borrow here from some powerful observations from someone who began to pay attention to silence in their life:

> It was in a large workplace meeting, the sort of meeting held in a stuffy, windowless room filled with too many bodies and chaired by an institutionally powerful man, that I first began to study silence. For as the silence in that packed room took root and spread – a silence fed and watered by the burble of the chair's meaningless utterances – I realised that there is such a thing as a silence comprised entirely of people refusing to say aloud what they are thinking. This was not the awkward silence which follows an inappropriate remark. This was a thick and muddy silence. It was a silence suffused with an intensely swampy acceptance that nothing could be said to stem the tide of fantasy-babble flowing from that man's mouth. Beneath his words our silence gathered and deepened. His world bore no relation to ours. How often does this happen? (Tatman, 2018, pp. 67–68)

Beyond this, the author identifies a number of other silences imbued with rich meaning as she goes about her personal and professional life. She speaks of the silence that emerges in the face of a truth that cannot be denied but which all the conversationalists desperately want to will away, which appears as '…a momentary gash in a conversation' (Tatman, 2018, p. 68). She offers insight into silences that descend when everything has been said but no common ground has appeared. And she offers the following insight, a powerful observation about our psychic relationship with silence:

> It is not possible for some of us to maintain our sanity if we do not retreat to our own silence on a regular basis. If we remain solely within our own silence for too long, we lose our sanity. This is not a nice conundrum. (Tatman, 2018, p. 69)

These explorations offer us a platform on which it is possible to build an understanding of silence in organisational life, something which has been at the forefront of our minds since the Covid crisis struck in earnest in March 2020. The pillars on which this platform is built can be summarised as follows:

1. Silence is not merely an absence of sound. It is never truly soundless
2. Silence is intimately related to speech rather than simply to noise
3. Silence and speech are seamlessly interrelated, with speech absorbing silence in order to shape its structure – like the gap between the stick hitting the drum in the creation of a rhythm – and silence speaking out in a number of contexts
4. The speech that appears out of voice or silence is intimately connected with power – the spaces in which we find the opportunity to connect with others, the way in which the power of others acts upon us and how at the same time we are a vehicle for power

References

Risser, J., 2019. Speaking from silence: On the intimate relation between silence and speaking. *Journal of Applied Hermeneutics*, Volume July, pp. 1–14.

Ross, A., 2017. *Searching for silence: John Cage's art of noise.* [Online] Available at: https://www.newyorker.com/magazine/2010/10/04/searching-for-silence [Accessed 20 September 2021].

Tatman, L., 2018. Silences. *Cultural Studies Review*, 24(2), pp. 67–74.

Voegelin, S., 2010. *Listening to noise and silence: Towards a philosophy of sound art.* New York: Continuum.

Wittgenstein, L., 1922. *Tractatus Logico-Philosophicus.* London: Kegan Paul, Trench, Trubner & Co Ltd.

Wragge-Morley, A., 2018. *What happened when I walked into the world's quietest place.* [Online] Available at: https://www.theguardian.com/commentisfree/2018/dec/24/what-happened-when-i-walked-into-the-worlds-most-silent-place [Accessed 20 September 2021].

5

SILENCE AS RITUAL

It is noteworthy how silence is seen as intrinsic to a number of rituals that have importance for human beings. Within organised religion one finds a commitment on the part of adherents to the practice of silence. For example, within the Christian tradition, the practice of silence is central to Quakerism, as the following explains:

> In Quaker worship there are no ministers or creeds. We first gather together in silence to quiet our minds – we don't have set hymns, prayers or sermons. In the stillness we open our hearts and lives to new insights and guidance. Sometimes we are moved to share what we discover with those present. We call this "ministry". We listen to what everyone has to say to find its meaning for us. Anyone can give ministry, including visitors. In the quiet we look for a sense of connection. This might be a connection with those around us, with our deepest selves, or perhaps with God. As we feel this sense of encounter grow stronger, we may begin to see the world and our relationships in a new way. Our worship may take us beyond our own thoughts and ideas to help us respond more creatively to the world around us.   (Quakers in Britain, 2021)

DOI: 10.4324/9781003296683-7

This suggests the embrace of silence as a positive act, wherein it is possible to become open to new ideas. Silence is seen as a stillness, whereas often when we are pushed into silence it generates for us a high degree of psychic turmoil and agitation. For example, we might consider the traditional English language idiom of "buttoning one's lip"; there is a strong sense of compelling force in this, even though we are said to be doing it to ourselves. The physical act of doing up a button, grappling with it to force it through a buttonhole, has a brutal edge when applied to the idea of fastening one's mouth together.

It is also suggested that the silence allows those sitting quietly to be better able to hear the divine, particularly in light of the one Biblical instance where God – whilst able to speak through the wind, fire, and earthquake – opts to approach the prophet Elijah using what is referred to as '...a still small voice' (1 Kings 19: 9–12). This is a salutary reminder to us all – and, in particular, to those in corporate positions where they are said to be leading – that to truly hear others, we need to silence ourselves. This means not just refuting the constant temptation to speak, to say things as others are seeking to say things, but to aim for a level of personal stillness that renders you receptive to actually hearing that other person as they find their way to give voice to their experiences, thoughts, and ideas.

Buddhism also has a strong attachment to silence as a religious practice. Indeed, some comparison has been made between Quakerism and Buddhism in this respect, with one writer observing that

> ...the identity of each community is defined partially through the emphasis each places on the existential and moral importance of silence. For each it is a moral as well as a religious imperative to discipline the ego in order that what we gloss as the numinous be realised. It is moral in the sense that only through such realisation can our true humanity be manifested: it is Good as well as good to be silent.   (Bell & Collins, 1998, p. 18)

Obviously, in Buddhism, silence is intimately related to meditative practices. Perhaps more interestingly, there is a discussion of the way in which the Buddha met a series of metaphysical questions with silence, actively refusing to offer responses to each of them – and the debate about "the silence of the Buddha" on these matters is an intricate one. Hence, one commentator on this topic suggests: 'Sometimes it is far more interesting to conjecture what a prophet might have meant if he [sic] had spoken than to listen to what he actually said' (Organ, 1954, p. 127). Again, for those who feel the need to lead, the refusal to speak when people patently expect you to respond but when you do not feel equipped so to do is a powerful act; it is a silence that opens a space for other opinions, should they choose to occupy it. And it reflects a humility sadly lacking in many of those who aim to lead. They fail to see that the prophet's standing is unaffected by their choice not to make some deep and meaningful response to everything that they are asked.

When it comes to Buddhist retreats it is often seen that every aspect of the time spent there is posited on silence – which also serves to create a meaningful linkage between seemingly disparate elements (Huszár, 2016). This runs the gamut from sharing meals together through to the practice of meditation. Similarly, silence is used in social situations to signify a collective acknowledgement of some shared quality. The biggest example of this in the UK is the two-minute silence that is "observed" (as the phrase goes) at 11 am on 11 November each year to mark the armistice at the end of the First World War.

Since the use of silence as commemoration first began back in 1919, the practice has expanded and is used in a wide range of circumstances. Indeed, there is now visible a counter-practice of commemoration, where an agreed short span of time is experienced not as a silence but as a round of applause. But when it comes to the former:

> The purpose of the silence is divided between remembering the past – the dead who sacrificed their lives – and marking the legacy of this sacrifice in the present [...] Thus not only was this reflection performed collectively, in public, but the object and the very structuring of the individual thoughts themselves were supposed to be co-ordinated in concert.   (Brown, 2012, p. 240)

The Foucauldian notion of a social technology drawn upon here can be used to interrogate other taken-for-granted practices, that have quickly become incorporated into the various contexts of the quotidian. Hence, Purser's (2019) critical interrogation of the ubiquitous practice of "mindfulness", an intensely individualised activity potentially attractive to a workforce that is heavily burdened by the expectations of them in their workplace and stressed by constant demands for faster and improved performance and productivity. As a practice it is ripped free from its religious grounding to offer something akin to spiritual succour to the overworked and overburdened. And it does not feel insignificant that this activity compels upon the practitioner a silence – their voice is quieted so that they might attend better to their interior state.

A collective and activist approach to the oppressive qualities of the modern workplace might well be built on voice or the active and collective withdrawal of voice, rather than a corporately approved form of individualised silence. But an activity like mindfulness – tucked away in a portfolio of support for people's corporate "health and wellbeing" – instructs people that remediation from the stresses of work lies within the gift of the individual and their personal relationships with voice and silence, rather than the collaborative clamour of people coming together in active dialogue.

To draw some threads together here, we need to recall that the composition of 4'33" by John Cage, discussed earlier, was preceded by him developing a deep and abiding interest in Zen Buddhism, the version of the religion that developed in the move from India through to China. Given his exposure to Zen at this time, it is argued that Cage began to explore and experiment with three key facets of the religion, which led him to a musical piece consisting of silence, namely '…the honouring of all things, the refusal of intention, and the embracing of the unpredictable' (Timmerman, 2009, p. 45).

This reinforces the idea of silence as a practice that is not merely the absence of sound, a noiselessness that arises where speech is absent. It is present in a range of formal activities of humankind – and so has value not merely as a negative to the positive of speech. With this in mind, we can see silence as part of our repertoire of ways of communicating. This means silence can be a choice that we make as a means of saying something.

We alluded earlier to the way in which silence can assert itself as a part of what is sometimes called the "talking cure", that is any psychodynamic therapeutic relationship where a person seeks to make sense of their experiences and feelings about their life in the company of someone who assumes some professional position in relation to this dialogue. This intense connection links someone assuming the role of healer and someone who, often by their own definition, needs healing. It is argued that power is structurally implicit within that relationship and so would be better talked about explicitly (Totton, 2018), while others focus on a Foucauldian interpretation of the ways in which subjectivity is crafted in relation to power/

knowledge, with psychotherapy being a site where such exploration might take place (Brown, 2007) or, indeed, where resistance might manifest itself (Guilfoyle, 2005).

This theoretical framing takes us to another site of interest in developing a panoramic perspective on voice and silence. As we note, the interplay between these two aspects of connecting and communicating is crucial in the therapeutic consulting room. But, in terms of filling a perceived gap in the Freudian schema on the precise mechanism of repression in the unconscious, upon which so much of the theory is built, it is argued that it is through speech, specifically where we stop ourselves speaking, that repression occurs. Hence, it is argued that: 'No other species has language, and no other species needs to develop habits of repression. This is no quirk of fate, but language is fundamentally both expressive and repressive' (Billig, 1999, p. 72).

In a practical sense, this can be understood when we compare how repression in Freud's work sits at the crucial juncture between instinct and civilisation, a delicate intersection between desire and the morality that arises to contain it. This dynamic can be said also to be present in speech, in regard to the way in which our communication depends on a degree of politeness: we are eager to say it how it is but recognise that the way in which we talk to one another is heavily structured. From here, it can be observed that polite as opposed to uncontrolled speech takes longer and involves the effort of restraint in terms of managing what can and cannot be said – and how it gets expressed (Billig, 1999, p. 91).

Notwithstanding the extent to which this construct plays a part in psychoanalytic theory and practice, which is the sort of metanarrative that needs to be viewed through the postmodern perspective of incredulity (Lyotard, 1984, p. xxiv), these observations helpfully open up the idea of how we manage our voice and embrace silence as both strategy and tactic in day-to-day life.

References

Bell, S. & Collins, P., 1998. Religious silence: British Quakerism and British Buddhism compared. *Quaker Studies*, 3(1), pp. 1–26.

Billig, M., 1999. *Freudian repression: Conversation creating the unconscious.* Cambridge: Cambridge University Press.

Brown, C., 2007. Situating knowledge and power in the therapeutic alliance. In: C. Brown & T. Augusta-Scott, eds. *Narrative therapy: Making meaning, making lives.* Thousand Oaks, CA: Sage, pp. 3–22.

Brown, S. D., 2012. Two minutes of silence: Social technologies of public commemoration. *Theory & Psychology*, 22(2), pp. 234–252.

Guilfoyle, M., 2005. From therapeutic power to resistance? Therapy and cultural hegemony. *Theory & Psychology*, 15(1), pp. 101–124.

Huszár, O., 2016. The role of silence at the retreats of a Buddhist community. *KOME – An International Journal of Pure Communication Inquiry*, 4(2), pp. 59–73.

Lyotard, J.-F., 1984. *The postmodern condition: A report on knowledge.* Manchester: Manchester University Press.

Organ, T. W., 1954. The silence of the Buddha. *Philosophy East and West*, 4(2), pp. 125–140.

Purser, R. E., 2019. *McMindfulness: How mindfulness became the new capitalist spirituality.* London: Repeater Books.

Quakers in Britain, 2021. *How Quakers worship.* [Online] Available at: https://www.quaker.org.uk/about-quakers/our-faith/how-quakers-worship [Accessed 22 September 2021].

Timmerman, P., 2009. Uncaged: Buddhism, John Cage and the freeing of the world. *Canadian Journal of Buddhist Studies*, Issue 5, pp. 39–57.

Totton, N., 2018. Power in the therapeutic relationship. In: R. Tweedy, ed. *The political self: Understanding the social context for mental illness.* Abingdon: Routledge, pp. 29–42.

6

SELF-SILENCING

There are inevitably times when we choose to "bite our lip". Civility and the essential to and fro of social intercourse demands that we consider what we say and when we say it. We have all come across people who introduce themselves by explaining that 'I say it like it is', which invariably means that their speaking is just about them and they have no concern as to how what they pronounce might be experienced by others. It is a crude declaration of aggressive linguistic individualism, whereas our view is that the individual can only find and define themselves by their presence and agency in a collective context. One needs to find a way of being in that context, rather than antagonising those around you who – through the dialogue – will enable you to embrace your personhood.

However, these observations notwithstanding, the phrase about biting one's lip underscores the violence required to stop our voice from bursting out when we pressingly feel we have something to say. To invert and revise the phrase, restraint can often be forced upon us, and in that situation, we can find ourselves being instructed to "button our lip" or "zip it".

DOI: 10.4324/9781003296683-8

This offers linguistic insight into how silencing ourselves takes considerable effort and – in one way or another – will be painful to do.

We can no doubt all think of experiences where, on reflection, we concluded that we should have said something. So much in our daily exchanges with others goes unsaid and this effect is particularly pronounced in organisational settings, even where the leadership there is seeking to force a climate where people are actively and explicitly encouraged to speak up. This prompt rings particularly hollow where the conduct of those leaders and the culture of the organisation in which we find ourselves seem to countermand this position. This is where we find corporate leaders 'instructing' people to speak up, which is a faintly ridiculous position in which to find oneself – as a leader or as part of the workforce.

The social nature of some of that opting to be silent – particularly when viewed through the prism of gender – is offered in Jack's (1991) exploration of the relationship between women silencing themselves and depressive illness. Elsewhere, this author posits that

> ...cognitive schemas about how to create and maintain safe, intimate relationships lead women to silence certain feelings, thoughts, and actions. This self-silencing contributes to a fall in self-esteem and feelings of a "loss of self" as a woman experiences, over time, the self-negation required to bring herself into line with schemas directing feminine social behaviour.
> (Jack & Dill, 1992, pp. 97–98)

The original work in this field built on the key notion of the role of women with respect to sustaining specifically romantic relationships. But there are others who are of the mind that this self-silencing – and its deleterious health impacts – arises out of women's efforts to maintain all social relations, not just the romantic ones, and their absorption into the image of femininity that assumes dominance in our wider social context (Maji & Dixit, 2019). This speaks, then, to Butler's (1999) idea of women having to perform femininity to a script not of their making.

It is not our intention here to allow men to colonise this very specific idea of women assuming a social role that requires them to silence themselves and hence to adversely affect their well-being. This is a particular phenomenon that arises out of the gender relations in our society. Nevertheless, there does seem a possibility to offer a parallel in corporate life, where the "good employee" is expected to remain silent in the face of what is tacitly taken to be the overall "interest" of the firm. A performativity is discernible that defines that "good employee", a subject that emerges from the mesh of power that resides in the workplace. The "good employee" – docile, engaged, conscientious, responsible, attentive, organisationally aware, dedicated to the firm's vision, purpose, mission, and values – represents a normalcy that, in turn, guides us to a notion of Otherness.

We have highlighted the notion of self-silencing here, something that we make an individual choice to do but often within a context that constrains and controls our free will and our capacity to exercise agency. But there are other ways of thinking about voice and silence in a more social and connected sense. One of those is the idea of the spiral of silence, which is of particular significance when we think about speaking up in organisational contexts.

Spiral of silence

John recently had a conversation with two people about the way in which corporate constraints make unethical people of us all. For his interlocutors the tension arose for them as people of colour experiencing very specific negativity in meetings to their contributions, an experience that was seemingly unnoticed but certainly unacknowledged by the white participants. Outside of the meeting the black and minority ethnic attenders spoke about it, collectively discussing the way in which what felt to be very individual experiences were reassuringly visible to them as a group.

The conversation took a rich turn, as they spoke about how we are all trained to bracket off things we know we should speak out about, hiding behind the veneer of professionalism expected in any given context. There was a discussion about how we are all tacitly aware of how we should appear and behave in various organisational settings. As well as being managed by others in the workplace, we actively manage ourselves, reminding us again that power does not merely act upon us but inserts itself within us. Indeed, it is perhaps at its least pernicious when it is experienced directly and between agents in a hierarchy. More perniciously, power inveigles itself into our interior lives and shapes our ways of being while claiming not to be present. This, of course, challenges the corporate narrative which innocently advocates that we bring our whole selves to work while always being true to our authentic identity.

Hearing from John about this exchange reminded Mark that his subjectivity is determined and defined by power, including the wash of power in which we find ourselves at work. The respectful professional person is ceaselessly mindful of context and hierarchy; they are complaisant but in reality are constrained by power as it pulses through the capillaries of the space wherein we rub along with others in order to do our work. How do we find the chance to speak up when the subtle tentacles of internalised power reach up and down our embodied subjectivity largely unnoticed and subtly strangle our voices?

Mark was acutely mindful at this juncture of something that he had been slowly acknowledging as he engaged in his own practice in a critical and reflexive way. He had spent over 25 years of his career in workplace development encouraging people to apply organisational awareness and to hone their political skills so as to navigate that context. He had, in essence, urged them to play the game, in order to blend in better with the beige and grey that dominates corporate décor and thinking. Inadvertently, he had acted as a conduit for the very power that he seeks to expose and critique.

Others have sought to make sense of how people find themselves in the midst of situations where they decline to speak out and become immersed in a collectively determined silence. For example, there is a serious body of work arising out of political attitudes and how their outward expression is constrained by what is called "public opinion" (Noelle-Neumann, 1993). The crucial underpinning of this theory of the spiral of silence relates to the way in which we all – as individuals who crave social connection – interpret our chances of isolation in terms of outwardly expressing opinions that we hold. Our calculations in this regard are manifold and include: how we subtly assess the deployment of opinion and trends relating to it; how we manage our voice in terms of calculating present and future dominance of opinion; how we are likely to assess dominance in the present to predict dominance in the future (Noelle-Neumann, 1974, p. 45).

One anecdotal example gives richness and texture to these notions. Working as she did in Germany, Noelle-Neumann spotted one of her students wearing a badge for the Christian Democratic party. In conversation, the student announced that she was not a supporter but wanted to experience what it felt like to wear it. Yet when they met a few hours later, the student had removed the party favour, declaring that it had been too awful an experience. This led to the following observation, which brings to life an insight that lies at the heart of the spiral of silence idea:

> Followers of the Social Democrats and of the Christian Democrats might be equal in numbers, but they were far from equal in energy, enthusiasm, or willingness to express and display their convictions. Only Social Democratic buttons and emblems appeared publicly, so it was no wonder that the relative strengths of the two parties were incorrectly assessed.
>
> (Noelle-Neumann, 1993, p. 4)

Mark spent much of his 20s ridiculously festooned in badges, pithy declarative demands for "Jobs Not Bombs", "Benn for Deputy", and (latterly) "Defend the Bromley 10". Undergirding this very public announcement of his politics was the implicit assumption of the rightness of his positions; when you feel you're on the right side of history and the direction of socio-economic progress is pre-determined, one feels moved to find every opportunity to give voice to your opinions. But it is almost certainly the case that not one person that Mark knew, or met in passing, at this time changed their attitudes in response to his sloganistic badge-wearing, other than perhaps to decide that they would keep their own opinions to themselves so as to avoid conflict.

On one hand the idea of public opinion can be considered as the liberated citizen making informed judgements about political matters. But it can also be interpreted as a form of social control, where it is not about dialogue or reasoned exchange but rather is about a deployment of power, wherein one side might be seen to be able to threaten the other with isolation (Noelle-Neumann, 1993, p. 228). This, in turn, directs us to a disturbing conclusion, in terms of our perspective on voice, silence, and – indeed – activism:

> Voicing the opposite opinion, or acting in public accordingly, incurs the danger of isolation. In other words, public opinion can be described as the dominating opinion which compels compliance of attitude and behaviour in that it threatens the dissenting individual with isolation, the politician with loss of popular support. Thus the active role of starting a process of public opinion formation is reserved to the one who does not allow himself [sic] to be threatened with isolation
>
> (Noelle-Neumann, 1974, p. 44)

To challenge the common place and the taken-for-granted is an individual and ethical act in itself; to do so by offering a counterpoint or complete alternative is to embrace activism. To do that as a lone individual is to risk being categorised as a **problem**, which needs to be managed, or as a **maverick**, who can be subtly incorporated so as to allow the corporate setting to appear more tolerant than it actually is. Such presence and its perception in organisational life is cross-hatched, of course, with relations of power: whether we are embraced as an amusing maverick or "othered" as a problem for the company in which we work is invariably not to do with the behaviour itself, which can often be the same in both instances – but rather by who is behaving in this way. All of this means that we are back at the Foucauldian notion of *parrhesia*, a commitment to speak out regardless of the negative impact that such a pronouncement is likely to have on one as an individual (Foucault, 2019). But a lone voice has to sound so that other silenced voices can find the courage to speak up – and to join together as an active collective to disrupt the dominant discourse – and offer an alternative to displace it.

Silence, judgement, and action (pluralistic ignorance)

If we acknowledge that we slip into spirals of silence as part of an anxiety about isolation, we also need to take into account the communicative environment in which we find ourselves. As explained above, we individually make interior judgements about speaking out or keeping silent in terms of myriad tiny calculations of our context. There is, however, a further argument that intimates that we are likely to consistently misinterpret the strength of dominant positions and thence to assume our perspective to be subaltern, peripheral, and the opinion of a minority.

Here, we are in the realm of what is called "pluralistic ignorance". This is closely linked with the notion of "bystander effect", wherein it is observed that the more people who witness an incident, the less likely anyone of those individuals will intervene in the situation in order to offer assistance (Darley & Latane, 1968; Latane & Darley, 1968). Beyond this the following offers a helpful and tightly drafted description: 'Pluralistic ignorance is a situation that occurs when an individual has a kind of attitude in public that is different from his individual beliefs because he mistakenly believes that most of his peers have an opposite opinion' (Mendes et al., 2017). This complicity with a consensus that does not exist serves to render us silent at precisely the time when our voices are perhaps most needed.

While the spiral of silence foregrounds the human concern around isolation, the idea of pluralistic ignorance posits the idea that this concern is often completely without foundation. Indeed, the anxiety around being ostracised is so profound that we are content to labour under the assumption that we are out of step and hence remain silent. Worse than that is the idea that we will actively and publicly subscribe to – and sometimes espouse – the position that we assume is held by those around us, even though we personally take an entirely contrary view. It is not difficult to connect the dots to follow the line to see where this has led and might lead again. For evil to flourish, after all, simply requires the good to stay their hand.

This internalisation is important but is amplified where the practical evidence of the enforcement is visible. The question being: '[I]s it possible that, ..., groups can become trapped in a self-enforcing equilibrium in which they pressure one another in order to cover up their own private doubts?' (Willer, et al., 2009, p. 452). The conclusion from this research was that: 'The theory of false enforcement goes beyond herd behaviour and pluralistic ignorance to explain why. False beliefs become much more stable when backed up by expectations of enforcement that are confirmed when someone deviates' (Willer, et al., 2009, p. 482).

To our mind, the false enforcement of unpopular norms is merely an element of the collective silence that swirls around what can and cannot be said. A visible act of reinforcement may be undertaken by a human agent enmeshed in this regime of voice and silence, actively compelling others to toe a line to which they themselves do not subscribe and secretly perhaps oppose. This is the second layer of internalisation, a particularly pernicious absorption of the overall regime and its active reinforcement.

References

Butler, J., 1999. *Gender trouble: Feminism and the subversion of identity.* 2nd ed. New York: Routledge.

Darley, J. M. & Latane, B., 1968. Bystander intervention in emergencies: Diffusion of responsibility. *Journal of Personality and Social Psychology,* 8(4), pp. 377–383.

Foucault, M., 2019. Parrhesia: Lecture at the University of Grenoble May 18, 1982. In: H. Fruchard & D. Lorenzini, eds. *Discourse and truth & Parrhesia*. Chicago, IL: University of Chicago Press, pp. 1–38.

Jack, D. C., 1991. *Silencing the self: Women and depression*. Cambridge, MA: Harvard University Press.

Jack, D. C. & Dill, D., 1992. The silencing of self scale. *Pyschology of Women Quarterly*, Issue 16, pp. 97–106.

Latane, B. & Darley, J. M., 1968. Group inhibition of bystander intervention. *Journal of Personality and Social Psycholoty*, 10(3), pp. 215–221.

Maji, S. & Dixit, S., 2019. Self-silencing and women's health: A review. *International Journal of Social Psychiatry*, 65(1), pp. 3–13.

Mendes, A., Lopez-Valeiras, E. & Joao Lunkes, R., 2017. Pluralistic ignorance: Conceptual framework, antecedents and consequences. *Intangible Capital*, 13(4), pp. 781–804.

Noelle-Neumann, E., 1974. The spiral of silence: A theory of public opinion. *Journal of Communication*, Issue Spring, pp. 43–51.

Noelle-Neumann, E., 1993. *The spiral of silence: Public opinion – our social skin*. 2nd ed. Chicago, IL: University of Chicago Press.

Willer, R., Kuwabura, K. & Macy, M. W., 2009. The false enforcement of unpopular norms. *American Journal of Sociology*, 115(2), pp. 451–490.

7

SILENCE AT WORK

Silenced. We fear those who speak about us who do not speak to us and with us. We know what it is like to be silenced. We know that the forces that silence us because they never want us to speak differ from the forces that say speak, tell me your story. Only do not speak in the voice of resistance. Only speak from that space in the margin that is a sign of deprivation, a wound, an unfulfilled longing. Only speak your pain.

(hooks, 1989, p. 23)

The workplace represents the key arena where the interplay of voice, silence, and power is most pronounced currently. This is to do with the ideological commitment in most corporate settings encompassing the idea that the workforce is actively encouraged to speak up, whilst the actual experience is that voices remain very tightly managed. The research that John has undertaken with colleagues over recent years focuses on how it feels to speak up – and what it means to listen up (Reitz & Higgins, 2017; Reitz et al., 2019). One effect of this is to make leaders in senior positions of organisations acutely aware of their responsibility to be seen to be listening. Corporate

DOI: 10.4324/9781003296683-9

leaders are expected to open up their office doors; hold town hall meetings; and walk the floor, just as they have been told – so as to be in a position to tilt their heads and nod encouragingly in the ways that create the illusion that they are genuinely hearing what is said, by whom, and how.

The pandemic threw into sharp relief for many the contrast between what leaders in organisations say that they are doing in terms of their listening compared to what is actually being said by the voices of those who deliver the business of the business, which seems to go largely unheard. In at least one session Mark ran for staff to discuss their positive and negative experiences through the pandemic and how power had manifested itself, respondents whilst largely focused on the positive also spoke about "Receiving directives with no conversation". There was a resurgence of judgemental and discriminative behaviour amongst managers, the emergence of bullying and coercion, and the observation that managers became more reactive, showing a tendency to say one thing and be seen to do another.

This should not be a surprise. The workforce in healthcare faced an unprecedented circumstance in the modern age, one for which no level of planned preparedness could truly leave us prepared. Indeed, the hubris of trying to plan everything organisationally to the nth degree finally met its nemesis when it collided with a microscopic bundle of insentient RNA. Whether one was working in an intensive care setting or from an office where you endeavoured to coordinate a collective effort, none of us were ready for what hove into view in March 2020 and proceeded to unfold in ways we could not have imagined. As the Cynefin Framework seeks ceaselessly to remind us, trying to manage simple circumstances is in a different order of practice to trying to find one's way through complexity and indeed chaos (Snowden & Boone, 2007). Increasingly, there is a literature emerging that makes clear the ways in which Cynefin can be applied to clinical practice – which then makes it slightly easier to make connections between the framework and management practice in healthcare (Gray, 2017; Lane et al., 2021).

Elsewhere, we are less inclined to be so understanding and forgiving. The respondents talked about greater leadership visibility – but this was seen to emerge from their embrace of command and control as a blanket response to every managerial challenge that crossed their desks during the crisis. Others contested the idea of improved visibility, arguing that remote working had diminished the felt presence of senior leadership, while line managers were more evident in the day-to-day of the workplace, whilst those at more senior levels seemed even more distanced from the actuality of the organisation. Others made observations that those with power stopped listening to what was being said in this context, which presupposes that they were hearing what was being said in the first place.

Our view on the basis of all of the recent conversations we've had with individuals and groups in a variety of contexts is that the workplace has developed into a space where voice and silence, alongside listening and actually hearing, are in intensified tension. This is borne out by research undertaken on how people felt about leadership in the healthcare system during the pandemic. This included the observation that, while voices were invited in, the clamour of noise coming from the top of the organisations meant that they could only contribute through formalised methods, such as 'How are you feeling today? Please click here' (Bristol Leadership & Change Centre, 2021).

Here's how overall we feel all of this is shaping up.

Silence is the default

There is an overwhelming expectation that people will hold their tongues and not speak unless and until they are spoken to. The only voices in such circumstances come from above and echo down, layer upon layer, until finally absorbed by the floor of the organisation. A colleague of John's tells the story of a manager she had who would literally scream red-faced at all of the people in their virtual meetings. At one point, having shouted in cruel and crude terms at everyone in a meeting, he was seen to bury his scarlet face in his hands and shake his head. He belittled staff and could not even stir himself to generate the illusion of modern staff engagement. For those who worked with and to him, the expectation was that there would be silence until such time as he bellowed at someone to speak. This story is not historical; it was happening over the course of the very recent past. And we're not convinced that it's all that exceptional.

In another similar instance, we heard of someone publicly welcomed by a senior leader to an online meeting, after they had electronically raised their hand to contribute to the discussion taking place. This staff member felt daunted by the circumstance; they told us that they had joined the meeting to represent their team and had no intention of contributing. However, a topic unexpectedly came up about which they personally knew a great deal. The welcome offered by the senior leader actually came as an acknowledgement of the staff member's raised hand, although that recognition was folded into a conversational power-play in which the senior leader said that they would come to the staff member in just a moment after they themselves took another opportunity to add to the conversation which was already dominated by their voice. Here, voice seemed to be welcoming voice, but – in so doing – was putting the latter into silence until such time as it was invited back.

A colleague of the staff member was also on this call. After the meeting they expressed exasperation and irritation at the fact that – when the staff member did finally get to speak – the senior leader allowed them just five words before interrupting. The colleague knowing the habit of this leader, took the time to count them. In this case the speaker kept going, ignoring the interruption. We gather that the staff member took a chance, disregarded this intervention, and opted to speak over the senior leader, who had already seized a great deal of the airtime. However, we would posit that this persistent pattern of over-speaking by the senior leader, whilst not quietening the staff member's voice, had – from the perspective of the audience, taking their cue from the verbal ebb and flow and power in play in this context – silenced them.

There are silences up and down any workplace

The organisations in which we work can be said to have four types of presence, which can be described thus:

Physical

From the portico and parquet of some corporate spaces to the glass and steel stacks soaring into the skies of the commercial centres of cities like London, we find ourselves enmeshed in spaces and places whence it is possible to draw and interpret meaning. In an analysis of the design and presence of court houses, for example, it is asserted that,

> The architecture of the courtroom stakes out the territorial boundaries of judicial power. The idea of the court as conceptually 'open' co-exists with

a clearly enforced spatial closure. At the same time as court architecture produces a rigid spatial segmentarity, it frames a space wherein the legal imperative involves a rigid separation of truth from falsehood, reason from madness and so on.   (Dovey, 2010, p. 128)

It would seem logical to assume that the physical environment where we work is a form that follows its corporate function – which is also a cultural text rich with meaning about what it means to be in that building and working there. In this it impresses itself upon us in order to shape our organisational selves – both accidentally and knowingly, as thinking around organisational management embraces architectonics (Kornberger & Clegg, 2004) – with a strong emphasis on its role in change management (van Marrewijk, 2009) and in those hubristic efforts around culture change (Skogland & Hansen, 2017) about which senior leaders get so animated and enthused.

One of the reasons that managers at the top of organisations have been so eager to march people back into the office workspace in light of the Covid-19 pandemic – generating what one research group has described as an "executive-employee disconnect" (Future Forum, 2021) – is precisely because it allows for greater surveillance of that workforce. In particular it also enables a moulding of the individuals in a space and time that they occupy that is very different to the notion of home. Working at home has the potential to remind us that – existentially, as human beings – it is home that truly matters and where we derive genuine "health and well-being" (as opposed to those corporate efforts at the remediation of the pressures and stresses of corporate life that are so familiar these days) …and that it is work that is the burden that denies the opportunity to spend our lives alongside family and friends.

Human

Our experience of working during a pandemic has brought to the fore the notion that companies are less about location and more to do with connection. The way in which we collectively mobilised key elements of technology to create communities of connection is noteworthy. We recognise the shortcomings of this remote working for some people but, at the same time, celebrate and preserve the fluidity of that moment. It disrupted taken-for-granted ideas about where business gets done and how people can connect to do it. It reminded us of the importance of our working together collectively – and the need to rethink getting things done in society. It left the very idea of corporate leadership contested.

Once we let go of the idea that a firm has to have a location, then we are perhaps better able to take on board that vital distinction between organising and organisation (Weick, 1969). Organisation is the rigid structuring that accretes around the dynamic, organising activity of people coming together to get things done. Organisational structures can be argued to inhibit the productive qualities of that human connecting – and hence inadvertently prevent timely and legitimate change from occurring organically. Meanwhile leaders who sit at the apex of that formal construction seek to demand change through organisation rather than enlivening organising (Tsoukas & Chia, 2002).

It seems self-evident that the critical means by which organising takes place is through the connection and conversation that arises between human agents. And it is pertinent to highlight here that there are instances where organising is having to work against and through the constraints of the organisation. In such circumstances voice and silence have particular relevance, for example where the rigidity of organisation serves to mute voice, so it may find other channels of expression. In the course of the pandemic, as we sat on Zoom or Teams calls, how many of us spoke with one another via WhatsApp groups that arose organically as our remote working developed? How many of us were in those virtual gatherings, toggling between WhatsApp channels and making observations and critiques as to what was happening in the main meeting? For many people, WhatsApp replaced the water cooler as the place where people spoke to one another under the organisational radar.

Structural

Organisations and their leaderships are transfixed by structure. Executives and their assistants devote much of their energies to the epiphenomena of organisational life, meaning those ethereal notions of vision, mission, purpose, strategy and values. They also devote themselves to the practice of reorganisation, badged as "transformation" so as to make it sound more rational and progressive, which is considerably more impactful on the day-to-day lives of people than the fluff of cookie-cutter corporate values and endless "visioning". This focus on structure and the change associated with it can be contextualised thus:

> The early approaches and theories to organisational change management suggested that organisations could not be effective or improve performance if they were constantly changing. It was argued that people need routines to be effective and able to improve performance. However, it is now argued that it is of vital importance to organisations that people are able to undergo continuous change.   (Todnem By, 2005)

It would seem that this is an area of focus for many occupying significant management roles because it is the most mutable aspect of company life and is imbued with the idea that it can have a causal effect. The production of an organisation chart creates the practical categorisation of the business and directly impacts the people that sit in the roles that constitute this pattern. To that extent it suggests a linearity, with action (a) generating outcome (b), reassuring people that the world is both plannable and manageable. However, the success here derives purely from the internal logic of this approach, although the practicalities of this type of endless structural fiddling are to involve the people in a churn of where they fit, what they do, who they do it with, and what reward accrues from that engagement.

Alongside these instrumental justifications for senior managers' enthusiasm for this type of activity, there is a persuasive case to be made that the embrace of change as a core contemporary management practice is also significantly ideological:

> Despite all assurances by the proponents of new public management that the new agenda is solely about rational strategic responses and "technical" aspects, organisational politics imply otherwise. Strategic change initiatives, their formulation and implementation are much about influence, power and control.   (Diefenbach, 2007, p. 135)

In light of this assertion and research into change management in higher education – this author lays out a series of critical observations that serve to make sense of the enthusiasm for change management and its intimate relationship with managerialism. This begins with corporate leaders presenting the change they envisage as a necessity rather than a choice, in response to what they perceive to be an altered business environment (Diefenbach,

2007, p. 138). This chimes with the first three management myths that we recently observed constraining management thinking, namely that: all is fixable; only perfection will do; and there is one true path to follow so as to achieve that state (Cole & Higgins, 2022).

Beyond the leadership assertion that "there is no alternative" (TINA), Diefenbach argues that change managers create an atmosphere of fear wherein the environment in which their organisation exists is presented to the workforce (and perhaps to shareholders) as inhospitable and dangerous. This creates an enemy without – and those within the boundaries of the company who contest this notion and resist the change quickly become badged as an enemy within (Diefenbach, 2007, p. 138). Both TINA and the label "enemy within" were successfully politically mobilised by Thatcherism, setting the terms of public debate for decades to follow.

Lastly, resistance is then seen as a justification for the proposed change being needed. This requires a more abrasive intervention into the workforce so as to persuade them of the rationale and the practicalities of the change. Indeed, the whole exercise – from identifying the business reasons for the change through to using managerialist processes to "make the case" in the face of suspicion and reluctance – reinforces the hierarchy within organisations, with only senior leaders truly equipped to navigate these treacherous waters. Resistance in this schema is not seen as potentially a sensible reaction, instead those who object to the change are Othered and sometimes pathologised, so that they can be fixed. And, off the back of all of this, comes the final stipulation, namely that those who reject this change management exercise must now either "adapt or go" (Diefenbach, 2007, p. 138).

Considering all of the above, it seems reasonable to conclude that the structural aspect of organisation is a vital space in which power is asserted and subtly enforced through the warp and weft of leadership practice, despite the sheen that overlays that in terms of engagement, involvement and empowerment.

Systemic

Whenever we see some elegantly designed diagram that notionally maps the structure of an organisation, we are immediately mindful of two things. First, we feel acutely aware of the titles, positions, and possibly pay cheques of those who populate this imaginary space – and hence conscious of the hierarchy from which some seek solace and others feel oppressed. This first glance at the structure hints at the deployment of power – and who is meant to be doing what in the company.

Second, notwithstanding all that we feel able to read off from this crude schematic, we recognise that beneath this scaffold, which locates people in a fictionalised representation of their corporate world and how that construct fixes them by title and status, there is the ordinary reality of the system where people are interconnecting (or organising) to get work done. In our experience of speaking with people working in the NHS during the Covid-19 pandemic, we have frequently heard how the obstacles, barriers and conduits that were structurally mandated simply evaporated as the inter-connected social system asserted itself to get things done in a timely and innovative fashion. For example, one clinician spoke about how patient transfers had previously often taken three days to organise, whereas – at the start of the pandemic – their willingness to engage with people as people, rather than worrying about positional status, meant transfers could safely be expedited in half a day.

Drawing together these threads

Our purpose in offering these observations about how we see organising and organisation is to open a space to consider how these various elements might intersect and overlap. No one perspective should be privileged, although a good deal of so-called "management science" focuses almost exclusively on the structural, while leadership studies endeavours to colonise the human with its own particular take on relational dynamics. The rolling interconnectedness of these four ways of envisaging organisation, the Physical, Structural, Human, and Systemic, nudges us towards being able to think about how voice and silence are present in these various configurations.

John recalls speaking to someone charged with producing a monthly report for their company board. In light of this, they were expected to attend each of the board meetings, albeit alongside their line manager. At the meetings they were expected to place themselves in a physical location – the Board Room – and to position themselves (often literally) alongside the person who sat above them in the organisational structure.

At this intersection of the physical (a corporate space imbued with positional power, indicating perhaps the tip of the hierarchical pyramid) and the structural – appearing before the senior leadership, sitting alongside the person who manages them, and enmeshed in the overbearing processes, procedures and practices that cluster under the rubric of "governance" – this person explained to John that they were not allowed to speak at the meeting about the report that they prepared. This privilege was preserved for the person who sat above them (structurally) and alongside them (physically, at this point).

This person producing the report was seen to be a mere instrument, the "human resource" deployed to produce the material that the "great and the good" looked over in their regular meetings. They were always present yet constantly silent in the course of the conversations (such as they were) that took place. This serves as a grotesque reminder of what gets taken for granted in corporate life and that it's not simply about an overall organisational climate around voice and silence when it comes to who gets heard and who doesn't. Instead, we need to recall that voice and silence shifts and changes over time, depending on the configuration of elements that constitute what we think of as organisation.

Elsewhere people come together unintentionally and create a situation where voice is heard: the kitchen or the coffee point in the corporate office block, where people congregate for one purpose and find scope for another; the smoking point, where people find themselves thrown together almost as a pariah group. Such exchanges in these physical locations can be seen to be negative, with the discussions not just running on what might be called small talk but encompassing rumour or gossip. In the latter respect, it is possible to see this as a more positive element of organisational discourse than the term ordinarily is seen to imply:

> Gossip is a type of storytelling discourse that exists in the "unmanaged spaces" of organizations and is a form of emergent story. It is a way of talking—and by talking we mean written or spoken texts—that enables the communication of emotions, opinions, beliefs, and attitudes about the experience of work and organizational life. (Michelson et al., 2010, p. 373)

There is also a negative side to gossip, where people from particular groups are Othered and ostracised by its action (Carrim, 2016). However, these liminal spaces – part of the workplace but separate from the work – are also sites of vocal resistance, which is expressed informally and through a vernacular. These are voices leaders do not want to hear, because what is being said there will not have gone through corporate rinsing, sanitising the sentiments. Here the voice is being heard unbidden in a location that is occupied by the human agents that make up the organisation. And some of the exchanges that take place in this context may also serve to encourage more effective connection around the system that actually gets the work done.

Senior leaders quite possibly secretly recognise that little of what they do and for which they are paid has any meaningful impact on the way in which the work of their company gets done. And some will recognise that effectiveness arises out of this type of systemic connectivity, over which they have little direct control. So, we do find the more instrumentalist of that less blinkered group trying to urge their people back to the office, so as to reinstate the kitchen, cooler, lift, lobby and smoking point as connective nodes – not realising that human agents are prone to seek out that sort of network for themselves, even in a virtual context. As ever with leadership practice, the moment that you call out some notion deriving from grassroots efforts at *autogestion* – describable as greater control of work and the workplace by those in the workforce that is, in turn, prefiguratively impactful in terms of our wider society (Lefebvre, 2009, pp. 138–151) – you denature it and efforts to incorporate that into organisational life relegates it from praxis to lifeless technique.

The ways in which we conceptualise organisation and how we can talk about them create a particular speak-up culture, which includes what is and isn't discussable. And those ever-changing spaces open up room for voice – sometimes sanctioned, occasionally unofficial – and also create silences. However, this idea of voice and silence cannot simply be read off from an articulation of a cohesively whole organisation: we also need to recognise that concerns around speaking out and being silenced persist at a microscopic level as well.

I feel silenced

Mark's job as an operating department orderly in the early 1980s saw him as one of two union shop stewards at the hospital in which he worked. The logic of that kind of representation is inescapable, given the disparity in terms of authority and capacity to act that exists between employees and employers. Employees must band together with others in solidarity and allow someone to step forward as a spokesperson, to marginally redress the imbalance of power. Management and workforce do not meet as equals, despite the shroud of equality that is cast over that relationship in law. A single voice can barely be heard in a context such as this, whilst a collective voice might at least be listened to – and may obtain some concessions out of those exchanges.

That notwithstanding, when responsibility is assumed by one voice to speak on behalf of many, it has the potential to diminish the dialogic richness in terms of listening to all of those voices and may lead to some going unheard. This is at its most pronounced in union arrangements that have over time succumbed to bureaucratisation, which is the experience of most recognised trade unions around the globe. What has been noteworthy recently is the presence of an increasing number of small unions with a strong orientation towards solidarity, mutual support, and – crucially – action.

Largely, this is seen to reflect shifts in the workforce composition across the whole economy, with large numbers of people now in precarious work in terms of the so-called "gig economy". The Independent Workers of Great Britain (IWGB) trade union mounted a significant campaign with respect to the status and rights of those working on behalf of the Deliveroo platform (see https://ridersroovolt.com/). As the IWGB themselves explain,

> The IWGB was founded in 2012 by Latin American cleaners organising for better working conditions. Since then, we have grown to thousands of members across the country. From outsourced facilities staff to gig economy workers, IWGB members are key workers on the frontline of the fight against poverty pay and insecure work. The IWGB organises couriers, cycling instructors, charity workers, yoga teachers, cleaners, security officers, video game workers, nannies, university workers, foster carers, private hire drivers and more. Through strikes, legal action and public pressure, we're fighting for workers' rights and decent pay and conditions. The IWGB is taking on the corporate giants of the gig economy like Deliveroo and Uber. Gig economy companies deny workers basic rights like the minimum wage, health and safety protections and sick pay. In 2020, the IWGB defeated the UK Government in the High Court over health and safety rights for gig economy workers.   (IWGB, 2021)

Their democratic practice and an orientation to those marginalised in society and enduring intense employment insecurity stand in sharp contrast to what goes on in more recognisable trade unions in the UK. In the 2021 election for a new General Secretary of Unite The Union, the successful candidate was elected with 46,696 votes, 37.7% of the 124,147 turnouts. This victory was achieved by around 4% of the entire membership of this enormous general union casting a ballot in favour of the successful candidate (Unite The Union, 2021). To our mind, this establishes some distance between the multitude of voices in the organisation and the one key voice that seeks to represent them.

In the face of structural issues such as this, it is unsurprising that people might feel silenced as a result. It's true to say that even the most ossified union structure offers a space in which people can organise collectively with some degree of safety, although those bureaucracies have always felt uncomfortable with any kind of wildcat action, as their corporatist function is premised on both representation but also on the instillation of discipline across the membership. And trade union legislation in the UK over the years has also worked to constrain the freedom of working people to withdraw their labour safely.

As a militant shop steward, Mark recognised that his voice was the loudest amongst the members who so diligently paid their subs. He stood on walls to denounce the management and gushingly celebrate the dignity of labour. As noted earlier, he rattled along as all the badges he wore clattered together on his lapel. He mimeographed and distributed dense screeds of agitation and propaganda. He hectored and denounced in the course of public meetings. The presence of this voice was predominant – and the position it occupied closed down the space for other legitimate voices to be heard in that workplace and within the trade union branch as well. It seems self-evident now that others around him will have felt silenced, just by the volume and assertion of what Mark was saying.

But eventually, the imbalance between capital and labour reasserted itself in some small way in the context of Bromley Hospital. The management decided that enough was enough. Gradually, through a number of episodes that occurred at work, Mark was brought to heel through a variety of formal procedures and a studied lack of support from his local full-time Union Officer. His life as an activist concluded with around six weeks to go when a final written warning was put on his personnel file. The silencer was now silenced, as he cravenly toed the line to tick down the clock until he could leave to take up a college place.

Sometimes the silencing occurs due to what a voice does or does not say. If someone shouts to you by name across the street, you immediately become the person they are calling – to them, to you, and to those around you. Their "hailing" lands you in a communicative context that gets you seen as the person you are. Their calling across the street creates a social reality for you – and the language that they use will serve to define how you are seen by others and crucially by yourself (Althusser, 1970/2008).

In matters of racial identity, one author working in the field of education draws a fascinating conclusion. In the school where she worked, it was noticed that there were a significant number of students who were seen by faculty to be wandering the halls when they should have been in lessons. This situation generated the following considerations:

> While publicly framing the hall wanderers as predominantly "black" could seem explicitly "racist", public silence on the hallway's racial demographics effectively allowed black students to miss class disproportionately, an institutional allowance that to many seemed no less "racist". Adults seemed somewhat less aware that the combined effect of whispering the word "black" in private and knowingly deleting the word in public was actually to *highlight* the perceived relevance of blackness to the hallway "problem".
> (Pollock, 2004, p. 174)

There is an interplay here between voice and silence, reminding us how individual or collective presence can be silenced by the ways that people speak about us. What is said, how it is said, and where it is said can efface us in social settings making us both silent and invisible. As the researcher notes: 'Knowing silences…are themselves actions with racializing consequences: actively deleting race words from everyday talk can serve to increase the perceived relevance of race as much as to actively ignore race's relevance' (Pollock, 2004, p. 174).

All of which suggests that it is possible to leave people feeling silenced not in terms of those individuals making a choice to withhold their voices but instead through the use or absence of speech that serves to deny their presence.

I choose silence

There are two workplace circumstances where people might opt as an individual not to speak and so remain silent. The first is where there is a sense that, despite appearances to the contrary, the manager is unlikely to hear what is being said, even if they create the pretence of listening. That pretence manifests itself in three ways: making regular public and self-serving invitations to staff to speak, through ceaseless surveys, focus groups, town hall meetings, and so on; simulating attention, through cues such as tilting one's head and nodding and making noises of encouragement; and responding in ways that are not about what has actually been said but are instead crude reactions to the superficial performance of speech and listening, the most painful of which is the "You said, we did" list so beloved of internal communication teams.

The second is perhaps more pernicious, where we mute ourselves in the face of a regime of silence that arises tacitly in and between work groups. Such regimes might be said to create a collective complicity with what is and what is not sayable, which emerges from the interrelatedness of the people involved. These regimes reflect not a positive development in terms of communication but instead reflect the demise of dialogue.

At this point it's worth touching on two concepts which have increased in currency in light of our intensified engagement with social media:

> An epistemic bubble is a social epistemic structure in which other relevant voices have been left out, perhaps accidentally. An echo chamber is a social epistemic structure from which other relevant voices have been actively excluded and discredited. Members of epistemic bubbles lack exposure to relevant information and arguments. Members of echo chambers, on the other hand, have been brought to systematically distrust all outside sources. In epistemic bubbles, other voices are not heard; in echo chambers, other voices are actively undermined. (Nguyen, 2020, p. 141)

We find this a compelling argument, not least considering the experiences over recent years in politics across the Atlantic, and indeed in the UK, with respect to the algorithmic operations of platforms such as Twitter (Kitchens et al., 2020). However, it should not go unremarked that these are contested terms, with at least one commentator making the point that to focus on them is to put the cart before the horse; we should instead be concentrating on the drive to the binary extremes in the practicalities of our day to day democratic politics and the way in which individuals identify so very strongly with these intensely antagonistic positions (Bruns, 2019). It is a human rather than a technological closure, reflecting some of the practices we have been discussing here.

An illumination with respect to regimes of silence arises out of the fraught and emotionally charged debate around the rights of trans people. This is an area that has been unhelpfully mobilised by a progressivism that is built on an identarian politics. In a report of an extensive consultation undertaken on how best to navigate the issues around supporting transgender people in sport, the following datum was offered:

> A significant number of interviewees said that they would only be involved if anonymity was assured because people were afraid to say in public what they privately believed. The overwhelming majority of people who considered fairness and safety could not be achieved with transgender inclusion into female sport did not feel confident to voice these opinions. Some said that they had been threatened with sanction or disciplinary action if they spoke out. Many of the interviewees who held positions with sporting agencies said their personal opinions were in direct conflict with that of their employer or agency's stated position, many felt they had no option but to remain silent in order to keep their job. This was a frequently voiced frustration which regularly reduced the interviewee to tears or hostility.   (Carbmill Consulting, 2021, p. 15)

Wrapped into this contentious space is a binary opposition with two perspectives compelled to the epistemic boundary by being in forced tension with one another. Those who embrace a progressive worldview and politics generate a powerful cohesion and a refusal to brook any perspective that might be seen to deviate from the defined orthodoxy.

Some from within those politics – especially those with an anarchistic as opposed to Marxian grounding – have found the courage to give voice to concerns about the way in which so-called "cancel culture" is used not only on those outside of those politics, but also to manage the membership within progressivism. There is a recognition that these practices are seen to be useful for a subaltern group to challenge what the voices of the powerful are saying, but there is seen to be negative side. In conversation with her comrades on this important topic, adrienne marie brown (2020) noted,

So many people unveiled the ways they'd either been called out or participated in call outs they later felt were ungrounded, or were grounded but didn't actually stop or change the problem. I heard about how often things are turned into public campaigns of shaming and humiliation before it is even clear if the thing is a misunderstanding, mistake, contradiction, conflict, harm or abuse.   (brown, 2020, p. 22)

This author pithily describes in outline how this process works in practice. By its nature, it relies on a partial (and oftentimes partisan) declaration about a particular circumstance. Woven into the fabric of this initial declaration is an expectation of immediate action, in some fashion of another: the person identified as a "miscreant" faces a demand to do something, such as immediately apologise; or the wider group (and sometimes society beyond) is forcefully called upon to pile in to add to the pressure. By this time the accusation has wriggled free of the immediate interlocutors and has developed an autonomous presence in the wider discourse. The punishment has begun for the focus of this attack, which could quite comfortably be referred to as "mobbing".[1] The more who become involved – often engaging so as to reinforce their position as a recognised progressive – the more the episode becomes both reinforced and (at the same time) further removed from reality (brown, 2020, p. 41).

Out of this "mobbing" flow consequences, which can only be avoided or mitigated if the person at the centre of this storm accepts that they must give voice to a form of speech defined by this ideological hazing. This is the territory of the cloying apology, particularly when it is delivered through social media (which has helped to amplify this practice). The alternative to this obeisance will include '…loss of job, community, reputation, platform. Sometimes there is just derision, and calls for disappearance' (brown, 2020, p. 41). It is no mere sophistry to observe how closely this description mirrors the experience of those who have endured life in totalitarian societies.

This may look to be a rash assertion, an instance perhaps of Godwin's law. A thoughtful analysis of totalitarianism observes that theorists in this field might be said to be promoting either a strong or a weak model of this structuration of society: the former hinges on the assertion that totalitarianism is defined by its successful brainwashing of the population so that they are absorbed by a new view of the world; the latter argues that it is the construction of technical checks, balances and surveillance in a totalitarian society that generates compliance. The former sees ideology as a totalising force; the latter focuses on a totalising structure (Tormey, 1995).

What might be said to undergird all of this? After all, there is an argument to be made that a liberal democracy can be seen to be totalising, with respect to the dominant discourse that asserts itself as a "common sense" view of our world. We would acknowledge the way in which a new modality of power works to smooth off the sharp edges that exist in our polities and wider societies. However, when envisaging more instrumental tyranny, we concur with the following:

> Totalitarian regimes are never happy merely with securing obedience or compliance: simply carrying out the commands of the authorities is never enough to guarantee a person's safety as it would be in most other forms of dictatorship. What the regime demands is a change in the entire outlook on life, the opinions, beliefs, values and aspirations of ordinary people. The corollary of such a demand is thus that individuals must give up their autonomy, their independence. They must conform rigidly and absolutely with the role defined by the regime. Freedom as the capacity of individuals to set their own goals is entirely anathema to the totalitarian outlook. It is in essence a threat to the order and regimentation of life that they require.
> (Tormey, 1995, p. 169)

This leads the author to observe that totalitarianism seeks to destroy that which presently prevails and to build a new status quo, often in the service of a millenarianism which sits beyond contestation, let alone active refutation. This reflects the origins of progressivism in the Enlightenment, although the contemporary manifestation of this politics uncomfortably yokes together a Whiggish expectation of history with the clumsier aspects of relativism that one finds in post-structuralist theory. This line of inquiry leads to this powerful conclusion: 'Totalitarian is thus borne above all of radicalism, a discontent with the present that is translated into a longing for the new' (Tormey, 1995, p. 169).

An additional element that also appears is the sense in which politics and religiosity intersect and interact. Progressivism in its present manifestation inadvertently invokes a number of practices to be found in the formal business of communing around a faith. To that extent, it mirrors the idea highlighted above that radicalism is both destruction and renaissance, in that it is a politics that carries within it both Apocalypse and a Promised Land. It pivots around the notion of unquestioning belief – and that the uncritical espousal of that belief buys one into the ranks of the chosen people. In all of this, we are reminded that 'The language of politics is always interspersed with the ecstasies of religiousity and, thus, becomes a symbol in the concise sense by letting experiences concerned with the contents of the world be permeated with transcendental-divine experiences' (Voegelin, 2000, p. 70).

The drive that arises out of the radical motivation to destroy the old and embrace the new can oftentimes create organisational spaces where silence is a default state. The history of the 20th Century reminds us of the power of these regimes of silence – and our obligation as voices to comply with them. There is a plausible equivalence between the way in which the state security apparatus in what was laughably called the German Democratic Republic (GDR) created a surveillant infrastructure where people were actively informed about family and friend and the way in which progressivism now defines what can and cannot be said. The full horror, though, of the system in the GDR is outlined thus:

> The Stasi's most important tool of surveillance and suppression, and its "main weapon against the enemy" was the dense network of spies called unofficial collaborators. Spies were recruited from the population and instructed to secretly collect information about individuals in their own social network. Being friends, colleagues, neighbors or sport buddies of the individuals they spied on, collaborators were able to provide valuable personal information that complemented the Stasi's knowledge of the population and helped creating an overall picture about anti-socialist and dissident movements and hence guaranteed surveillance of the society's everyday life. At the same time, the threat of being denunciated and the concealed presence of the state security caused an atmosphere of mistrust and suspicion.   (Lichter et al., 2015, p. 6)

There is an argument that says that a crucial element of surveillance and compliance in the GDR consisted of encouraging the populace to demonstrate "tokens of allegiance", meaning participation in ritualised events in support of the state. Every citizen was expected to demonstrate their commitment not just to the regime but to its notion of socialism through active involvement in massified events that nowadays only really exist on the parade grounds of Pyongyang. So, in the GDR, it has been suggested that the

> Stasi typically got wind of "missed opportunities" to pay allegiance through its countrywide web of secret informants which deeply pene-trated all organizations in the GDR. Once suspect of questionable loyalty, Stasi began to investigate the reputation of citizens, inquiring about them at work and in the neighborhood.   (Glaeser, 2013, p. 12)

Let us not presuppose that this is some Stalinoid aberration that arises in real life and real-time experiments with "actually existing socialism". As we shall explore, actions around voice and silence might be said to scope and shape the very idea of "community". Before the horrors of Jonestown deep in the Guyanese jungle, Jim Jones's People's Temple – built in California on a rich honeycomb of socialistic thinking, powerful notions drawn from Christianity, and an unusually egalitarian approach for the time – subjected members of its governing council to a tortuous encounter process where the person "on the floor" was subjected to vicious criticism by their close circle (Kilduff & Tracy, 1977, p. 34).

When it came to that fateful day in 1978, serious scholars of this vile episode in which more than 900 people (including 300 or so babies and children) perished through taking poison have offered the following assessment:

> The mass suicide description was never accurate, of course, since the three hundred infants and children could not choose to die in any mean-ingful sense. Nevertheless, early eyewitness accounts indicated that most adults voluntarily took the poison. An audiotape made at the time revealed that only a single person, Christine Miller, verbally dissented, and she was shouted down by the crowd.   (Moore, 2013, p. 306)

What has this to do with silence in the workplace? These extreme exam-ples offer a warning as to how things can speedily unfold – and how the spaces that we occupy with others can suddenly end up as locations where there is a tacit list of things that can and cannot be said. This may not derive from explicit prohibition; where such constraint exists, resistance is far easier. Instead, it arises out of a burgeoning collective silence which, in turn, justifies itself through our individual willingness to tolerate it.

Silently in such circumstances, we are subtly making a personal calcula-tion as to how personally harmful it might be if we were to give voice in a spirit of dialogue.

This should not be interpreted as an intervention on the side of what is ingenuously referred to as "free speech". As is the case in so much public debate, we are presented with an impossible choice between progressivism and a classical liberalism which pointedly disregards (and hence shrouds) the complexities of power. The latter is ably demonstrated by one of its key contemporary advocates: 'Free speech is the marrow of democracy. Without it, no other liberties exist…Unless we are able to speak our minds, we can-not innovate, or even begin to make sense of the world' (Doyle, 2021, p. 6). This formulation assumes a social contract founded on equality, where one voice is as valued and carries as much weight as another. It unhelpfully effaces the idea of dominant voices and subaltern voices, a treacherously complex place when viewed through a global prism:

> Outside (though not completely so) the circuit of the international divi-sion of labour, there are people whose consciousness we cannot grasp if we close off our benevolence by constructing an homogeneous Other referring only to our own place in the seat of the Same or the Self. Here are subsistence farmers, unorganized peasant labour, the tribals and the communities of zero workers on the street or in the countryside. To con-front them is not to represent (…) them but to learn to represent our-selves.   (Spivak, 1994, p. 84)

This offers an insight into just how labyrinthine the debate around voice, in terms of where people find themselves and how they are seen in the warp and weft of power. There is no parity of esteem that would enable us to valorise each and every voice equally. Hence, a classical liberal position is, for us, as problematic as that of the contemporary progressivist; indeed, one might conclude that, in the circumstances where public discussion is in such a parlous state, we are pinched between two ideologised perspectives that forcefully occupy the space where human beings might ordinarily find space and time to engage meaningfully with one another.

One does not need to cast back far in history to discover a time when voice and the freedom to speak was a central concern of progressivism. For example, Berkeley, a prime locus for 1960s radicalism and the students' movement, experienced what has been described as a "free speech crisis" in September 1964 as the university administration interceded to prevent student groups from engaging with the university population in a key campus location (Cohen, 2015). In seeking to capture the meaning of the Free Speech Movement (FSM) that sprang up in light of this, Hirsch (2004) quotes a speech from December 1964 delivered to a protest by Mario Silvo, one of the prominent players at this moment in US history:

> There is a time when the operation of the machine becomes so odious, makes you so sick at heart, that you can't take part, you can't even tacitly take part, and you've got to put your bodies on the gears and upon the wheels, upon the levers, upon all the apparatus, and you've got to make it stop. And you've got to indicate to the people who run it, to the people who own it, that unless you're free, the machine will be prevented from working at all.   (Hirsch, 2004, pp. 12–13)

Hirsch's commentary – delivered originally as a speech in 1994, 30 years after these events – focuses on the way in which this somewhat all-encompassing movement was built out of several responses to the seemingly arbitrary way in which the administration chose to clamp down on the student voice on campus – and beyond. It was mired in the politics not merely of the campus but of its adjoining communities and, indeed, of California itself (Draper, 1965/2009). Hence, for Hirsch, 'It was an insistence on engaging in substantive politics over sandbox politics' (Hirsch, 2004, p. 3), but also a rebellion with a cause and – importantly for the argument being advanced here – in its questioning of authority, 'The Free Speech Movement was a demand that the First Amendment be in force at UC, that admission to Cal not [sic] require a forfeiture of Constitutional guarantees. It was a co-mingling of our thoughts with the Founding Fathers' (Hirsch, 2004, pp. 4–5).

This resonates with the positions assumed by those behind the Iron Curtain that descended at the close of the Second World War who spoke out so bravely against the oppressive control of the Soviet Union and their proxy regimes. Beneath fluttering red flags emblazoned with symbols of the working class, these grotesque bureaucracies exercised totalitarian control and sought to strangle voice and silence debate. The dissidents tried to give voice in the face of a social silence that prevailed, a silenced orchestrated thus:

> The manager of a fruit-and-vegetable shop places in his window, among the onions and carrots, the slogan: "Workers of the world, unite!" Why

does he do it? What is he trying to communicate to the world? [...] I think it can be safely assumed that the overwhelming majority of shopkeepers never think about the slogans that they put in their windows, nor do they use them to express their real opinions. That poster was delivered to our greengrocer from the enterprise headquarters along with the onions and carrots. He put them all into the window simply because it has been done that way for years, because everybody does it, and because that is the way that it has to be [...] It is one of the thousands of details that guarantee him a relatively tranquil life "in harmony with society", as they say.   (Havel, 1978, pp. 5–6)

Returning to our contemporary context we perceive an intrusion into dialogic space of unyielding ideologised thinking and contend that the workplace is one of those locations where it might reasonably be expected that meaningful exchange between human agents might take place. However, through a process of active silencing that arises from managerial precepts and imperatives and via the intrusion of collective regimes of silence, the room for voice is diminished. Setting aside for one moment the purist notion of a "free speech" disentangled from the mesh of inequalities and power deployment, we are still confronted with a circumstance in a society that notionally assumes tolerance as a foundation wherein:

A recent survey by the Cato Institute and YouGov found that nearly two-thirds of Americans feel compelled to keep their views to themselves out of fear of causing offence, while a third are refraining from sharing their political opinions because they believe their employment prospects would be endangered if they did so.   (Doyle, 2021, p. 28)

What practical and qualitative difference exists between Havel's greengrocer and the American respondents here? And what comparisons can be reasonably made between the regime that Havel describes that induced the greengrocer to comply and the ideologised corporate circumstances in which we presently find ourselves? In the latter we are faced with acculturation through a complex overlay of company values alongside illusory programmes of empowerment, so ably described by Hugh Willmott (1993) in his comparisons of totalitarianism and corporate practice in capitalism, and other silences that emerge amongst the workforce. This will be explored later in the section that interrogates silence as a secret password.

I am invited to speak. I seem to be listened to. (I am not heard.)

Imagine that you are an actor in a stage drama, about to perform on the opening night. You have spent weeks with the script, learning the words until you were "off the book"; you have performed those words in relation to your fellow actors; you have embodied those words in order to give shape and volume to your character and thereby develop a verisimilitude; and you have been through your "blocking", working out how this performance will play out in the limited physical space of your stage.

If all of this preparation comes together effectively, there is a good chance that your audience will suspend their disbelief and allow themselves to be absorbed by the drama to the exclusion of real life for that moment. And, depending on your preferences in terms of acting styles, you may efface yourself in favour of the character that you have worked so hard to create. But, in most instances, you will – through your stagecraft – have an acute awareness of yourself being immersed in a performance. Your speech in that context is that which was previously on a page and is now tripping from your lips; the speech of others will not consist of words that constitute a dialogue and will instead simply be lines to which you attend merely as cues to that which you are primed by the script to say next.

This would be a dramaturgical performance – but performativity is a key feature of our social life and there are instances where our lives can feel scripted, particularly in relation to our respective psychologies and the roles that we assume. In this regard, the theories surrounding transactional analysis (TA) offer us some insight as to how this might work through the idea of the life script, a repertoire of behaviours that crystalise in light of a range of formative experiences (Steiner, 1990). Undergirding TA is a cluster of ur-roles – the parent, the adult, and the child – and attitudes and behaviours associated with each; we then enter into a schema as to how these respective states would interact as played out by two people, which offers additional insight into scripting (Solomon, 2003).

Creeping into this space comes the fascinating notion of the performative role-oriented idea of leadership, which is something in corporate life that lacks the tangibility of management and occupies a somewhat ethereal space floating above the grounded practicalities of the work done to deliver what the business offers to its clients. We speak about this as *leadership distance*, something that has arisen in organisational life, where those leading the firm are not properly part of it. But that disconnect leads to practical and cultural challenges in the business and is a characteristic of the way in which leadership has now supplanted management – and in which organisational structures have grown so much bigger.

As leadership drifts on thermals and air pockets above the hard terrain of getting things done, it assimilates and renders more technical core human activities such as listening. Hence, one study offers this conclusion about what arises out of leadership engaging in listening in the workplace: 'We can express our key finding in terms of a formula: (1) mundane act carried out by (2) a manager and (3) labelled leadership means (4) an expectation of something significant, even "magical" being accomplished' (Alvesson & Sveningsson, 2003, p. 1455).

Listening is precisely one of those mundane acts. Our organisations, as we have suggested and as the theory of the communicative constitution of organisations (CCO) foregrounds (Cooren & Martine, 2016), are built upon voice and listening, which is integral and often unnoticeable in human organising. But only someone with a formal leadership position would elevate this essential human practice to a place where it is seen to be one of their main contributions to the world of work. This process of what has been called "extra-ordinarisation" is important in terms of the structuration of power in the workplace because: 'The ideology of managerialism and the discourse of leadership is such that what managers do, what can be labelled as leadership, is (potentially) highly significant' (Alvesson & Sveningsson, 2003, p. 1455).

Here we have a familiar day-to-day activity, namely listening, that is implicit in human connectedness, so commonplace in social intercourse as to be largely unnoticeable. But, when managers engage in this behaviour, it acquires an additional quality that helps the listener to embrace the idea that they are a leader. And so, in the grim circularity that loops us back to the uncertainty of what is meant when we speak of leadership and the industry that asserts that it is uniquely equipped to develop this capacity, a putative leader understands for that label to be justified they need to demonstrate they recognise the corporate importance of listening and hence the need to be doing it – and to be seen to be doing it.

The act of listening, ordinarily simply part of the back and forth of people communicating, can then be argued to acquire a magical quality – and, at the same time, it is denatured and ideologised. We end up in a situation where leaders listen because listening is discursively recognised as a facet of leadership. They know they're meant to listen and know what listening looks like... but what is done is a simulacrum of listening, because they are invariably not actually hearing what is being said. It is performative leadership, obsessed with gestures that merely reinforce position and superficially appears to be honest and engaging. But it is merely listening without hearing − and, in many instances, it is actually just the appearance of listening, so as to placate the workforce rather than actively and meaningfully engaging with them.

This is leadership practised without criticality and reflexivity. It appears like the person on stage with whom we opened this section, so entrained and engrossed by the role they perform that they are listening simply for scripted cues rather than hearing what is actually being said by the person − or people − in front of them.

This ushers the employee into a profoundly dishonest organisational space. The invitation to speak seems to be there; the leader by all appearances seems attuned to the important things that the employee is trying to say; but little if any of what that employee says is genuinely heard, because the conversational drama is all, rather than the content of the exchange. And, just as listening is deemed to be key to leadership so leaders are keen to be seen to be doing it, so the enticement to use voice serves an ideological purpose, reinforcing the idea that people are free to speak and the leaders are attuned to listen.

You are actively encouraged to speak so the workplace can shroud itself with the claim that its culture is open and equal. But beneath this claim lies the simple fact that what is said is often not heard. The leader has looked like they were listening, as they are told these days to do, and have given the appearance of being attentive to what might have been said, but they have no real intention of engaging with it. They have done enough to create the impression that power in the organisation has shifted and is somehow different, while it remains a constant although its expression may shift and change so that it appears to be less oppressive.

To be asked to speak and then not heard is perhaps even more painful than never being told that your opinion matters. In the next section we look at the role that voice and silence can play in actively defining the boundaries of a range of social groupings − and the way those groupings have a tendency to end up as regimes of silence, to the detriment of all.

Note

1. The following offers insight into what is meant by this important term in working life:

> Psychical terror or mobbing in working life means hostile and unethical com-munication which is directed in a systematic way by one or a number of persons mainly toward one individual. There are also cases where such mob-bing is mutual until one of the participants becomes the underdog. These actions take place often (almost every day) and over a long period (at least for six months) and, because of this frequency and duration, result in con-siderable psychic, psychosomatic and social misery. This definition elimi-nates temporary conflicts and focuses on the transition zone where the psychosocial situation starts to result in psychiatric and/or psychosomatic pathological states. (Leymann, 1990, p. 120)

References

Althusser, L., 1970/2008. Ideology and ideological state apparatuses (Notes towards an investigation). In: *On ideology*. London: Verso, pp. 1–60.

Alvesson, M. & Sveningsson, S., 2003. Managers doing leadership: The extra-ordinarization of the mundane. *Human Relations*, 56(12), pp. 1435–1459.

Bristol Leadership & Change Centre, 2021. *No going back! Learning and unlearning about NHS leadership practice and development in the wake of COVID-19*. Bristol: University of West of England.

brown, a. m., 2020. *We will not cancel us – and other dreams of transformative justice*. Chicago, IL: AK Press.

Bruns, A., 2019. *Are filter bubbles real?*. Cambridge: Polity.

Carbmill Consulting, 2021. *Project report: SCEG Project for Review and Redraft of Guidance for Transgender Inclusion in Domestic Sport 2021*. London: Sports Council Equality Group.

Carrim, N. M. H., 2016. 'Shh…quiet! Here they come.' Black employees as targets of office gossip. *Journal of Psychology in Africa*, 26(2), pp. 180–185.

Cohen, R., 2015. Teaching about the Berkeley Free Speech Movement: Civil disobedience and mass protest in the 1960s. *Social Education*, 79(5), pp. 301–308.

Cole, M. & Higgins, J., 2022. *Leadership unravelled: The faulty thinking behind modern management*. Abingdon: Routledge.

Cooren, F. & Martine, T., 2016. Communicative constitution of organizations. In: K. B. Jensen, R. T. Craig, J. D. Pooley & E. W. Rothenbuhler, eds. *The international encyclopedia of communication theory and philosophy.* Chichester: John Wiley & Sons, pp. 307–315.

Diefenbach, T., 2007. The managerialistic ideology of organisational change management. *Journal of Organizational Change Management,* 20(1), pp. 126–144.

Dovey, K., 2010. *Becoming places: Urbanism/architecture/identity/power.* Abingdon: Routledge.

Doyle, A., 2021. *Free speech and why it matters.* London: Constable.

Draper, H., 1965/2009. *Berkeley: The new student revolt.* Alameda, CA: Center for Socialist History.

Future Forum, 2021. *Future forum pulse: The great executive-employee disconnect.* [Online] Available at: https://futureforum.com/pulse-survey/ [Accessed 16 November 2021].

Glaeser, A., 2013. Power/knowledge failure: Epistemic practices and ideologies of the secret police in former East Germany. *Social Analysis,* 47(1), pp. 10–26.

Gray, B., 2017. The Cynefin framework: Applying an understanding of complexity to medicine. *Journal of Primary Health Care,* 9(4), pp. 258–261.

Havel, V., 1978. *The power of the powerless.* [Online] Available at: http://havel.fiu.edu/about-us/publications-and-resources/the-power-of-the-powerless.pdf [Accessed 18 October 2021].

Hirsch, J., 2004. *What was the Free Speech Movement?.* [Online] Available at: https://fsm-a.org/FSM%20Documents/2004%20What%20Was%20The%20Free%20Speech%20Movement%20by%20Jeff%20Hirsch%20OCR%20optimized.pdf [Accessed 18 October 2021].

hooks, b., 1989. Choosing the margin as a space of radical openness. *Framework: The Journal of Cinema and Media,* Issue 36, pp. 15–23.

IWGB, 2021. *About Us.* [Online] Available at: https://iwgb.org.uk/en/page/about-us/ [Accessed 3 November 2021].

Kilduff, M. & Tracy, P., 1977. Inside peoples temple. *New West,* 1 August, pp. 30–38.

Kitchens, B., Johnson, S. L. & Gray, P., 2020. Understanding echo chambers and filter bubbles: The impact of social media on diversification and partisan shifts in news consumption. *MIS Quarterly,* 44(4), pp. 1619–1649.

Kornberger, M. & Clegg, S. R., 2004. Bringing space back in: Organizing the generative building. *Organization Studies*, 25(7), pp. 1095–1115.

Lane, P. J. et al., 2021. Creating a healthcare variant CYNEFIN framework to improve leadership and urgent decision-making in times of crisis. *Leadership in Health Services*, 34(4), pp. 454–461.

Lefebvre, H., 2009. *State, space, world: Selected essays.* Minneapolis: University of Minnesota Press.

Leymann, H., 1990. Mobbing and psychological terror at workplaces. *Violence and Victims*, 5(2), pp. 119–126.

Lichter, A., Loeffler, M. & Siegloch, S., 2015. *The economic costs of mass surveillance: Insights from Stasi spying in East Germany – IZA Discussion Paper No. 9245.* Bonn: Institute for the Study of Labor (IZA).

Michelson, G., van Iterson, A. & Waddington, K., 2010. Gossip in organizations: Contexts, consequences, and controversies. *Group and Organization Management*, 35(4), pp. 371–390.

Moore, R., 2013. Rhetoric, revolution, and resistance in Jonestown, Guyana. *Journal of Religion and Violence*, 1(3), pp. 303–321.

Nguyen, C. T., 2020. Echo chambers and epistemic bubbles. *Episteme*, 17(2), pp. 141–161.

Pollock, M., 2004. *Colormute: Race talk dilemmas in an American school.* Princeton, NJ: Princeton University Press.

Reitz, M. & Higgins, J., 2017. *Being silenced and silencing others: Developing the capacity to speak truth to power.* Berkhamstead: Hult Research.

Reitz, M., Nilsson, V. O., Day, E. & Higgins, J., 2019. *Speaking truth to power at work: How we silence ourselves and others – Interim survey results,* Berkhamstead: Hult Research.

Skogland, M. A. C. & Hansen, G. K., 2017. Change your space, change your culture: Exploring spatial change management strategies. *Journal of Corporate Real Estate*, 19(2), pp. 95–110.

Snowden, D. J. & Boone, M. E., 2007. A leader's framework for decision-making. *Harvard Business Review*, 85(11), pp. 68–76.

Solomon, C., 2003. Transactional analysis theory: The basics. *Transactional Analysis Journal*, 33(1), pp. 15–22.

Spivak, G. C., 1994. Can the subaltern speak?. In: P. Williams & L. Chrisman, eds. *Colonial discourse and postcolonial theory: A reader.* New York: Columbia University Press, pp. 66–111.

Steiner, C. M., 1990. *Scripts people live.* New York: Grove Press.

Todnem By, R., 2005. Organisational change management: A critical review. *Journal of Change Management,* 5(4), pp. 369–380.

Tormey, S., 1995. Totalitarianism in perspective. In: S. Tormey, ed. *Making sense of tyranny: Interpretations of totalitarianism.* Manchester: Manchester University Press, pp. 167–190.

Tsoukas, H. & Chia, R., 2002. On organizational becoming: Rethinking organizational change. *Organization Science,* 13(5), pp. 567–582.

Unite The Union, 2021. *Sharon Graham announced as Unite's new general secretary.* [Online] Available at: https://www.unitetheunion.org/who-we-are/structure/unite-2021-general-secretary-election/ [Accessed 3 November 2021].

van Marrewijk, A. H., 2009. Corporate headquarters as physical embodiments of organisational change. *Journal of Organizational Change Management,* 22(3), pp. 290–306.

Voegelin, E., 2000. The political religions. In: M. Henningsen, ed. *The collected works of Eric Vogelin Volume 5: Modernity without restraint.* Columbia: University of Missouri Press, pp. 19–74.

Weick, K., 1969. *The social psychology of organizing.* Reading, MA: Addison-Wesley.

Willmott, H., 1993. Strength is ignorance; Slavery is freedom: Managing culture in modern organzations. *Journal of Management Studies,* 30(4), pp. 515–552.

8

SILENCE IS A PASSWORD

The notion of community has developed considerably over recent years. It has a rich currency in current discourse: 'Community is one of the best-loved terms in political discourse; even the "defense community" softens its image with the word' (Corlett, 1993, p. 16). Previously, there was a strong sense that community was defined largely by geographical location, extended to encompass the idea that the people in that locale were in some way meaningfully connected. This is where we find the urbanism of Jane Jacobs and her "sidewalk ballet", where community envelops both place as a physical location and the way in which it is constituted, in terms of its routines and facilities. The latter, of course, arises out of the physical material of that neighbourhood and the myriad interactions with the physical and social environment amongst all those who reside or pass through there (Jacobs, 1961/2000).

The relation to the physical has become somewhat frayed in contemporary thinking about community. The argument now advanced is that community is formed in response to needs for membership; influence (in terms

DOI: 10.4324/9781003296683-10

of mattering); integration and fulfilment of needs; and a shared emotional connection. In terms of membership, this is suggested to have five attributes: 'boundaries, emotional safety, a sense of belonging and identification, personal investment, and a common symbol system. *These attributes work together and contribute to a sense of who is part of the community and who is not'* (McMillan & Chavis, 1986, p. 11 [Emphasis added]). Suddenly, community feels less like an organic collective than a club to which one might apply for entry.

In a community context unity should be premised on a centrifugal rather than a centripetal orientation, reaching out to encompass and connect more. As Mary Parker Follet (1919) explains:

> The urge to unity is not a reduction, a simplification, it is the urge to embrace more and more, it is a reaching out, a seeking, it is the furthest possible conception of pluralism, it is a pluralism spiritually not materially conceived. Not the "reduction" to unity but the expansion to unity is the social process. (p. 583)

Contrariwise, then, community without unity is interiorised and self-referencing and this is now the dominant model, whereas it seems more positive to follow the argument that leads us to think of '...community as mutual appreciation of differences by deconstructing oppositions – such as nonwhite-white, inside-outside, and especially deconstruction-(re)construction' (Corlett, 1993, p. xvi).

It seems reasonable to speak of a shift in terms of community from locational to transactional. Meeting the needs related to community means that maintaining a position within that formation is critically important to the members. In light of this, those inside the community have a tendency to speak with the same voice and say the same things. There would seem to be two possible reasons for this: first, because those individuals intrinsically agree with the shared discourse of the community and its espoused values (and values-in-action); or, second, because they trade adherence to these shared perspectives for their unchallenged continued community membership. Herein, we trace in outline the concepts of the spiral of silence, pluralistic ignorance, and the like – and acknowledge the way in which these practices shape voice and silence, particularly in the workplace.

There are a number of perspectives that look to make sense of the individual's relationship with a group in terms of the dynamics of membership.

Social Identity Theory, derived largely from the work of the psychologist Henri Tajfel, seeks to go beyond the individual in the group to look instead at the group inside the individual (Trepte, 2006, p. 255). A person's self-esteem is said to be linked with their membership of a group – and the group on which they depend in this way is defined by them as an in-group, standing in contrast to outgroups (Abrams & Hogg, 1988, pp. 317–318).

Research in this field suggests something that resonates strongly with the ideas on community that we are advancing here:

> [I]ndividuals endorse attitudes that increase their proximity to the stereotypical group position, even in the absence of direct group pressure and when attention is focused on the group boundaries they strive harder to distinguish their own group from other groups.   (Abrams et al., 1990, p. 99)

Work by Moscovici and their collaborators looked at the way in which groups generate social representations that serve to bind them together. These are said to be 'the ensemble of thoughts and feelings being expressed in verbal and overt behaviour of actors which constitutes an object for a social group' (Wagner et al., 1999, p. 96). Elsewhere, there is discussion of BIRG, an acronym for "basking in reflected glory". Research with respect to this shows people's willingness to associate with a group if it is seen to be successful or effective (Cialdini et al., 1976).

We need to be mindful of the work that undergirds the notion of "groupthink", a term that has passed into everyday language with a strong negative connotation. It is said to be '…the mode of thinking that persons engage in when concurrence-seeking becomes so dominant in a cohesive ingroup that it tends to override realistic appraisal of alternative courses of action' (Janis, 1971). The Challenger disaster in January 1986 is seen to be an example of how groupthink can lead to terrible outcomes. In analysing how this arose, a number of features of groupthink have been identified, which include: belief in the inherent morality of the group; collective rationalisation; outgroup stereotypes; illusion of unanimity; and direct pressure on dissenters. (Janis, 1991)

Lastly, the insightful synthesis of anthropology and sociology in the work of Pierre Bourdieu has much to say in terms of the ways in which we rub along together. He also makes some sense of how those social connections can both liberate and constrain us. His notion of habitus is explained in terms of playing a game of football: the pitch, the rules, and the expectations of others around us constrain how we can behave…but this simultaneously offers us the space to play the game in the way that we choose. It is usefully summarised here:

> The habitus is a set of *dispositions* which incline agents to act and react in certain ways. The dispositions generate practices, perceptions and attitudes which are "regular" without being consciously coordinated or governed by any "rule". The dispositions which constitute the habitus are inculcated, structured, durable, generative and transposable.
> (Thompson, 1992, p. 12)

Bourdieu's focus on the tension between context and individual leads him to offer a wide array of fascinating insights as to the extent of our agency – and the constraint of the social, which speaks to the way in which community works. He suggests, for instance, that

> Because the subjective necessity and self-evidence of the commonsense world are validated by the objective consensus on the sense of the world, what is essential goes without saying because it comes without saying: the tradition is silent, not least about itself as a tradition.   (Bourdieu, 1977, p. 167)

Much around us in social situations is so familiar as to be invisible. Our immersion in these spaces means that such things end up unnoticed and unquestioned, hence taken for granted. It is not possible to step out of this, so as to be able to dispassionately "look" at it. This indulges the fascination with the idea that we can treat our social relations as an abstraction, something that can be put under a microscope and studied like a rock, a plant, or an insect. We cannot. Instead, we need to interrogate the circumstances in which we find ourselves individually and also in dialogue with those around us.

These are some important insights on humans in groups that need to be acknowledged, as we describe our thinking about community. Within its bounds, we see *zealotry* and *complicity* at work, the former reflecting the fact of members being unquestioningly committed to the knowledge and practice that ties the community together and the latter indicating the willingness of members to silence themselves even in the face of things about the community with which they personally disagree. Hence, we have two types of member: one who wholeheartedly buys into the community and the ideas that bind it together; and one who – for the sake of that membership and in fear of ostracism – tolerates views and attitudes with which they fundamentally disagree.

In light of this, it is apparent that the community can be distorted by its leadership, in terms of those who enjoy an accorded positional power in the community – or to whom some sense of positional power accrues in light of the way that these people come to enjoy a dominance of voice (notwithstanding the idea that they would likely be thought of as first among equals in this relational space).

Community members for whom zealotry or complicity either does not apply or has come not to hold sway any longer are faced with a choice around *voice* (which manifests as either opting to leave or speaking their own truth into the community power, apparent through the apparatus of a "regime of silence") or *silence* – which means to reintegrate complicity into their subjectivity and thereby disappear again into the community. This leads to the conclusion that conversation in a community context which eschews unity in favour of constrained collectivity is not actually dialogue but is merely a currency exchanged by members to secure their continued presence within that tightly defined club. The exchanges between members who wish to remain as members are performative exchanges, designed to reinforce the non-expansionary community as opposed to opening up to speak out and up.

While there is speech in this context, it says nothing and merely binds the members together: it is, in essence, a noisy silence. It is a script, delivered solely for the purpose of ensuring that the players recognise the importance of the drama in which they are committed to playing a part. In this context, a community member who speaks out and fractures the cohesion of that "regime of (noisy) silence" is of necessity driven to the edge of the community, where they unwittingly serve the vital purpose of creating an essential boundary. The boundary defines membership of the community – but this is only established by voices that do not sit comfortably within that regime – and that articulate conversational perspectives that cannot ever be seen to have currency within that community.

The community member who surrenders that membership in order to give voice to ideas and opinions that defy the "regime of (noisy) silence" finds themselves on a boundary of their own creation. They have greater value now to that community insofar as they bound the interiority and exteriority of that community. In this peripheral place, they may initially seek to make a conversational appeal to those within the community – although this merely adds value to the mainstream conversational currency and its conversion into a sense of belonging. Eventually, they may appeal to those outside of the community, which finally signals the transition from marking the boundary to being beyond the boundary.

One of the key places where we nowadays obtain our sense of community is in the workplace. Notwithstanding what we saw across the pandemic in terms of mutual aid and neighbourhood initiatives springing up, it is difficult to find the sort of connection that we associate with community in many of the localities in which we live. Neoliberalism and its implicit individualism have compelled us into "property-owning isolation tanks", where we live atomised existences focused on back garden barbeques, Sky TV packages and boundless video gaming. Instead, the workplace provides us with various communal elements, which can be summarised thus: the provision of a network of friends; the opportunity to work in a functional sub-group on common tasks; the organisation itself as something to which people feel that they belong; connections that exist in terms of profession, occupation or job class; and, lastly, the ability to go to a place of work (Klein & D'Aunno, 1986).

It is also the case that the notion of community has been politically occupied over the recent period, particularly by those who presume to hold a progressive perspective. Whilst traditionally the historical focus of the Left has been on the importance of unity, as expressed with respect to solidarity and trade unionism, the mobilisation latterly is more fragmentary. In this contemporary world view, the notion of community is ceaselessly calibrated, with each fresh assessment tightening its defining elements to establish and shrink the boundaries and the population therein. This ends up feeling like community without unity, which segments and constricts membership rather than one with an expansive sense of solidarity. And it should not escape our attention that one of the key practices that undergird the new modality of power that Foucault so elegantly describes (Foucault, 1991) is fragmented categorisation, a widely accepted and uncommented habit that segments populations to render them susceptible to governmentality. The old idea of "divide and conquer" is seen through fresh theoretical eyes.

Let's ground these observations around community boundaries, voice and silence in an example drawn from Mark's experience. In 1980 – a year after Margaret Thatcher had formed her first administration – Mark joined the Labour Party, throwing himself into political activism. He attended myriad meetings at the H G Wells centre in South London, went door to door with leaflets and petitions, canvassed during elections, pounded the streets of cities across the UK in support of jobs, became a shop steward in the health service, stood for election, and spoke at meetings. He even sold Leftist newspapers (at least one of which was alleged shamefully to be supported by the Gadhafi regime in Libya) and was moved on occasion to write for them. He marched with the miners, visited pit villages and protested with the print workers.

This world of political activism is small and reassuring. It draws together often disparate groups of people who share a particular world view. This is the vernacular of such tightly defined groups – something which binds them as one and sets the boundary in terms of fixing who is inside and outside. The conversation within this community threads around the people who find themselves in this space and ties them together. The politics of the Labour Party at that time, from Mark's experience, defined itself very clearly in contradistinction to Thatcher and her government(s). This was the common language that people within that community used with one another in order to reassure themselves as to the cohesion of the group of which they were a member.

But there was another feature of Labourism at that time, something that continues to overshadow the party and the cohesion it requires to get things done in the world. This was an intense factionalism, perhaps at its most pronounced during the campaign for the deputy leadership of the party between Denis Healey and Tony Benn. On a jobs march in Cardiff, Mark recalls the relish he experienced when, at the rally to close the event in a local park, he began booing Healey even before the politician had made his way properly to the microphone. The park echoed with the sound of noisy people booing, although it was not necessarily the majority, and a spectacularly florid Healey vainly battled on to offer his remarks to the throng.

In terms of the community with whom Mark identified at this time, Healey's voice – and what he had to say – was not something to which to listen and certainly did not merit being heard. Instead, the politician was driven to the border of that community, where the public challenged his opinions and their expression served to reassure everyone else that they were collectively in the right place, where right was on their side. Healey's voice served to define the edge of a group shaped by a common opposition to everything for which he stood. Within that group, if anyone felt anything akin to sympathy towards Healey – or, more importantly, what he had to say at that time – their membership of the community depended on them remaining silent in that regard. And those members derived all manner of social goods from their position within the group, so their silence seemed a small price to pay when they were handsomely paid in the currency of belonging.

Meanwhile, the noise within this not-Healey community – seen as dialogue in that space at that time – represented merely the constant exchange of approved verbalisations. However, this chatter did not define the group; it veiled what was going on by creating the illusion of conversation and meaningful exchange. Energising group definition came from voices such as Healey's – or anyone who broke ranks and expressed sympathy for positions deemed unacceptable – that served to define the boundary between the group and the rest of the world.

The person who expressly verbalised an alternate perspective to the one that labelled the group had a moment on the boundary to decide which way to go: they could recant and return to the fold or they could embrace their new perspective and leap into another communal context. But that moment of hesitation was the exact time in which that community was visibly defined. And the apostate, jumping free of one set of discursive constraints and oftentimes landing in another, became utterly *persona non grata*. Mark recalls that the opprobrium he held towards his so-called comrades in meetings of his Constituency Labour Party's General Management Committee (GMC) far exceeded the loathing he felt towards the Tories in the Town Hall and the central government.

As Monty Python memorably suggested, in the skit from their *Life of Brian* about the People's Front of Judea, it is the Left that is primarily afflicted by all of this (Monty Python, 2012). These are extremely ideological spaces where adherence to a set of beliefs in its purest sense is crucial. Hence, the silence that these communities generate and sustain amongst their memberships. Being complicit with that collectively shared perspective – and suppressing positions that could be seen to be contrary to that overall schema – is essential, when the alternative is the centrifugal force that accompanies the expression of a contrary viewpoint. Mark can think of numerous positions when he suppressed an opinion that ran counter to the group position; more than that – and perhaps worse – he would then give the appearance of being a zealous adherent to the ideas with which he fundamentally disagreed. This is a circumstance where conversation super-ficially looks to be the currency of exchange amongst the members – but where both voice and silence are being actively managed by every indi-vidual in this context.

At that time, Mark was regularly taking part in weekly protests about the NHS in the suburban High Street where he lived. There was a campaign to prevent the closure of a local hospital for elderly people, which led to Mark and a colleague building a large wooden coffin, which they painted black and daubed in white with the letters "NHS". These High Street protests would involve a tiny band of people, their presence horrendously amplified by a megaphone and a snare drum.

On reflection, Mark realises it is entirely likely no one amongst the pro-testers really thought these embarrassingly small and cacophonous activi-ties would influence any passer-by. Instead, it served to do two things: it allowed the protestors to feel superior to those who did not share their views on these issues; and it bound together this community in a ceaseless pursuit of activity rather than of inquiry. To see this as serious politics – the opportunity to engage with others, to dialogically persuade them that one's opinion has virtue and is worthy of further exploration – was (and remains) delusional.

To underscore this point, a woman called Jenny and her husband were shopping in the High Street one Saturday when they saw the band of noisy activists processing down the carriageway, incommoding drivers and offending pedestrians. The coffin, as ever, was there, borne on the shoulders of four sombre-looking people. Mark – festooned with Leftist badges – was marching along with the drum, mindlessly thumping it somewhat arrhythmically as he went. The husband looked disdainfully at the crew and said: 'Look at that bloody idiot with the drum'. Whereupon Jenny, the anaesthetics secretary in the operating theatres where Mark worked at the time as a porter, defensively responded, 'That's not an idiot, that's Mark from work'.

The intemperate observation of Jenny's husband is an attitude with which Mark now has considerable sympathy, after years of reflection on his politics, the sort of world he'd like to see, and whether those two things meaningfully connect. But our contemporary situation makes this more than a personal anecdote. What informed Mark's need to make a noise, beyond the narcissism of youth, is still with him and us. How can we go about engaging with the deeply embedded inequities of the socio-economic system that we unwittingly inhabit, while both envisaging and collectively building a different way of being?

A few years ago, an analysis of the ways in which progressive politics organises and acts took a healthily critical view of the strategy and tactics of the Left in a capitalist society. It's an analysis that supports the idea we are promoting here as to how voice and silence foster the constraints that act as boundaries for groups, particularly groups that feel besieged by the wider set of conditions. To start with, it is suggested that

> [M]any of the tactics of the contemporary left have taken on a ritualistic nature, laden with a heavy dose of fatalism. The dominant tactics – protesting, marching, occupying, and various other forms of direct action – have become part of a well-established narrative, with the people and the police each playing their assigned roles.   (Srnicek & Williams, 2016, p. 6)

It is possible to build from this observation and acknowledge that the assigned roles mentioned are the reassurance the people seek – and that **voice** (agreeing with the discourse that binds these people together in a community, or speaking out against it and hence assuming a liminal position in terms of the ongoing definition of its boundaries) and **silence** (relishing the community connection and keeping quiet about elements of the binding discourse with which one disagrees) are the key practices that shape a politics that is performative and definitely not prefigurative. This latter term deserves some explication: 'By "prefigurative", I mean the embodiment, within the ongoing political practice of a movement, of those forms of social relations, decision-making, culture, and human experience that are the ultimate goal' (Boggs, 1977, p. 7).

This is to argue for a different form of politics, one that turns away from both reformist demands on the state and vanguardist efforts to overthrow that state. It is seen in particular through the distinctive ways in which social movements manifest themselves, their practice showing that '…prefiguration does not privilege the ends to the exclusion of the means of political struggle' (Maeckelbergh, 2016, p. 122). This chimes with one of the maxims offered by Myron Rogers in terms of change in workplace settings and beyond, namely that the process you use to get to the future is the future you get (Atkinson, 2016).

The authors go on to say that these acts are symbolic and ritualistic, yet give the individual the reassurance that they have done something, regardless of how vacuous, self-serving, and unhelpful they are in terms of building bigger and more effective dialogic coalitions to explore change (Srnicek & Williams, 2016, p. 6). Banging a drum in Bromley High St gave Mark a sense of being part of a small group that had something important to say… but, rather than do the diligent work of connecting with people one by one, Mark filled the space where voice might have been heard with the self-satisfied thumping of a drum.

The individualistic satisfaction that arises out of engagement with the gestural – and the associated sense of a membership of a small and pure community – is amplified in our current circumstances. Neo-liberalism has surreptitiously shaped progressive politics so as to encourage it to focus on the individual and segment its constituency into ever finer calibrations rather than opting for the difficult task of seeking to build a grand coalition. This is made worse by our reliance on individualistic channels through which we engage with others. This seems especially apparent when we reflect upon the following:

> The contemporary landscape of social media…is littered with the bitter fallout from an endless torrent of outrage and anger. Given the individualism of current social media platforms – premised on the maintenance of an online identity – it is perhaps no surprise to see online "politics" tend towards the self-presentation of moral purity.   (Srnicek & Williams, 2016, p. 8)

One can detect these important themes in contemporary stories. At the time of writing, the self-styled Colston 4 have just been acquitted after they toppled a statue in Bristol and rolled it into the harbour. Notwithstanding what we might feel about Colston and how committed we might be to uniting with others so as to tackle the iniquities of our society, it remains the case that this was merely gestural politics – and in our dichotomised society, the two camps are forced to one of two opposed positions, for or against. For progressive politics, being "for" the Colston 4 and their act is the default and acts as a litmus test in terms of membership of that community.

Once again, though, this example offers deep insight into the power of voice and silence – and the importance of applying a critical and reflexive approach to language and practice that is so taken for granted that it is never interrogated. For example, in light of their acquittal, one of the four was quoted in the press as saying that the verdict was '…a victory for anybody who wants to be on the right side of history' (Humphries, 2022). The defence teams had indeed urged the jury to be 'on the right side of history' (Humphries & Grylls, 2022).

This decidedly eschatological conceit, drawn directly from the Whiggish sensibilities of the Enlightenment, seeks to segment the world into two camps, one "good" and one "bad". It implies a march of history and does so through a particular progressive prism. Those with whom one disagrees are seen as not merely holding a different opinion but as espousing a position that runs counter to something seen to be historically inevitable. Their arguments are said to be "outdated" or looking "backwards", which means it is not being engaged with what is actually being said. It is possible to dismiss these perspectives on the basis that they look regressive if one assumes one's positions are in some way progressive. No dialogue is deemed necessary with those who seem to be on the wrong side of history.

The voicing of this sentiment establishes the discourse within that specific community and determines its boundaries on the basis of promoting an agreed orthodoxy amongst community members (and a silence if any one of those people has ideas that might be seen to run contrary to that perspective). At the same time, it accommodates any openly expressed alternative positions by driving them to the boundary in order that they might also serve a definitional purpose. In such an arrangement the idea of dialogue effectively disappears.

Supplementing this ideological certainty, and hence rigidity, is the reported response from one of the four that: 'We didn't change history, we rectified it' (Humphries, 2022), which seems to resonate with the antihumanist practice of airbrushing people from photographs in order to seemingly re-write the past. One is forced to think of those pictures from the Russian revolution in 1917, where Lenin is on a platform addressing an audience, alongside a space where in earlier versions one would have seen Leon Trotsky.

Echoing the rigid certainty of the so-called "democratic centralism" of Leninist political practice, in reality, more centralised than democratic, they were also quoted as saying that their act was justified because from their perspective: '…"democracy had well and truly broken down" after years of political deadlock in [Bristol] about what should be done with the statue…' (Humphries & Grylls, 2022). This throwback to "vanguardism", where a small, self-declared and quite possibly wholly unrepresentative group of a class or community substitutes itself for those on whose behalf it says it is acting, is an example of a voice speaking over the voices of a wider population, some of whom are then silenced by this supplantation. As democratic leftists used to chide the Leninists: "If you want to be a vanguard, go and join Securicor!"

The refusal to embrace the idea of unity as part of an expansive notion of community has been a feature of entrenched positions across history. But the "death of dialogue" that seems especially noticeable in contemporary circumstances is generating more and more corrosive antagonism as people lock into the model of "community" that we have analysed above. In this regard, the story of Kristine Hostetter is illustrative and worth exploring.

Hostetter is a fourth-grade teacher in a town called San Clemente in Southern California. Her politics by all accounts were conservative and sympathetic to Trumpism, which resulted in her joining the March on the Capitol on 6 January 2021. It's unclear how active she was in the disorder that unfolded, but – as the following explains – her "community" was rent in twain by her involvement:

> But it was not until Ms Hostetter's husband posted a video of her marching down Pennsylvania Avenue towards the Capitol on Jan. 6 that her politics collided with an opposite force gaining momentum in San Clemente: a growing number of left-leaning parents and students who, in the wake of the civil-rights set off by the police killing of George Floyd, decided they would no longer countenance the right-wing tilt of their neighbours and the racism they said was commonplace. That there was no evidence that Ms Hostetter had displayed any overt racism was beside the point – to them, her pro-Trump views seemed self-evidently laced with white supremacy. So she became the cause.   (Rosenberg, 2021)

In the midst of the clamour generated by two competing communities of shuttered thinking, there were a number of pertinent observations with respect to this diminution of dialogue. The first was that one of the antagonists who felt moved to start a petition for Hofstetter to be dismissed was an erstwhile student of this teacher. In the New York Times (NYT) report, this person was moved to observe on her time as a student that '[S]he has only warm memories of her time in Ms Hostetter's class and cannot recall being mistreated or singled out for being black' (Rosenberg, 2021). Here the desire to give voice, and be part of a collective voice, supersedes experience, which meets community needs but does not serve either side of the discussion in terms of initiating space for dialogue.

The second observation pivots around the following:

> Complicating matters is Ms. Hofstetter's relative silence. Apart from appearing at protests and the incident at the beach [where it is alleged she was seen at a public face mask burning], she has said little publicly over the past year, and did not respond to repeated interview requests for this article. People have filled in the blanks.   (Rosenberg, 2021)

There is a subtle demand implicit in the passing observation that she failed to reply to the NYT when they approached her clearly more than once. Here is a demand for voice, made by a powerful element of the Fourth Estate. In this instance – and in regard to others seeking to read the situation – Hofstetter's silence is not allowed: whatever she means by her silence is overwritten by what others read into it. It cannot just be a silence; wordlessness here is seen as a vacuum that draws in the words of other.

This reminds us that listening to react is nowhere near listening to hear, regardless of how uncomfortable what we might then hear might make us. In an analysis of the way in which right-wing politics in Germany is arguing that the dominant (liberal) discourse is denying them the opportunity to say contrary things, Schröter (2019) moves from scholarship to partisanship. It leads them to this observation, which is worth consideration through the prism of voice and silence we have outlined:

> The present-day German anti-political correctness discourse evolves mainly around claims by the New Right to have been silenced in a left-liberal discourse hegemony. I will describe anti-political correctness discourse as a language ideological debate and claims to have been

> silenced as strategic metadiscursive moves which seek to shift public
> discourse to gain legitimacy for the New Right's ideological positions
> and, most of all, to delegitimise the left, which is framed as censoring
> other views.   (Schröter, 2019, p. 168)

In this formulation, the author ascribes a motive to the way in which she
sees her political opponents behaving without any evidence other than her
individual interpretation. Her articulation of this offers no room for the idea
that perhaps those opponents genuinely feel that their voice is denied – and
that it might actually be the politics of the Left that is constraining dialogue.
And, even if the agenda being promoted by the Left can be construed as
fairer and more decent, it remains a partisan view that should not inhibit
speech, regardless of whose opinions one might then be forced to entertain.
This is why the sneering attitudes of many who see themselves as in some
way progressive in their politics towards those who in the UK supported
Brexit, and in the US who continue to find Donald Trump an appealing candidate, seems so problematic. If you demonise those with whom you disagree, you are left only with exorcism as opposed to conversational exchange.

A school inspection by Ofsted at the end of 2021 underscores the tension that exists as the agenda of pursuing the betterment of the world col-
lides with a political insistence that such betterment requires that no one
should be openly allowed to take a position that is contrary to that. The
institution was strongly committed to equality and inclusion, but the following was recommended, in light of the fact that 'A significant number
felt that their voices are not encouraged or, in some cases, are suppressed'
(Ofsted, 2022):

> While recognising the importance of promoting equalities, a significant
> minority of parents and pupils told inspectors that a culture has devel-
> oped where alternative opinions are not felt welcome. In some class-
> rooms, teaching has not allowed for questioning or for the balanced
> presentation of opposing views.   (Ofsted, 2022)

Here we see how voice and silence interplay in the context of a collective built on social and political acceptability and intention. We offer this
not to denigrate the efforts of the school to tackle head on quite legitimate challenges around equity and fairness. It does however offer an excellent instance where the best of intentions can become subsumed by a

community superstructure that denies voices other than those deemed to be acceptable. This in turn silences thoughts and expressions of a range of perspectives that are deemed alien to that specific context.

Some observations drawn from Foucault offer some further illumination as to how a community collectively generates its boundary. The boundary is constructed through the interconnectivity of (i) respectable/acceptable speech (that which is zealously embraced or performatively said); (ii) expected silence (the literally unspoken agreement that community members tacitly holding views in mind that run contrary to what is seen as respectable/acceptable speech within the community boundary will keep their peace at all times); and (iii) outlandish expression (wherein a member of that community can no longer keep silent, which drives them to the edge of the community where they personally teeter – and, by their presence there, reinforce the boundary-edge of the community and oftentimes the strengths of the binds that tie together all of its other members).

This schema leads us to Foucault's orientation to the idea of experience and his core notion that power is discernible not merely where one person seeks to control and/or influence others but where one epistemic perspective assumes the mantle of normalcy, whilst others subsumed by it acquire the status of Other. Foucault mobilises a particular notion through which to articulate this:

> [T]here is the idea of a "limit-experience," a foundational gesture by which a culture excludes that which will function as its outside – in this case, the exclusion of madness and unreason by reason...Foucault suggests that one could do a series of histories of these limit-experiences, which might include the construction of the Orient as other to the West, the fundamental division between reason and dream, and the institution of sexual prohibitions.   (O'Leary, 2008, p. 8)

In later work, Foucault enriched this perspective by asserting that '...a "limit-experience" is an extreme experience which transgresses the limits of a culture – an experience, that is, of the sort that Bataille both describes and conjures' as opposed solely to an event wherein a society builds a boundary between in and out (O'Leary, 2008, p. 8). As Foucault explains:

> The idea of a limit-experience that wrenches the subject from itself is what was important to me in my reading of Nietzsche, Bataille, and

Blanchot, and what explains the fact that however boring, however eru-
dite my books may be, I've always conceived of them as direct experiences aimed at pulling myself free of myself, at preventing me from being
the same.   (Foucault, 1978)

This expansion of Foucault's thinking so that limit-experience can refer
to both the way in which a society sets its boundaries and to the way in
which people might opt at an individual level to test those boundaries is
important. The former perspective resonates with our thinking as to how
communities define themselves through the self-management of voice and
silence. The latter offers empowerment to the human agent to either suc-
cumb to the numbing consensus on which community is so often founded
or to move to the boundary in order to test it openly.

   This latter practice finds an echo in the sociology of what is called
edgework. This refers to specific spaces where certain people actively seek
out and pointedly engage in risk-taking activities, such as skydiving and
the like. It is suggested that this can best be understood as follows: '...
the opposition between spontaneity and constraint is at the heart of many
important problems that confront members of modern postindustrial society. An exploration of the spontaneity-constraint dialectic holds the key to
understanding why people pursue edgework' (Lyng, 1990, p. 865). It is
suggested that edgework tends to include activities that involve a threat to
well-being or to an ordered sense of self. Hence, we suggest that breaking
silence and giving voice in a constrained context can quite reasonably be
thought of as edgework, proceeding from our analysis of Foucault's use of
the concept of limit-experience.

   But we must never disregard the comfort that derives from being part
of a community, as opposed to teetering precariously on its boundary or
finding oneself entirely outside of it. We have spoken already about how
persuasive the fear of isolation can be. A voice from Communist Albania
draws upon Kafka's writing to speak about their experience, noting that,
for Kafka's characters, in titles such as The Trial and The Castle, they endure
a lack of freedom but also isolation at one and the same time (Rejmer,
2021, pp. 44–45). No one comes to support the individual; nobody con-
curs with their analysis of the absurdity of the circumstances in which they
are trapped; not one other person comes to show solidarity in the face of a
manifestly oppressive situation.

Our anxiety over isolation is supplemented by a counterpoint with which it interacts, namely our delight in being part of something social, such as a club or an association. As a sidebar, we may also be considering how we fit into the inevitable hierarchy that will exist in such circumstances: we may want to demonstrate our ambition to achieve higher status in that context by saying regularly and loudly what is accepted and thereby contributing to the regime of silence that prevails in that space. Recent research, for example, found that '…low-status individuals compared to high-status individuals are more likely to use jargon in the communication and conversation with others' (Brown et al., 2020, p. 287), which they label as *compensatory conspicuous communication*.

We are often fearful of being cast out – but we are equally enamoured of just the reassurance of the crowd, of being inside. And that can lead to our silence – and our collective silencing of others.

References

Abrams, D. & Hogg, M. A., 1988. Comments on the motivational status of self-esteem in social identity and intergroup discrimination. *European Journal of Social Psychology*, 18, pp. 317–334.

Abrams, D. et al., 1990. Knowing what to think by knowing who you are: Self-categorization and the nature of norm formation, conformity and group polarization. *British Journal of Social Psychology*, 29, pp. 97–119.

Atkinson, J., 2016. *Myron's Maxims*. [Online] Available at: https://www.heartoftheart.org/?p=1196 [Accessed 24 June 2022].

Boggs, C., 1977. *Marxism, prefigurative communism, and the problem of workers' control*. [Online] Available at: https://syllabus.pirate.care/_preview/library/Carl%20Boggs/Marxism, %20prefigurative%20communism, %20and%20the%20problem%20of%20workers'%20control%20(439)/Marxism, %20prefigurative%20communism, %20and%20the%20-%20Carl%20Boggs.pdf [Accessed 24 June 2022].

Bourdieu, P., 1977. *Outline of a theory of practice*. Cambridge: Cambridge University Press.

Brown, Z. C., Anicich, E. M. & Galinsky, A. D., 2020. Compensatory conspicuous communication: Low status increases jargon use. *Organizational Behaviour and Human Decision Processes*, Issue 161, pp. 274–290.

Cialdini, R. B. et al., 1976. Basking in reflected glory: Three (football) field studies. *Journal of Personality and Social Psychology*, 34(3), pp. 366–375.

Corlett, W., 1993. *Community without unity: A politics of Derridian extravagance.* Durham, NC: Duke University Press.

Follet, M. P., 1919. Community is a process. *The Philosophical Review*, 28(6), pp. 576–588.

Foucault, M., 1978. Interview with Michel Foucault. In: J. D. Faubion, ed. *Power: Essential works of Foucault 1954–1984.* New York: The New Press, pp. 239–297.

Foucault, M., 1991. *Discipline and punish: The birth of the prison.* London: Penguin.

Humphries, W., 2022. Bristol jury clears protestors who toppled Colston statue. *The Times*, 6 January, p. 1.

Humphries, W. & Grylls, G., 2022. Colston verdict 'isn't licence to destroy statues'. *The Times*, 6 January, p. 5.

Jacobs, J., 1961/2000. *The death and life of great American cities.* London: Pimlico.

Janis, I. L., 1971. Groupthink. *Psychology Today*, pp. 84–90.

Janis, I. L., 1991. Groupthink. In: E. A. Griffin, ed. *A first look at communication theory.* New York: McGraw-Hill, pp. 235–246.

Klein, K. J. & D'Aunno, T. A., 1986. Psychological sense of community in the workplace. *Journal of Community Psychology*, 14(October), pp. 365–377.

Lyng, S., 1990. Edgework: A social psychological analysis of voluntary risk taking. *American Journal of Sociology*, 95(4), pp. 851–886.

Maeckelbergh, M., 2016. The prefigurative turn: The time and place of social movement practice. In: A. C. Dinerstein, ed. *Social sciences for an other politics: Women theorizing without parachutes.* London: Palgrave Macmillan, pp. 121–142.

McMillan, D. W. & Chavis, D. M., 1986. Sense of community: A definition and theory. *Journal of Community Psychology*, 14(January), pp. 6–23.

Monty Python, 2012. *Life of Brian – The People's Front of Judea.* [Online] Available at: https://youtu.be/WboggjN_G-4 [Accessed 24 September 2021].

Ofsted, 2022. *The American School in London.* [Online] Available at: https://reports.ofsted.gov.uk/provider/27/101168 [Accessed 15 March 2022].

O'Leary, T., 2008. Foucault, experience, literature. *Foucault Studies*, Issue 5, pp. 5–25.

Rejmer, M., 2021. *Mud sweeter than honey: Voices of communist Albania*. London: MacLehose Press.

Rosenberg, M., 2021. *A teacher marched to the Capitol. When she got home, the fight began*. [Online] Available at: https://www.nytimes.com/2021/04/10/us/politics/kristine-hostetter-capitol.html?referringSource=articleShare [Accessed 26 April 2021].

Schröter, M., 2019. The language ideology of silence and silencing in public discourse: Claims to silencing as metadiscursive moves in German anti-political correctness discourse. In: A. J. Murray & K. Durrheim, eds. *Qualitative studies of silence: The unsaid as social action*. Cambridge: Cambridge University Press, pp. 165–185.

Srnicek, N. & Williams, A., 2016. *Inventing the future: Postcapitalism and a world without work*. London: Verso.

Thompson, J. B., 1992. Editor's introduction. In: J. B. Thompson, ed. *Language and symbolic power – Pierre Bourdieu*. Cambridge: Polity, pp. 1–31.

Trepte, S., 2006. Social identity theory. In: J. Bryant & P. Varderer, eds. *Psychology of entertainment*. New York: Routledge, pp. 255–271.

Wagner, W. et al., 1999. Theory and method of social representations. *Asian Journal of Social Psychology*, 2, pp. 95–125.

9

LESSONS FOR CORPORATE LIFE (ON SUSTAINING CLIMATES OF SILENCE AND VOICE)

In Kafka's parable on Ulysses, we are told that the silence of the Sirens is more perilous than their song, and that Ulysses – who realized, as his ship neared them, that the Sirens were silent – put on an act to protect himself from this silence, plugging his ears with wax and having his men tie him to the mast. In Kafka's retelling of the tale, the silence of the Sirens represents a zero degree of song and, following a stubborn tradition that sees in absence the most extreme form of presence, also represents an at once zero and ultimate degree of reality. In this sense Heidegger could write that we truly experience language precisely when words fail us. (Agamben, 2012, p. 96)

Speech can be persuasive, as can silence. Silence can be chosen and also inflicted. The two are intimately intertwined and are experienced in specific social contexts that are always and inescapably riven with power. We may opt to speak – and, in doing so, run counter to the expectations of the milieu in which we find ourselves. We may appear to choose not to speak, when we secretly know that the idea of choice is a contested one in

DOI: 10.4324/9781003296683-11

general – and all the more so when we consider the environment where we might wish to use our voice. Our refusal to say something may be a choice in name only, a situation that feels to be inescapably forced upon us.

But what does all of this mean for us all in our corporate contexts? The organisation in society makes great pretence to be egalitarian yet is infested with hierarchy; it cleaves to the notion that it is democratic, whilst – at the same time – tightly managing the conversational economy that exists within its boundaries. It announces itself as a place where there is a parity of esteem, when we know that some voices "matter" whilst others are deemed not to be of value, despite the seemingly endless invitations to speak up so that our voices can be heard. And, importantly, it is a terrain where there is a delicate interplay between everyone in terms of voice and silence, particularly with respect to the workplace community or communities to which we seek to belong or maintain our membership in.

More than anything else, it is a space wherein an assemblage of human agents interact through language, through its outward expression and its subjugation. It is an arena where meaning accrues to speech as an act – and to what is said, by whom, and where. Equally, silence in this domain has meaning for all involved, and it can be subtly enforced, gently encouraged, or personally chosen, although none of these exist outside the context where communication takes place.

To provide a few practical observations in response to this exposition on silence, in particular, we offer another live example, to consolidate the ideas outlined above.

*

> "It was like living in *The Trial*," said Shehu. "You were hauled out of your house for interrogation and asked, 'What do you have to say?' You hadn't done anything wrong, but the authorities had their own opinion about you, and were particularly resolute about inflicting punishment on suspects and innocent people. You need only to have said something at a committee meeting that someone else found disturbing. You might not have realised it yet yourself, but they already knew you were having doubts.   (Rejmer, 2021, pp. 36–37)

In 1984, Mark was a student of industrial relations and trade union studies at Middlesex Polytechnic. It was another foray for him into formal education, after an undistinguished result in O Level Sociology at a night class in Orpington College and an engagement with an A Level in Physics at the same institution, aborted after one painfully embarrassing lesson which reinforced how his O Level achievement had been (as his physics teacher had rather pointedly remarked) pretty much a fluke. He was a full-time student at Middlesex and was feeling rather pleased with himself.

It was the time of the miners' strike and – even though the class was exclusively made up of socialistic trade unionists who were all (some of them very) mature students – it very quickly split down the middle, between ardent supporters of the industrial action and those who took a more measured, even sceptical, perspective on the dispute. The two factions sat across from one another in the classroom, the supporters in one back corner of the room and the sceptics in the other. In crude outline, the supporters' group was heavily metropolitan – indeed, London-centric – and, because it was a post-graduate certificate, largely made up of graduates. Only Mark had been an active shop steward prior to joining the programme. Contrariwise, the sceptics tended to hail from towns and cities outside the capital, particularly those in the Midlands and the North. Most – if not all – had been employed in working-class occupations and had been union stewards.

The two groups scowled at each other across the room and seemingly converted every topic of scholarly conversation in the class into a tightly scripted exchange about the National Union of Miners, its leadership, and the strike. There was no real intellectual to and fro, certainly no space for give and take. It was merely the thoughtless parroting of well-rehearsed (and completely uninterrogated) positions between the two groups – with the sceptics, in truth, perhaps just a little more willing to show some curiosity and engagement in a meaningful debate about the most significant industrial relations dispute for a good many years and the politics that surrounded it.

Someone from the supporters' group brought in a copy of The Face magazine, which had a piece on the strike. Mark and a friend avidly tore out the full-page pictures of Dennis Skinner and Tony Benn that illustrated the article – and churlishly stuck them on the wall high in the corner, so our "heroes" could be seen to be glowering down on our foes, acting as religious icons who would directly impact the thoughts and positions of those on the other side. In truth, of course, not one of us on the supporters' side truly imagined that appending these portraits to the wall would make the slightest difference in terms of the discussion we might find our way to have about this important topic. They were put up to piss people off, something of which Mark is now somewhat ashamed.

Even the faculty was judged – particularly by the supporters' group – as to whether they were "on the side of the angels" (that is, agreed with the pro-strike position) or not. At least one was seen to pass the litmus test while another seemed non-committal, although we cut them some slack due to their history in the movement. But one seemed to turn our litmus paper Tory blue rather than pink or red, and so the supporters took against them in a quite significant fashion.

On one occasion, late in the academic year, we heard from one of our numbers that this "blue" faculty member had behaved inappropriately towards her in a one-to-one tutorial. Even now the notion of this crude abuse of power between a lecturer and a student sticks in Mark's craw. But this legitimate complaint, which should have been raised through the college channels to be properly investigated, was quickly seized upon by Mark and his colleagues as a political campaign not solely about this specific misbehaviour but about the politics of the lecturer, which were taken to inform directly the wholly inexcusable behaviour that was said to have taken place. The woman's complaint was wrest from her and instrumentalised as a means of attacking the faculty member.

Mark and another man from the supporters' group took responsibility for the drafting of a collective letter to the course leader. They spent hours on it, while the woman who had originally made the complaint was barely involved and showed little interest in the line that was being taken. Eventually, the letter was produced and signatories from the supporters' group put their names to it. It was passed to the course leader – Mark's view now being that the politicised content that filled the letter drowned out the woman's voice of concern about the way in which she felt a man had behaved towards her, in the context of a professional as opposed to a personal relationship.

All of this reinforces our assertions as to how voice and silence interconnect to generate community boundaries – and in so doing can diminish the real opportunity for dialogue to appear. For Mark, the drafting of the letter had slipped free of the instance that sparked it. Instead, it was something that served to prove that Mark was worthy of his membership of the supporters' group. In social circumstances such as these, founded as they so often are upon a notion of purity, truth and faith, members need constantly to assert the positions which are seen to bind that group together. This is complicity rather than conversation, a way of saying the thing that is required to be said – as opposed to a truth that has to be said.

Obviously, it would also have been possible to stay silent so as to reinforce the boundaries of that tight-knit community of which Mark was so desperate to be a member. Crucially, though, espousing a perspective that ran counter to the dominant discourse of that particular collective would have seen the speaker teetering on the precipitous edge of that community. The other community members would have looked at this individual and marked the boundary that the person speaking out in a contrary fashion served to define. Their voice would no longer be the reassuring voice from within but instead their speech would serve to guide what and who were in and out.

The outspoken person cannot forever remain on that boundary, having seen it defined by their voice in this instance. They are likely then to fall into a liminal space between a range of communities, such as it might be said to have existed between supporters and sceptics. But this limbo is an isolation that is too much to bear for most human beings, so it seems more likely that the liminal is simply a slight gap across which they leap to join another community. In this regard, we are endlessly giving voice to perspectives that merely buy us into – and thereby give shape to – a collective, rather than ever truly speaking out.

This leads us to the idea that, had anyone in the supporters' group wanted to do anything other than reinforce their membership of the group and thereby strengthen its boundaries, their expression of a view that ran contrary to the accepted one would have left them at the very limit of that collective. Concern over isolation and estrangement from an environment that was reassuringly homely for them would perhaps have led them to stay momentarily in the liminal space before crossing over and possibly joining the sceptics' group. The courageous alternative, of course, that which embraces the Foucauldian notion of parrhesia, would be to remain in the liminal space, using their speech to attract others to perhaps form a new community. But that idea of the "lone voice", endlessly echoing in the void but obtaining no other response than the diminishing sound of their own voice, is about saying the heretofore unsayable – and being able to bear the idea that one might be alone and isolated in a wider silence between other communities.

So, how does this translate into a corporate context? Here are a number of observations arising out of the exploration and examples offered in this chapter thus far:

1.   We create a collective climate around voice and silence

Let us focus, to begin with, on the "we" here. Certainly, those who occupy positional power – especially the people who define themselves as leaders in an organisation – have a significant impact on how people speak up and on their silence. Most bosses now are attuned to the idea that they should be listening to their workforce; however, the experience of many of the people with whom we have spoken over recent years is that few of those bosses actually listen to hear – and that act of hearing and acknowledging what is being said, regardless of how unpalatable it might at first appear or how quick the listener might be to dismiss it, is the stepping off point for meaningful dialogue at work and an honest exchange.

The first advice for those in leadership positions can simply be stated thus:

Listen to hear – and, if you don't intend to hear, then don't pretend to listen

The need for more honesty in organisational life recurs again and again for us as we explore the experiences of people from our shared perspectives of both practitioner and writer. We are not much sold on the notions of "authentic leadership" or similarly on the admonition that everyone should "bring their whole self to work". The workplace is an unnatural place where we perform the role for which we are paid; corporate demands that seek to insert the workplace into our interiors – that intrudes to enfold our hearts and minds – have at best surveillant ambitions and at worse carry the stench of totalitarianism.

Let's return to that "we", which is there to implicate us all in corporate life. The two of us have argued throughout this chapter that our location in a community – particularly a collective group in the workplace – is dependent on the ways in which we subtly manage our voice and silence in that context. Self-censorship is a foundational element of tolerance, respect and civility. But the litmus test is the extent to which we manage speech and restraint through the lens of our personal ethics – or, instead, how we echo that which we hear around us and bury attitudes that run counter to the socially defined discourse. So, some advice for us all in corporate life is:

Be aware of both your own ethical compass and the collective constraint that surrounds you...and create the space in yourself to allow those two perspectives to encounter one another

We have also endeavoured to underscore that silence is not merely the absence of noise. In particular, silence should not be thought of as the thing that arises when people are not speaking. Instead, it is implicit in human communication and intrinsic to speech itself, which is constructed through the rich weaving of voice and silence. Silence may be something people chose – or which they feel to be imposed. Either way, that silence is saying something to you. You must listen to that silence in its wider context instead of just rushing in to invite those who have opted for quietness to abandon it. Silence in corporate settings is not noiselessness that must be filled. It can arise out of reluctance or resistance, from discomfort or constraint. And it is not something that you have a right to interrogate or penalise.

If someone decides to be silent – whether in light of an individual decision or because they do not feel as though the context in which they find themselves would welcome what they would really want to say – they are involved in an act of communication as opposed to a withdrawal from the wider space of discussion. In light of this, the following precept can be acknowledged:

People will personally choose when to speak and when to keep silent. It is no one else's job to compel someone to give voice – as much as no one should create conditions where people feel compelled to stay silent.

Corporate life has developed an obsession with making sure that people feel able to speak up – but has failed to acknowledge that this is meaningless without careful and meaningful attention to the organisational environment, its communicative climate, and the delicate issue of psychological safety, despite this linkage being clearly acknowledged (Edmondson & Lei, 2014). This is important in light of what is seen to be the vitality of voice and silence to businesses:

> Voice in particular has been discussed as a critical mechanism for employees to improve working conditions and enable them to change or remove aversive personal outcomes that they may otherwise experience, such as "exhaustion" and "withdrawal". In contrast, repeated decisions to remain silent can increase such aversive personal outcomes. Therefore, "burnout"—"a form of occupational fatigue that is characterized by both exhaustion and withdrawal"—is an important employee outcome that has been theorized to have opposite relations with voice and silence.   (Sherf, et al., 2021, p. 118)

If your world view is one that privileges the idea of business outcomes rather than one that seeks to put humans at the centre of the organisation, there is evidence that indicates how creating an environment where voice can find space, and silence is not mandated, offers you a bottom-line payoff. That said, if you're lacking an ethical orientation, then – in all honesty and with the best will in the world – you simply won't have the heart to generate the required supportive context. Your efforts will be transparently insincere and crudely instrumental.

2. Leadership involves opening up space for dialogue not managing voice

Let's give some substance to this assertion. Simply, no one is fooled by the shameful performativity of a great many senior leaders. John tells the story of the way in which a group of staff seemed oddly interested to ask questions in the town hall meetings that their CEO convened. When he asked someone leaving one such meeting why this was, the response was simple: it's better to be sitting in comfort in a boring meeting than standing in the plant doing the boring work.

It would seem that everyone involved in this supposed act of communication is seeing through its performative nature. There is the concern that those people at the top of the tree begin to believe their own hype, surrounded by people who are unlikely to ever draw attention to this and are simply entranced by the appearance of these meetings. Nothing feels more reassuring and personally gratifying for a senior leader than the semblance of having followers. But those followers may not all be as passive as it appears; you may be being played by your people… and no one would blame them for that. This leads us to the following claim:

If you refuse for whatever reason to attend properly to those around you in your organisation who speak up, they may opt for silence – or use their voice as resistance. But you won't know what's going on.

The world is weary of leaders across society being seen merely to listen but not necessarily to hear. Three years before Mark was born, the bible of boring management was busy ideologising the idea of listening as one of the facets of modern management, which saw a 14-point checklist for executives to establish a listening improvement programme (Nichols & Stevens, 1957). At one point, four processes are suggested for mental activities that distinguish what makes a good listener. Interestingly this model suggested that the executive would not actually be listening so as to hear what it was that was being said in the moment. Instead, the first activity was defined thus: 'The listener thinks ahead of the talker, trying to anticipate what the oral discourse is leading to and what conclusions will be drawn from the words spoken at the moment' (Nichols & Stevens, 1957, p. 88).

Most people would see that as leadership condescension, effectively indicating that the executive is consumed by a need to second-guess what is being said to them rather than actually clearing their head to hear what is being said and how. It suggests that the subaltern voice is not something of value in itself but merely offers material that has to be mentally leapfrogged so that the leader gets what they want as soon as possible. This is rather than getting to where the speaker wants to be, regardless of how long it may take them to get there, given who they're speaking to and the power context in which that exchange is taking place. Here writ large is how most staff engagement exercises are experienced, as the encouragement of a chorus of voices that can be interpreted as being in support of a dominant organisational narrative. All of which leads to the following stipulation:

Voice in organisation is not simply a leadership resource, something to be sanitised and absorbed – and then crudely put to work in the service of the corporate narrative.

Indeed, it is often a counterpoint to that narrative, something that needs to be heard in order to challenge the taken for granted. This needs everyone to listen and to hear, not just to listen and utilise. This means leaders need to set aside the ideas that they hold about listening – why it's important and how to be seen to do it – and go back to first principles. These actively privilege the vitality of human dialogue and recognise that those in positions of power have a major responsibility to manage themselves in those engagements, acknowledging how power is being experienced and is shaping and directing the exchange.

Whereas "leadership" needs to be seen to be listening, so as to placate people in the workplace and foster the illusion of involvement, an ethical leader will be present in order to hear and value what is actually being said. The former is clumsily performative, with people looking like they are truly attending to what their interlocutors are working so hard to get across: the latter is a human-to-human endeavour to connect so that the opinions, ideas, concerns, and anxieties are actually heard in a corporate setting. This is also an active attempt to acknowledge the power that is invested in our workplace relationships, which is also the behaviour of an ethical leader.

A leader needs to make room for all of the voices, in particular those with which they disagree, and which run counter to their perspective.

3. Be intensely mindful of the social functions of voice and silence – and your impactful role in that context

We are mindful of a story from a very senior leader who describes how the merest flicker of emotion that passed across their face in a meeting, where someone was speaking to a document that they had drafted, became amplified by the dialogic emptiness of their organisation into a major drama. An entirely fictionalised account took wind and became common knowledge, wherein this executive had been seen to rip the document apart and tear the speaker off a strip.

In that respect then, the leader can be said to carry two key responsibilities. The first of those is as follows:

> *Foster and encourage through your exemplary behaviours and prefigurative practice an organisational space at the core of your business where people feel that their voice will be listened to, heard, and respected – even if you are then moved to contest what it is that they say.*

The fundamental faultline in liberalism is exposed here, of course, with respect to people being seen to say the unsayable. For example, as we were drafting this chapter, the story broke of Dr Steve James, a consultant anaesthetist working in intensive care at a London hospital, speaking up to the Secretary of State for Health and Social Care about mandated vaccination for NHS staff during a visit to this trust (Gayle, 2022). In this context, the politician notionally looked to be engaging with the people at the hospital and inviting them to express their opinions, particularly on this topic. The doctor's response was clearly unexpected, as he expressly mobilised arguments to suggest that there was limited scientific evidence to support the policy; moreover, the newspaper report suggests that, following his comments, other staff – in particular nurses as part of that party – did not respond to the Secretary of State's invitation to outline what they thought of the situation.

This intervention prompted a rapid contrary response, highlighting several issues, one of which was that, whilst Dr Steve James was entitled to a personal opinion about this specific policy, his comments were too generalised and cast doubt on the efficacy of vaccines in general. This is a somewhat nuanced perspective that is difficult to maintain, given how speaking up is always a deeply personal matter – and is about sharing the opinion that you hold as an individual as opposed to merely parroting a party line (Foucault, 2019).

The wider reaction took place amongst the broader professional community to which Dr James might be said to belong, with other doctors and clinical staff quick to respond in order to counter his view. Hence, a few days later, it was reported that:

> [H]is stance has provoked a backlash from NHS staff across the country. Dr Rich Breeze, an anaesthetist at University Hospital Lewisham, said: "I completely disagree with Steve James who told Sajid Javid that he didn't believe in vaccines. A deluded, irresponsible and dangerous intervention." Thousands of NHS staff took to Twitter with similar messages explaining why they had received both doses and a booster jab. Many said it was the "single most important thing" they could do to avoid being admitted to intensive care or dying from the virus.   (Gallagher, 2022)

Regardless of how unhelpful – and indeed unpalatable – we might consider Dr James's intervention to be, his reasoned intervention, obeying its own internal logic, needs to be heard, rather than dismissed based on the mental equivalent of a knee-jerk reflex and a deeply partisan adherence to what might be seen as a contrary position. Indeed, the framing that perceives our position to be diametrically opposed to that offered by Dr James is one that unhelpfully expands the gap between these perspectives. This gap then becomes so extended that it disallows people from reaching across to one another to create a foundation for dialogue.

We conjecture that Dr James may well have been complicitly keeping his counsel so as to maintain his comfortable position as part of the medical community to that point. When he did find an opportunity and the context in which to give voice to the contrary view that he must have been tacitly holding for some time, our thinking suggests that this drove him to the boundary of that community – and the reaction that it elicited served primarily to strengthen that boundary and reinforce the connectivity of those left inside it. Dr James hovers precariously on the edge, possibly having fallen into a liminal space outside of the community of which he was previously a member yet lacking the momentum or direction towards another alternative community, such as those who extend criticality to the whole question of Covid and vaccination. Indeed, he may end up in that awkward place – between the orthodoxy and the alternative perspective, the anti-orthodoxy – in perpetuity, given that he is unable to subscribe to either position wholeheartedly.

Our immediate response is perhaps to castigate, to isolate, and to marginalise someone expressing their opinions in this way. But that is a community action that, in turn, serves to bind us in our sense of rightness by identifying those outside of our boundaries. At root, we are enacting the elements that were attributed to the way in which the idea of the "crowd" asserted itself towards the end of the 19th century, which worked on the assumption that: 'The substitution of the unconscious action of crowds for the conscious activity of individuals is one of the principal characteristics of the present age' (Le Bon, 1896/2001, p. 4). This author identified three mechanisms that serve to bind us to the crowd, namely: the sense of invincible power that it offers to us and which disinhibits us so significantly; the contagiousness of life in a crowd, which makes it more comfortable for us to surrender ourselves to it; and the way in which our immersion in a crowd creates a state of fascination that is akin to hypnotic control, thereby rendering us puppets to a collective will rather than autonomous individuals. (Le Bon, 1896/2001, pp. 17–18)

This leads us to a summary of the second leadership responsibility, namely,

> *Your role is to foster unity in the face of the presence of potentially divisive community. And this needs you to invite, listen to, and hear all of the voices, particularly those who sound the least like yours – and then to encourage engagement with those sentiments rather than blithe dismissal.*

This feels as though it runs counter to the defensiveness that is a feature of so much contemporary practice in the field of Human Resources. Indeed, HR is the business activity that, despite its attempts to reorient and reposition itself, leads to the following conclusion:

> HR often gets trapped in a **policing** role, mediating employee grievances, monitoring compliance with employment laws, and enforcing codes of conduct. What's more, the function often has seen its mission as one of helping workers overcome deficiencies that hinder their performance. Without ignoring these tasks, the New HR concentrates on the positive. How can we enhance revenue by doing more to engage employees? (Breitfelder & Dowling, 2008)

We're not sure that anyone is taken in by the notion that poor old HR has somehow got trapped in the business of policing the workforce. Nor are we persuaded by the idea that this supposed entrapment is occasional, rather than constant in respect to what it is created to do and so actually does in a capitalist business. Moreover, we are compelled to note that HR has sought to transition in the way police forces now declare themselves to be police services; whether the HR functionary is breathing down your neck because you're not being sufficiently organisationally compliant, or badgering you for a sanitised version of your opinion in focus groups designed to generate the illusion of engagement, we are being policed.

So, our final recommendation is simply as follows:

As a leader, you need to tell HR to back off, because that policing function diminishes dialogue instead of encouraging it.

Let's conclude this initial section of guidance for leaders seeking to engage at a human and meaningful level with others in their organisational settings with a quick shuttle back to the 19th century, where a leading liberal can be found making the following observation about policing opinion and the importance of voice, silence, and community:

> Laws to punish differences of opinion are as useless as they are monstrous. Differences of opinion on politics are denounced and punished as seditious, on religious topics as blasphemous, and on social questions as immoral and obscene. Yet the sedition, blasphemy, and immorality punished in one age are often found to be the accepted, and sometimes the admired, political, religious, and social teaching of a more educated period. **Heresies are the evidence of some attempts on the part of the masses to find opinions for themselves**. The attempts may be often foolish, but should never be regarded as deserving of punishment.
> (Bradlaugh, 1878, p. 3)

For those who constrain themselves in a community of orthodoxy, determining perhaps that they are on the right side of history, as the people down in Bristol asserted, they will define their positions as the heresies that will displace the dominant discourse. In their minds, it will be inevitable that the rightness of their opinions will finally become widely accepted. However, what this disregards is that those who sit opposite them in our dichotomised public conversation will also see themselves as expressing a heresy – a heresy that also lays claim, of course, to the position of future dominance. And, lastly, the expression of those heresies has the function in the community that we have described here, encompassing complicity and zealotry in order to ensure that those who offer positions contrary to that which binds together the community are forced to the boundary and thereby make it more robust in terms of enclosing acceptable opinion.

Here, perhaps, we can perceive heresies arising in contrast to a heresy that itself seeks to become the dominant way of thinking. It reminds us that regardless of how right and unquestionable we take our opinion to be, there will be others who – legitimately – contest it or indeed take a contrary view. If we opt to simply shunt those contrary opinions (and those who express them) into a broad boundary position of being simply unacceptable in our community, we belittle their epistemology and deny the limited space for dialogue.

References

Agamben, G., 2012. Image and silence. *Diacritics*, 40(2), pp. 94–98.

Bradlaugh, C., 1878. *The laws relating to blasphemy and heresy: An address to freethinkers.* London: Freethought Publishing Company.

Breitfelder, M. D. & Dowling, D., 2008. *Why Did We Ever Go Into HR?.* [Online] Available at: https://hbr.org/2008/07/why-did-we-ever-go-into-hr [Accessed 11 January 2021].

Edmondson, A. C. & Lei, Z., 2014. Psychological safety: The history, renaissance, and future of an interpersonal construct. *Annual Review of Organizational Psychology and Organizational Behaviour*, 1(1), pp. 23–43.

Foucault, M., 2019. Parrhesia: Lecture at the University of Grenoble May 18, 1982. In: H. Fruchard & D. Lorenzini, eds. *Discourse and truth & Parrhesia.* Chicago, IL: University of Chicago Press, pp. 1–38.

Gallagher, P., 2022. *Medics react with fury to 'deluded' doctor who questioned Sajid Javid over Covid vaccine mandate.* [Online] Available at: https://inews.co.uk/news/health/covid-19-vaccine-medics-fury-over-deluded-doctor-who-questioned-sajid-javid-nhs-mandate-1391677 [Accessed 11 January 2022].

Gayle, D., 2022. *Unvaccinated NHS doctor challenges Sajid Javid over compulsory Covid jabs.* [Online] Available at: https://www.theguardian. com/politics/2022/jan/08/nhs-doctor-challenges-sajid-javid-over-covid-vaccination-rules [Accessed 11 January 2022].

Le Bon, G., 1896/2001. *The Crowd: The study of the popular mind.* Kitchener: Batoche Books.

Nichols, R. G. & Stevens, L. A., 1957. Listening to people. *Harvard Business Review*, Issue September-October, pp. 85–92.

Rejmer, M., 2021. *Mud sweeter than honey: Voices of communist Albania.* London: MacLehose Press.

Sherf, E. N., Parke, M. R. & Isaakyan, S., 2021. Distinguishing voice and silence at work: Unique relationships with perceived impact, psychological safety, and burnout. *Academy of Management Journal*, 64(1), pp. 114–148.

10

SILENCE DESCENDS

Throughout all of our work in this area we have been guided by the idea that voice and silence in organisations are both reflective and constitutive of power in that context. Importantly, though, we cleave to a view of power that departs somewhat from the traditional take in business thinking, which is often reflective of a foundational presumption of a hierarchy (French & Raven, 1959). This presupposes that power arises out of hierarchy, whereas we take the view that power precedes it and is actively colonised by hierarchy. This is the power equivalent of someone walking along the street and finding a fifty-pound note: the currency – with its value inscribed and its capacity for circulation amongst an entire population established – is not ascribed to a particular individual but is merely taken up and utilised by them.

Instead, we see power as a characteristic of the interconnectivity of human agents, a facet of the complex network of relationships that we sustain not least through our engagement with organising around a shared task in a corporate context. Power is not a resource in this picture, seized by one in order to constrain or compel another; it is not an instrument by

DOI: 10.4324/9781003296683-12

which one person can consistently inflict their will on others. Instead, it is something that is implicit in our efforts to connect and communicate with one another – and so we are both acted upon by power as we sit in the web of relations that exist for us all, but we are also a vector for power because of the way in which we reside in this context.

We may fixate on the structural aspects that quickly seek to inhabit and co-opt this mesh of power, such as the hierarchies (both visible and subtly invisible) in organisation, but this merely conspires to disguise the myriad ways in which each and everyone one of us is implicated in power. And, as intimated above, this is particularly the case when we surrender our individuality – and the criticality that seems implicit in terms of a person finding their way in the world – in favour of our absorption into a community, or perhaps a better term in this regard is "crowd".

Here it is useful to acknowledge the idea of the crowd as offered by Elias Canetti – a bounded group, drawn together by its connections. The crowd is emergent in terms of a congregation of people becoming one and perhaps dissipating as quickly as it appeared. And, in light of these attributes, the crowd is seen to be intimately related to power (Canetti, 1973, p. 16). Canetti goes on to offer an important view on power itself, which resonates with our argument through the following example:

> The cat uses force to catch the mouse, to seize it, hold it in its claws and ultimately kill it. But while it is *playing* with it another factor is present. It lets it go, allow it to run about a little and even turn its back and, during this time, the mouse is no longer subjected to force. But it is still within the power of the cat and can be caught again. If it gets right away it escapes from the cat's sphere of power; but, up to the point at which it can no longer be reached, it is still within it. The space which the cat dominates, the moments of hope it allows the mouse, while continuing however to watch it closely all the time and never relaxing its interest and intention to destroy it – all this together, space, hope, watchfulness and destructive intent, can be called the actual body of power, or, more simply, power itself. (Canetti, 1973, p. 327)

This means that we are holding two precepts in respect to power in organisational contexts as particularly important, specifically:

1. **Power can be felt in a wide range of human-to-human activity and not merely through one person applying pressure to another**

2. **We are all of us affected by power but – at the same time – are invested with power, particularly where we might subsume our individuality unthinkingly into a collective**

In practical terms this orientation underscores that power is not unidirectional, in terms of moving from top to bottom. Instead, it pulses through all of the connections that exist for us in a social context and means that silence is not merely compelled from above, but may subtly be demanded in relationships that exist for us horizontally and below us. This is particularly the case when we are facing a community that sustains itself by an orthodoxy that it also seeks to proselytise beyond its defined boundaries.

This is not to deny the ways in which dominant and subaltern voices interact. Instead, it simply contests the idea that dominance is determined positionally, in terms of its promotion by the uppermost levels of an organisational hierarchy. Dominance may be attained outwith the positional – but its origin as an overbearing perspective that permeates everything about the quotidian still serves to define voices that can be seen as Othered. Once we set aside the positional, the following observation seems to attain even more import:

> Whereas one form of silence is an absence of voices, another form of silence lies in the unspoken assumptions on which dominant stories are based. The stories that dominant groups tell about the way things are and ought to be in the world includes more than constructed representations of themselves. Dominant stories also include representations of people who are different: poor people, elderly people, women, people of color, and others. When stories about non-dominant groups are told from dominant perspectives, features of the dominant group are assumed to be natural or normal. Only non-dominant features are noted, or marked in stories that are told from a dominant point of view. Features of dominant groups remain unmarked because they are assumed to be normal – natural – not especially notable or worth mentioning.   (Amburgy et al., 2004, pp. 82–83)

To offer an example as to how this dominant/subaltern connectivity that exists outside of the idea of hierarchical social structure might be thought about in a practical sense, the response of The Observer newspaper in the UK to the intense confrontation that exists around transgender rights is illustrative. This, after all, is a significant voice of progressivism in the country, although both The Observer and The Guardian are titles that arose out of liberalism. Nevertheless, its editorial on the topic takes issue with the way in which key "community" positions can assert their dominance to negatively impact the lives of those who take an alternative view to their orthodoxy. The newspaper expressed these concerns thus:

> Freedom of expression is a fundamental human right and a cornerstone of democracy, which cannot flourish unless citizens can articulate their opinions and ideas without fear of retaliation, censorship or sanction. So it should concern anyone who claims to be a democrat that there is growing evidence that women who have expressed a set of feminist beliefs that have come to be known as "gender-critical" have, in some cases, faced significant professional penalties as a result.   (The Observer, 2021)

In light of this, it is important to acknowledge the connection between the leader and silence in an organisational context; as we've indicated, silence in the workplace often arises directly out of the presence and actions of the leader – and people's relationship with that leader. But, at the same time, leadership itself as a practice opens and closes the space for voice in a range of settings – and in particular where the terrain between the dominant and other subaltern voices needs to be navigated.

Hence, it is one thing for a leader to hold themselves and those around them to account in terms of seeking to ensure the opportunity for people to speak, to be listened to, and to be properly heard and acknowledged. But there is also a responsibility to intercede between the competing narratives – and thereby to interrupt unquestioned dominance, so as to encourage dialogue. Those who seek to lead must manage themselves, in terms of their presence, performance and practice in the work context. At the same time, they must speak truth to power where voices, even those from below in the organisation, have attained an unchallenged dominance and where those communities are rigidly shaped through acts of voice and silence, within their boundaries and at their edges.

This leads us to a simple axiom in relation to leadership as something into which anyone might be moved to step:

A person opting to embrace the responsibility of leading in a given time and circumstance needs to be driven not by ego but by a well-developed personal ethical orientation.

And this simple observation arose powerfully for us at the time of writing when the news was awash with stories of Boris Johnson demonstrating blithe disregard for the rules that his own government had introduced. Even when the narrative webs that he had spun were cast to the wind of scrutiny, his *amour-propre* and unbounded sense of privilege prevented him from recognising his ethical shortcomings.

Hence, **insight** is another crucial element of the person and their potential for leadership. And, as we have explored elsewhere, that is driven by a solid adherence at a personal level to **criticality** and **reflexivity** (Cole & Higgins, 2021), sitting alongside this personal commitment to an ethics of the self. It sounds boastful, perhaps hubristic, but our view is that, in the space of the past two paragraphs, we have offered a clear fresh direction for what is referred to as "leadership development"; stop teaching content and start creating space, time, and support for people to find their ethical selves – and if that potential doesn't exist inside them, do all you can to stop them becoming leaders.

We leave the concluding remark to Emma Goldman, the noted US anarchist activist who actively embraced the idea of free speech in light of the governmental constraints that were placed throughout her career on her voice:

> Mental shackles have never yet stemmed the tide of progress, whereas premature social explosions have only too often been brought about through a wave of repression.   (Goldman, 1908, p. 6)

References

Amburgy, P. M., Knight, W. B. & Keifer-Boyd, K., 2004. Schooled in silence. *Journal of Social Theory in Art Education*, 24, pp. 81–101.

Canetti, E., 1973. *Crowds and power*. Harmondsworth: Penguin.

Cole, M. & Higgins, J., 2021. *Stuck in the middle – and feeling the pinch*. [Online] Available at: https://radicalod.org/2021/10/12/stuck-in-the-middle-and-feeling-the-pinch/ [Accessed 13 January 2021].

French, J. R. P. & Raven, B., 1959. The bases of social power. In: D. Cartwright, ed. *Studies in social power*. Ann Arbor, MI: Institute for Social Research, pp. 259–269.

Goldman, E., 1908. *What I believe.* [Online] Available at: http://theanarchistlibrary. org/library/emma-goldman-what-i-believe.pdf [Accessed 12 January 2021].

The Observer, 2021. *The Observer view on the right to free expression.* [Online] Available at: https://www.theguardian.com/commentisfree/2021/ jun/27/the-observer-view-on-the-right-to-free-expression [Accessed 28 June 2021].

Part III

THIRTY-FIVE VOICES... AND BEYOND

11

THIRTY-FIVE VOICES

As part of our work, we used social media to invite respondents to complete a survey. In the course of that exercise, we felt privileged to receive thirty-five free text responses, where people spoke candidly about their experiences of organisational life and leadership therein over the period of the first two years of the Covid 19 pandemic.

When you do a survey, the temptation can be to dive into the numbers, turn what people have said into what passes as "hard" data, rather than stay with their words in the raw. Later on in this section we'll go that route because it has some value, but we want to lead off with the people who filled in the free-text box, who had the energy to write about their first-hand experience in their own words, freed of the set-piece questions and assumptions that were inevitably built into what we'd asked people to respond to using a sliding, numeric scale.

We want to engage with this work in a different and considerably more reflexive way, showing our "working out" so as to offer the reader insight

DOI: 10.4324/9781003296683-14

into the live challenge of moving from listening to hearing. So here are some initial thoughts that Mark had as he began to work with the work while considering his role in shaping and directing it.

Some important shared initial considerations – in Mark's voice

My initial and palpable reaction to reading the thirty-five voices is that what people have shared feels almost overwhelming, particularly as John and I have an explicit commitment both to listen and to hear what is being said. My experiences in organisation development nudge me towards trying to cluster the remarks, to bundle them under themes or topics. The problem is that this sort of approach is about me projecting my view of the world onto thirty-five separately and individually offered commentaries. In so doing, I squeeze out the vivid voices in favour of some sort of pseudo-scientific exercise. Once the themes become the focus of the exercise, the voices drift into the background – and the uniqueness of what they have said becomes lost.

Rather than starting with thematic buckets, another approach involves pulling out a selection of quotes, which inevitably privilege some voices over others, because what they say resonates with me. Some of this may simply be a superficial response to a particular level of fluency or the deployment of some *mot juste*. Perhaps I am drawn to some turns of phrase because I am experiencing some positive sensation that this person speaks like me. Am I – at a quite deep level – inadvertently responding well to voices that sound like mine? Perhaps it is even deeper than that: am I looking for people that seem to be speaking on my behalf?

This chimes with a conversation I was part of recently where people for whom English was not their first language spoke candidly about their experiences in British corporate life. These people recognised that they had come to this second language often considerably later than someone immersed in it since birth. Notwithstanding their competence in it, there will be some elements – such as idioms – that will pass them by. They also observed that they might be perhaps half a beat or so behind someone for whom it was their first language, so might appear hesitant in the midst of an exchange or indeed may take a little longer to process what has been said, to marshal their own thoughts, and articulate them. When we review the traditional so-called competence-based employment interview through the prism of this experience, we can suddenly see how it contains within it a structural inequality.

There is another layer on top of all of this, which is that – as I review the thirty-five voices and end up exploring what they say to me, rather than what they are saying to the world, my judgement may also be clouded by the idea that I want to anticipate what you, as the reader, have made of reading that section of this chapter. On the one hand, I might feel moved to reassure you – somewhat superciliously – that your responses are those of at least one of the authors of this book. However, on the other hand, I might be prompted to justify my authorial position and the power dynamic therein in relation to the reader by drawing out elements of the thirty-five voices that serve to demonstrate my analytic competence and worthiness to be writing a treatise such as this.

I acknowledge that the material has tended to substantiate the thoughts John and I were exploring prior to the release of the survey. This is reassuring, of course, in that it suggests that our reading of circumstances over the past two years has chimed with how others sensed things. The danger here is that I might be tacitly drawn to latch onto commentary that validates my view – and downplay remarks that might run counter to the perspective the two of us have already laid out. The question is: how would I have reacted to the material if it had by and large contradicted my point of view? And can I check and check again that I am not allowing my outlook to distort the material so that I end up using it instrumentally?

Why does this matter? Isn't it merely a rarefied exploration of research method, with no practical bearing on the world of business? Quite the contrary. These deliberations are intimately related to leadership in organisational life – and our very generalised statement that people need to listen to hear. In these discussions, we are actively exploring what it means to hear, whether voices are coming to you through a research instrument or from the shop floor.

Importantly, research practice is one area of activity where an ethical approach is expressly required. Hence, in research that aims to participate in improving and not just reflecting on the world of hidden experiences, it seems all the more important that ethics is central to the work and the way we approach it. John drafted the following statement of ethical intent in regard to practising in this way, which we feel summarises the position:

> Participative Inquiry has a distinctive ethical frame which emphasises the importance of critical self-inquiry. Since the participant-inquirer is not claiming to hold an objective position in relation to the context they're reporting on, to work ethically in this way requires explicit attention be paid to the subjective reality of the person or people involved in providing a commentary on events and experiences.

It is our contention that leadership practice needs to embrace the liveliness of such an ethical stand – a contention we'll describe in a more prescriptive way in Section "Mark's Engagement with the Thirty-Five Voices" for leaders who wish to embrace both listening and hearing.

My act of selection and curation of what people have written then might be seen to be an act of seizure, where I reach out and snatch snippets that echo my thinking and things I might have said in the past. They validate my understanding – and my authorial approval of these remarks might be seen to be adding value to what has been said. My homing in on the text of the comments tears them away from the voice that announced them and renders them manipulable as data in the service of an argument.

It is also the case that the survey appeared as an open invitation for people to speak so that they might be heard. But this invitation comes with its own constraints, which inadvertently shape what people might feel able to say. The survey was anonymous – the technology we used did not ask for any identifying data – but giving voice to the opinions that we have reproduced below will almost certainly have involved some sort of self-editing by the respondents: 'If I say this in this way, what if it appeared in the public domain and I could be identified in some way as having said it?'

No matter how safe the space might actually be in which people are invited to speak, our internal capacity for silencing on the basis of how sayable we consider our opinions remains. And this internal calculation for us as individual voices will be done in light of the social or organisational milieu in which our voice might ordinarily be heard. Hence, my initial reaction to the thirty-five voices is to acknowledge what they are saying – but perhaps to also wonder the extent to which they have edited and tempered those remarks.

The sense of the survey being a space in which one's voice is publicly heard is to be acknowledged. But it is important not to disappear down the rabbit hole of wondering what might have been unsaid. Another feature of inviting voice through a structure such as the survey is simply that the means by which people can express their opinions is controlled by the medium that is being used. It is not a free-form dialogue, clearly, but a call-and-response that is itself inscribed with power, as is the case with all surveys, such as those used to "involve" and "engage" employees. And the free text invitation that the thirty-five voices accepted so as to share their thoughts about their experience over the past two years is limited and limiting, in terms of how much might be said and how it might be expressed.

My final overarching concern is that it is important to hear what people have said before responding. Attending to someone's voice whilst, at the same time, mentally entertaining my immediate responses to it – and allowing those reactions to overshadow what is being said – is to deny that person the genuine chance to be heard. This represents a major psychological effort entrained as we are to listen so as to respond – and to use the comments of others primarily as a prompt for speech of our own. Every corporate meeting can be said to have this communicative distortion at its heart. And it is especially difficult to bracket oneself off from reacting to someone's voice when they are saying something with which we disagree.

With these considerations hopefully occupying some space in the mind of the reader – we offer an unedited reproduction here of all the comments people shared with us in the survey.

Thirty-five voices

1. My organization is extremely supportive. I feel that our senior leadership listens to us and takes action. If they're unable or unwilling to take action, they provide the "why" behind their decision. It has been my experience that not speaking up is a personal decision due to personal insecurities or personal experiences with prior employers who were not as proactive and employee satisfaction focused. It took me time to get comfortable with and trust that the culture talked about at my organization was the culture actually in action. To my surprise, it has been at all levels within the organization.

2. Working as an interim in an organisation I have more freedom than colleagues to speak up and not worry about the consequences. Over the period of the year I have been in the organisation, I have felt my motivation to speak up drop away, as I realise that although senior management may listen to me they don't want to hear what I am saying and don't want to act. My boss is nice (an exec director) but ineffectual. He almost refuses to make decisions because he doesn't want to create conflict, so he appeases people by saying he will address things but rarely does. Lots of people in his wider team are unhappy and performance and morale are pretty low, but we cover for him and his weaknesses. One way of doing this is not speaking up about them outside of the team. This may not be the most harmful experience of not speaking up, but it is draining as it means that, as a team, we spend a lot of time moaning about him and his behaviours to one another. We feel that if we raise it with him, it will just get ignored again.

3. Well, what's there to share? I was naive enough to think that the culture of silence can be broken.

4. Sometimes silence is a choice. When the cost of speaking up is high and the chance of it making any difference low.

5. I often feel there is a certain way of being and speaking that is allowed when discussing with senior leaders, and that makes me feel I cannot fully be myself or share what I am thinking or feeling because it is not appropriate or may lead to negative consequences e.g. I won't be considered for a promotion. It sometimes feels like a different language that is spoken at the top, that is more political and critical. It doesn't put me at ease. If I disagree with a senior leader I rather keep it quiet, than end up with a debate.

6. Working 100% remote in a different time zone from most management makes hearing and being heard very difficult for me. Added to that where I work management are not communicating much through any forms.

7. Certain topics fall on deaf senior ears. Burnout. Performance at all costs. Incivility – no appetite to effectively deal with this as perpetrators are powerful and not easy to replace

8. My management listens to me and always talks to me, however these days there is a pressure on everybody to say the same thing and not

to express the real feelings because we do not want to be different to others. It is OK as long as you agree with everything the majority thinks.

9. I am working on co-production and there has been a huge positive push in NHSEI

10. I feel quite comfortable raising issues myself and report to an executive director in my organisation and feel heard. Unfortunately, I have witnessed some junior and senior managers discourage their staff from speaking up and not allowing them access to support such as staff networks where they could share similar experiences and feel supported. Covid-19 pressures have been used as an excuse to disengage and make unilateral decisions in some cases to the detriment of some members of staff. I feel this is particularly the case for staff from BME backgrounds or for staff with disabilities.

11. During first wave of CV-19 hierarchy was flattened slightly and middle / senior level were trusted to manage operational aspects and make decisions. As time has passed, and life has begun to return to normal, noticed slipping back into top down/ autocratic leadership form senior leaders has crept back in

12. It is very difficult to voice out especially if you have been subjected to unfair comments or expectations. The voice of the management team is always stronger and if one speaks up it is considered "demanding or creating conflict".

13. As a senior leader I feel able to speak up, but I have to be cautious and careful about what I say given the politics and views of others. Cultural background plays a strong role in the ability to speak up as it's harder being in the minority, raising issues that don't always affect the majority if it's not their lived experience. I'm trying to be brave but also cautious, so this is the tension felt daily as a senior manager of colour in the minority in meetings I attend. I hope this helps explain my view and experience.

14. Interestingly the challenge posed by Covid allowed/necessitated me to have more conversations with my staff, e.g. I often had to listen to them about their home/family circumstances and health issues in order to support them. This in fact helped me to build relationships and consolidate my leadership role in the context I was a new manager, and overall contributed to my development. I think my input

has been largely appreciated by my staff, but this meant more time and effort on my part, whereas I don't have any extra time to do this. These also largely go unnoticed by the senior leadership. I think Covid highlighted/exposed strengths and weaknesses of organisations, management and leadership practices e.g. the lack of adaptability, clarity, procedures and the ability to respond to clinicians/managers' needs on the ground has compounded the challenges. I think in this time the organisations which value and know the importance of, and needs of, support for middle managers will thrive (and also ones which have been recruiting good managers purposefully). Unfortunately, I am not in one of these organisations, but having come from a very good one I can see/feel the difference support for managers makes. In my current organisation there is no support whatsoever, such as training or purposeful leadership-focused supervision/support for managers (there was a period many of us were left without any supervision). The communication with managers is largely based on criticisms of what we are not doing well rather than what is going well, we don't feel appreciated or trusted to make our own judgements whereas we are at the same time left to get on with the running of services and no support is offered when we request [it]. The Trust is in a dire situation and this is affecting our reputation and recruitment, but we are told this isn't the case (i.e. no listening), we are not allowed to recruit as there are financial uncertainties but it is the managers who get the blame if we are not delivering the same service with less staff. Poor corporate services are draining managers' time and affecting service delivery but there is no helpful response. As middle managers we are in a lonely position, we have to remain upbeat with our junior staff but with no support from the above we can easily burn out. The problem is there is no incentive on the part of the organisation to retain managers, they are reorganising and all managers are potentially at risk of redundancy and it works well for the Trust if we just go off sick, burn out or leave. In this context it is hard to speak up.

15.   I keep on editing and sending out a monthly newsletter to my group to keep them in touch. I encourage my group to voice out their prayer request. I have Zoom phobia therefore I avoid most virtual meetings.

16. Leaders have not led with often being scared to make decisions that will have an operational or strategic impact. The initial change during the first wave was commendable by senior leaders. However, within each subsequent wave senior leaders have hidden being bureaucracy and failed to listen to their teams.

17. It feels very risky to speak up about the lack of progress on issues relating to disabled staff and when we have any sort of organisational briefing progress on race is almost always discussed and nothing is said about disabled staff or other protected characteristics – this includes comments being publicly posted in the chat.

18. As a bilateral deaf person who relies on hearing aids and lip reading, the use of mask wearing has been incredibly disabling. As healthcare commissioning organisation, I have repeatedly asked that senior leaders on site visits both use and encourage use of clear visor masks to help those with disabilities/dementia/children. I have also recommended that we require our services to use these masks to prevent increasing inequalities for the deaf and hard of hearing community. None of these have got anywhere. I have also been actively pushing to get appropriate British sign language interpreters readily available, offered and used at all vaccination centres. This is slowly moving through the organisation teams involved with vaccinations, but so far, nil has changed.

19. Generally in the Organisation decisions are made at a senior level, contractors brought in and the existing staff are not fully listened to. Contractors/Consultants rarely tell us anything we don't know but somehow their "expertise" is listened to more than those who have worked in the organisation for many years. In the face of it the organisation is probably more open than it has been in many years but do they really listen? I am not so sure...

20. Offering different perspectives and constantly being told by line manager that I am afraid of uncertainty and I need to work faster. Being told by line manager that other colleagues have raised complaints about me but not asking for my account of what happened and not challenging colleagues' use of words/language which I felt were judgemental, not based on behaviour. Finding that whenever I tried to highlight an issue it essentially made things worse for me – like I was seen to not be cooperating or compliant. So now I keep quiet until I can make my exit.

21. Witness to a general degradation in the capacity of many senior leaders to sustain their ability to think, and especially to attend with compassion, concern and carefulness to the experiences of others; often this is accompanied by a tendency toward dismissive language 'time to put your big girl knickers on and get on with it' (direct quote said to some nursing colleagues) and at others cruel and demeaning behaviour. I have understood this as a toxic response to the dual challenges of people having extended power at a time of crisis and that of managing/tolerating the anxieties COVID has evoked in self and others – such that dismissiveness, contempt and cruelty become defensive responses to that which otherwise might be unbearable...

22. I always speak up if I feel I will be understood correctly. I am sometimes fearful of not being understood correctly and people making wrong assumptions.

23. Although the words of the exec and very senior team are always on message with the NHS People Promise and NHS constitution, the next rungs below can seem afraid to bring nutty issues to their (Exec and VSM) door. This is turn suggests that they (our line managers) don't want to hear it and definitely don't want to sort it...as they are just surviving themselves. I feel that this is because there is a culture to keep folks going, being aware of the operational pressures that we are all in and the impact of the pandemic. An example would be the reporting tends to be about the positives of what we have done, and how amazing we are for doing that...rather than what there is still to do to not leave anyone behind. I appreciate that this is really difficult to get the right balance – but for me on a down day, I hear insincerity and I feel isolation.

24. Changing organisations in the last year, I can see what a difference it makes when leaders commit to overtly giving people space and freedom to speak up. The six months before that was completely different, in a political organisation, where I was literally silenced by the most senior person advising me to "stop digging my own grave" when I challenged them. As a senior officer myself, it meant my role became untenable in this organisation and I had to leave. Whilst this is an extreme example, there are great leaders and organisations out there, it just takes the right acceptance to be human and not delude yourself by the trappings of assumed power.

25. I consider myself to be at the mid-level of seniority and have found access to senior levels open, listening and responsive. I have had occasion to encourage new-starters to speak out and express their strengths.

26. There is an unwritten, informal policy of not supporting secondments less than 12 months, which narrows opportunities for personal and professional development. Rather than this be a discretionary approach where each request can be considered on merit it means that I have felt that the glass ceiling that is above me has been reinforced and my opportunities are further narrowed. Unconsciously this is keeping me as a disabled employee at a lower level than perhaps my abilities and capabilities would warrant me being at. I have raised my concerns and they have disappeared into an arena of silence, for what I perceive to be fear of challenging executive decisions or rocking the boat. This is not the only time I have experienced a very top-down approach to our organisation's work, where it can be perceived to be very much the opposite of the 7 ways of working outlined in the NHS People Promise.

27. I have been fortunate to move from a team where senior managers didn't value my opinion. Am in a better placed team where senior managers are inclusive and take time to listen.

28. In the past 18 months I have experienced a call to lead. Having 16 hours a week extra to rest and do what I want to do has been invaluable. I have been using my programme management skills and assertiveness to deliver the day job. I have also used my campaigning skills to support the organisation to make changes. A senior leader recently said he thought I was operating under the radar.

29. I am a white middle-aged male typical of the so-called privileged cohort known as the patriarchy. I work in public service in a lower grade role. Any opinion I voice is immediately dismissed as "what would you expect from them". I am completely marginalised. Abandoned by white middle-aged men in senior positions – presumably for fear of being branded as prejudice or "looking after their own" and the inevitable career destroying backlash that comes with that. I am regularly treated as a second-rate employee because I do not fit the demographic of what the organisation would like to portray. This is not equality, or inclusivity, it is diversity at the cost of all else including,

I'm saddened to say, quality of service and value for money. I'm not opposed to EDI, exactly the opposite in fact. However, my employer has created a culture where it's OK to demonise middle-aged white males and deny us any voice. On a daily basis I feel reviled and disapproved of. Surely this cannot be progress.

30. I had a particular challenging relationship with my line manager, their micro-aggressions were invisible to other people in the team, and because my predecessor (who was mixed race) had a bad experience, it made me nervous about speaking up, in case the behaviour was sanctioned by senior leaders. In the end, my mental health was deteriorating and I felt there was nothing to lose, apart from more of myself if I didn't challenge the manager. It was the best decision I have ever made because their behaviour changed. Historically, I have left jobs because of managers but I now refuse to move on, until I am ready. I have had amazing leaders in the same organisation, so I know there are pockets of psychological safety.

31. Seniors recognise the importance of being seen to listen. However, this is always considered in the context of wider priorities e.g. delivering organisational priorities, supporting more senior stakeholders. The steps that need to happen for people to be felt they are heard include listening to be exemplified by seniors, actual understanding of what is said (and unsaid) and then actions are taken forward that at least address areas of concern. This often falls down at the first stage or at the understanding stage. Various layers of managers also act in the silencing piece if it is understood to be "career" limiting to try to speak about a topic that is trying to be silenced or moved on from.

32. I feel safe to speak up, but some topics have been difficult to talk about such as big changes and being loyal to decisions. Also speaking up as new to senior staff when you feel they are out of order in their behaviour and reactions.

33. We seem to have a listening culture with great support to equalities networks but, overall, we are a managed organisation with an output to deliver to a set time target. Output trumps all else.

34. Awful levels of racism that have gone unchallenged and many have been silenced. Morally bankrupt accountable officers and a total inept and incompetent HR service. Sad to see inequality and racism is thriving in the NHS at its highest levels

35. In the Trust I keep pointing out issues about resources. And whilst I
     felt they were initially heard; nothing has been done to address them.
     So when I try to speak about them now I feel they are ignored - or that
     I am becoming a broken record.

You have hopefully just attentively read what the thirty-five voices had to
say about their experiences, their reflections, and their fresh thinking in
light of voice in corporate life over the course of the pandemic. How did
you react to this close reading of the voices of others? How did it make
you feel? Did you find yourself responding in your head whilst supposedly reading? Were there things that were said you realise you did not hear
because your own mind was actively refuting it?

   Questions like these were precisely some of those that we tried
to challenge ourselves – and one another – with, so as to do justice to
what people had said, to bear witness to their bearing witness, and
to show how our thinking had developed in respect to a dialogic engagement with this material.

   The next section offers insight into the dialogue that we had as we listened to and worked to hear the voices who had offered us their insights.

John's engagement with the thirty-five voices

I could only hold back for so long before wanting to step into a curatorial
frame – a lot of my self-worth is wrapped up in my skill at synthesising
and working with a mass of qualitative data, at playing the game where
information is seen as best served in a condensed form, because people
don't have the time or inclination to work with the messiness of the whole.
Below then are the phrases and words that I was drawn to highlight as having particular significance. Once they've been presented, I'll then reflect on
what that says about my world view:

> '... for people to be... heard... [needs] actual understanding of what is said (and
> unsaid)'
>   'Changing organisations in the last year, I can see what a difference it makes
> when leaders commit to overtly giving people space and freedom to speak up'...
> 'My organization is extremely supportive... To my surprise, it has been at all
> levels'... 'I always speak up if I feel I will be understood correctly'... 'I have been

fortunate to move from a team where senior managers didn't value my opinion'... 'I know there are pockets of psychological safety'

'We seem to have a listening culture... but, overall... Output trumps all else'... 'I keep pointing out issues about resources... when I try to speak about them now I feel... I am becoming a broken record'

'Covid allowed/necessitated me to have more conversations with my staff, e.g. I often had to listen to them about their home/family... health issues in order to support them... but this meant more time and effort on my part, whereas I don't have any extra time to support them'

'...although senior management may listen to me, they don't hear what I'm saying'... '...there is a certain way of being and speaking that is allowed when discussing with senior leaders'... 'Certain topics fall on deaf senior ears'... 'Witness to a general degradation in the capacity of many senior leaders to sustain their ability to think... attend... to the experiences of others... such that dismissiveness, contempt and cruelty become defensive responses to that which otherwise might be unbearable'

'I was naïve enough to think that the culture of silence can be broken'... 'It is very difficult to voice out especially if you have been subjected to unfair comments or expectations. The voice of the management team is always stronger'... 'Being told by line manager that other colleagues have raised complaints about me but not asking for my account of what happened'

'... there is a pressure... to say the same thing and not express the real feelings because we do not want to be different to others'... 'There is an unwritten, informal policy of not supporting secondments less than 12 months'... 'I had a particular changing relationship with my line manager, their micro-aggressions were invisible to other people in the team'

'Covid-19 pressures have been used as an excuse to disengage... this is particularly the case for staff from BME backgrounds or for staff with disabilities'... 'Cultural background plays a strong role in the ability to speak up as it's harder being in a minority, raising issues that don't always affect the majority if it's not their lived experience'... '... any sort of organisational briefing progress on race is almost always discussed and nothing is said about disabled staff'

'I am a middle-aged male typical of the so-called privileged cohort known as the patriarchy... I am completely marginalised... my employer has created a culture where it's OK to demonise middle-aged white males and deny us any voice. On a daily basis I feel reviled and disapproved of'... 'Awful levels of racism that have gone unchallenged and many have been silenced'

'As middle managers we are in a lonely position, we have to remain upbeat with our junior staff but with no support from the above we can easily burn out'... '... senior leaders have hidden behind bureaucracy and failed to listen to

*their teams'... 'the words of the exec and senior team are always on message...
the next rungs below can seem afraid to bring nutty issues to their... door'*

*'Contractors/Consultants rarely tell us anything we don't know but some-
how their "expertise" is listened to more than those who have worked in the
organisation for many years'*

I read through this selection some weeks after identifying them, a deliberate
decision to give myself time to try and notice what it was I was noticing –
in most parts of my working life that has involved me formally belonging
to an institution, I am struck by how rare that is. Reflections are required
in the moment, and very rarely after some time has passed so that you
can encounter your choices and responses as if they had been made by a
stranger.

What I notice in what I have chosen is part of two recurring themes –
firstly the use and abuse of power, which I see playing out in the lack of
seriousness that I saw so many people reporting as being the response of
senior others to what was said. Secondly the impossibility of the context so
many people find themselves in, where personal agency and good will can
only get you so far in situations where custom, practice and process rule
the roost.

It is no surprise to me that this is what I choose to see – having worked
hard to try and step out of the psychic torment that came from being heavily schooled in the habits of the British social and international corporate
elites. I have the personal disposition, and background of familial incom-
petence, to be left feeling how inadequate these elite ways of knowing are,
how illiterate they are in their understanding of what it is to be human
being, rather than an economic or socially approved label.

Which is of course why I want to research in areas such as this, I am
deeply invested in the cliché of research as personal process. What I choose
to inquire into reflects an itch I have to scratch. My scratch is how to be
heard about what matters to me, not what I have been told should matter
to me.

Mark's engagement with the thirty-five voices

What follows is my selective engagement with elements from the thirty-five
voices that impacted me in one way or another. I will own those feelings

and give voice to what I have heard and how it has affected me. But, as the reader, I invite you to engage with my response with an acknowledgement that my curation and arrangement of this commentary arises out of me and should not be seen to carry any greater authority than the statements to which I am referring because of my authorial voice. In this exercise, I am adding a thirty-sixth voice, albeit one that is offering its remarks in personal reaction to what I have heard the other thirty-five saying. It is hopefully part of a dialogic process.

As this book has hopefully so far demonstrated, John and I are trying to articulate a nuanced view of voice and, in particular, silence. Our position arises out of our experiences in organisational life; our weekly conversations about what we have seen and what it prompts in each of us, and how we make sense of all of this as two people together – and as two individuals. In light of this, having heard all thirty-five voices, I was moved to think reflexively about how a number of those comments seemed to speak out on workplace silence.

The first voice that I struggled to hear was this one:

> I feel that our senior leadership listens to us and takes action.... It has been my experience that not speaking up is a personal decision due to personal insecurities or personal experiences with prior employers who were not as proactive and employee satisfaction focused.

This was a difficult comment for me to engage with and to accept because it offered a refutation of the standpoint that John and I had arrived at over the course of our deliberations. For that reason, it was even more important that I avoided merely *listening to react* and instead actively heard the speaker and what it was that they were saying. If I just *listened to react*, it would be to mobilise my habitual opinion.

As a reported experience it reminds me that silence can sometimes arise out of a general contentment, which is to say that only those of us with a contrary perspective to the status quo are moved to give voice. Discontent with the common place offers motivation to speak; satisfaction with existing circumstances means it feels like there is nothing to say. In light of this, it seemed all the more important to hear this person describing a level of contentment to which the schema that John and I have hatched didn't seem to offer space. And to recognise that others might feel similarly but are unable to articulate such opinions in light of a consensus that seems to say otherwise. Indeed, a consensus seems to shout in the face of someone who might want to say something contrary. It would be convenient for me to dismiss this as a lone voice…but can I truly presume to know that others do not feel the same way and feel silenced by the view that I seek to articulate, here and elsewhere?

As I worked to make sense of what I was hearing and how I was reacting to that first voice, another contribution reminded me of the silencing effect of consensus. In social and organisational life, consensus is so often seen to be something that we should actively pursue. It is portrayed as a universal good. But it can also be seen as an apparatus that silences. Once a consensus is declared, it is assumed that the discussions are done and there is a collective perspective to which everyone is expected to subscribe. Here's the voice I heard that led me to think more deeply in this regard:

> [T]hese days there is a pressure on everybody to say the same thing and not to express the real feelings because we do not want to be different to others. It is OK as long as you agree with everything the majority thinks.

My reaction to this comment is a warm and confirmatory one; I find myself basking in its content and the elegance of its expression. This means I need to take more time to scrutinise this than I might ordinarily do. The question being: am I hearing the speaker or listening to my reactive interpretation of their statement? And, in the context of this book, am I mobilising this opinion merely to substantiate the perspective that John and I are seeking to advance considering the work that we have been doing?

What I hear is a fellow human being articulating an opinion about the experience of being in the majority or the minority. I also hear them expressing this in a somewhat abstract fashion: the first-person singular does not appear, but I can hear the first-person plural and an indefinite pronoun. But I need to guard against stepping beyond what I hear into interpretation, which would say more about me than the speaker and what they were seeking to say in this instance. If they and I could be in dialogue in light of this statement, the opportunity to inquire would present itself; presently, though, an observation I might make beyond the confines of what has been said thus far would be a mere interpretative assertion.

There is sometimes the temptation to triangulate, to validate the view offered by someone by putting a number on how many others also said something like it or to draw upon another person's rich observation to demonstrate a connection. However, it does not seem unreasonable for me to juxtapose this person's experience with that of another with whom I spoke. In our conversation, she and I alighted upon a shared notion that we described as "corporate ventriloquism", where we find ourselves saying something that arises out of the culture of the organisation rather than out of our experience of being a human agent in that context. There are certain things that the good employee is expected to parrot, even when it runs counter to what they think and what they believe. This makes dummies of us all.

As a sidebar, the woman with whom I was privileged to have the conversation that led us to this conclusion lived in a context that meant – because of its surveillant and oppressive nature – she was understandably guarded with respect to what she felt able to say openly. It was possible to sense her self-censorship – and I too exercised caution in the course of the exchange so as to not introduce conversational topics that might lead her into a difficult place when trying to formulate a response. The conversation itself was context that meant that both sides of the exchange were tightly managed. Her circumstances were straightened in terms of the liberties that she enjoyed; mine were (at least notionally) far freer. Yet each of us approached the dialogue mindful of the other's situation – and so our discretion to exercise our voices was limited by the character of our connection.

Returning to the statement that speaks about people being pressured to say the same thing, this patently presents a potential to engage in an inquiry. But that would require anyone drawn to that exchange to accept what they had heard and to open up a reflective and inviting space for people to share further observations about the topic in itself and their reactions to it. This takes us beyond, "I agree" or "I disagree" (or, using a voice overwritten with power, "That's right" or "That's wrong"): it places us in a rich conversational terrain between "I hear" and "I think".

This takes me to the survey response which has been most impactful for me, in that it looks to be saying what should not be said. Certainly, I recognise that the person would almost certainly not openly give voice to this particular experience in their organisational setting, which makes them saying it in this context all the more important. They say the following:

> I am a white middle-aged male typical of the so-called privileged cohort known as the patriarchy. I work in public service in a lower grade role. Any

opinion I voice is immediately dismissed as "what would you expect from them." I am completely marginalised...I'm not opposed to EDI, exactly the opposite in fact. However, my employer has created a culture where it's OK to demonise middle-aged white males and deny us any voice. On a daily basis I feel reviled and disapproved of. Surely this cannot be progress.

I can imagine the visceral reaction that many will have to this. But I am keen to pause to hear what is being said in terms of that which is sayable and that which is unmentionable. This is not – as we sought to underscore in Part II – a reckless and insensitive adherence to the abstract notion of free speech as an ideological construct. But I am very taken by the feminist sociologist Dorothy E Smith's story that helped to inform her development of the standpoint approach to social research (Gurung, 2020), which I quote here at some length:

> Riding a train not long ago in Ontario I saw a family of Indians, woman, man, and three children standing together on a spur above a river watching the train go by. There was (for me) that moment – the train, those five people seen on the other side of the glass. I saw first that I could tell this incident as it was, but that telling as a description built in my position and my interpretations. I have called them a family; I have said they were watching the train. My understanding has already subsumed theirs. Everything may have been quite other for them. My description is privileged to stand as what actually happened, because theirs is not heard in the contexts in which I may speak. If we begin from the world as we actually experience it, it is at least possible to see that we are located and that what we know of the other is conditional upon that location as part of a relation comprehending the other's location also. There are and must be different experiences of the world and different bases of experience. We must not do away with them by taking advantage of our privileged speaking to construct a sociological version which we then impose upon them as their reality.   (Smith, 1974, p. 12)

The importance of this standpoint perspective is that it actively privileges the voice being heard and the experiences about which it speaks. No attempt is made to overlay it with active interpretation in regard to the researcher or some other authority, such as the corporate leader. However, whilst embracing the idea that one must attend to the voice as it speaks and what it is seeking to say, we need also to be mindful of the dangers that attend to an absolute commitment to this, with respect to the potential to slide into a morass of poststructuralist relativism.

Two perspectives can help to mediate this. The first of these is a way of thinking about how "somebodies and nobodies" (Fuller, 2004) end up in communication with one another bearing in mind the inequality between them. It is possible to summarise the underpinnings of this muted group theory (MGT) in three simple precepts:

1.   That differential power and status tend to interfere with the free expression of ideas from lower status people;
2.   That the inhibition of such expression reinforces the integrated but incomplete world views held by the powerful, by denying them access to alternative perspectives and to information that does not fit neatly into their cognitive models; and
3.   That one implication of the necessity of lower status peoples to adapt to the dominant models at the same time as they retain their counter-part models, is that greater cognitive complexity may be required of them for adequate life functioning than is required of elites. (Colfer, 1983, pp. 278–279)

MGT introduces the notion of a dynamic between the dominant and sub-altern, where the latter manages two world views at the same time: their own and that of the former. This is obviously burdensome – and, in prac-tice, can be seen in activities such as code-switching, a linguistic notion which relates to the capacity to move from one form of language to another (Nilep, 2006). But this is far from straightforward: with respect to gender, for example, it is suggested that 'Unable to symbolise their experience in the male language, women take one of two routes: one path requires inter-nalizing male reality – alienation; the other is being unable to speak at all – silence' (Wall & Gannon-Leary, 1999, p. 24). Elsewhere, the idea of footing is applied as a build on these ideas to describe the movement of people across various voices to accommodate in conversations of which they are part and with those with whom they are conversing (Goffman, 1981).

Meanwhile, the dominant, of course, organise the world through just one view – their own – and do not feel compelled to adjust at all. Hence, for those in senior positions, those who are dominant in corporate life, there is a need for them to actively embrace the notion of inviting subaltern groups to speak – and to ensure that they hear what is said without interruption or real-time interpretation, thereby recognising that people around them are seeing the world very differently. The dominant need to actively invite voice while the subaltern need to find their's otherwise,

> Silence reinforces the self-confidence of the dominant group and encourages the maintenance of the dominant, incomplete yet cohesive world view. (A major part of this incompleteness derives from the dominant group's lack of access to counterpart models, reflective of the life circumstances of muted groups.)   (Colfer, 1983, p. 278)

The second moderator in terms of engagement with voice, alongside MGT, is the idea of *verstehen*, which arose in response to the ways in which social science sought to shroud itself with the ideas and practices of natural science. We discuss this in more detail in the Postscript to this book, but it can be boiled down to the simple imperative to hear what people are saying and to work to understand it, rather than to interpret it. Hence, the argument goes, while we seek to *explain* the natural world, our responsibility is to work to *understand* the social (Martin, 2018, p. 10). This means that '... social phenomena have to be understood "from within"' (Martin, 2018, p. 2). This represents a significant shift in attention and means hearing what might seem unhearable, in terms of your personal view. We go on to argue that this concentration on – as opposed to refutation of – voice lays the foundation for dialogue, a dialogue that opens up our engagement with views other than our own.

The privileging of a particular perspective and voice, then, is not the sole preserve of the researcher. It potentially resides in us all, as individuals and as a collective. The corporate leader will often dismiss the perspective of others around them on the basis that these people are not privy to the whole picture. This is simply asserting that the pictures of others are less important than the ones constructed by the leader. Similarly, as we explored in Part II, a community can often use submission to a collective view of the world as a *sine qua non* for membership – and will define itself in contradistinction to perspectives that might arise within its boundaries, but which will quickly be marginalised and then deposed.

To hear a voice, rather than to listen to it so as to ready ourselves to dismiss it, entails a preparedness for the fact that the view expressed may not be one with which we agree – and which may feel to be contrary to the perspective that we hold. This is not to give licence to people to say things that are designed to offend us; instead, it is about a readiness on our part to hear the voice of others when they are speaking so as to bear witness to their experience. If we listen to react – or, in this instance, perhaps, listen to reject – we deny a space for dialogue where a range of voices come together in a collective inquiry, where we seek to understand the views of others and crucially find the chance to exchange views and so shift our presence in a social context.

In conversation, John and I explored our different responses to the comment from the person defining themselves as a "white middle-aged male". I was immediately taken by the fact that it was a voice speaking about its experience, an experience that most socio-corporate contexts would not necessarily wish to hear and which would therefore be present in the workplace but unheard. John, however, was so taken aback by what this voice was saying that his immediate reaction was to "disappear" the comment and exclude it from this text.

Both reactions are understandable – and our dialogue as we seek to practice in the realm of voice and silence allows us to engage with our own opinion critically and reflexively. It leads me to question how we can engage with voices that articulate perspectives that might feel contrary to our own? How do we find the room for our voice to be heard without simply countermanding the voice of the other? How do we turn up in a social setting with an active commitment to create the conditions for voices to be heard – and to guard against the complicit silence or articulation of a group perspective that serves to sustain, yet constrain, a community?

Where organisations might appear to be encouraging and supporting dialogue, a number of comments served to remind me it is not simply about an individual finding the internal resource to speak up and those around them being comfortable and prepared to move beyond listening to react to hearing so as to engage. Hence, the following particularly resonated with me in terms of my own experience of the quality of conversation in corporate settings and the ways in which this is conducted.

> It sometimes feels like a different language that is spoken at the top
> Certain topics fall on deaf senior ears.
>> [S]enior management may listen to me they don't want to hear what I am saying and don't want to act

[I]f one speaks up it is considered "demanding or creating conflict"
Seniors recognise the importance of being seen to listen.

This selection of excerpts from the thirty-five voices helps me make sense
of what I see in organisational life, which I can sometimes interpret simply as me being sensitive to certain things. The use of a particular type of
conversational style, with its own vernacular and idioms, is something that
to me seems particularly apparent when looking at managers speaking and
in particular at the senior leadership. The latter might argue that they want
to hear the voices of the workforce, but they will struggle to hear what is
being said if the language they use at the top is different to that which one
hears across the rest of the company. And it is the case that the professional
services companies are fluent in that senior leadership language (and,
indeed, reinforce through their use of it – think of the times that you've
seen a phrase in material produced by these companies and how quickly
you start to hear senior leaders parroting those ideas and expressions).

A different sort of language is by its nature not an inclusive way of having conversations. It is important to underscore that the "deaf" ears on
which some voices fall retain the capacity to hear if they so choose. The
euphemism of "deaf ears" delicately sidesteps the active choice of some
people to allow others their voice but to silence what it is that they have
said. They are not impaired and are not deaf in a physical sense: they are
choosing not to hear, whilst appearing to welcome people speaking up.

The other thought these remarks spark for me as I attend to what is being
said, before thinking through the implications and considering the extent
to which the statements resonate with my own experience, is how what
is often spoken of as "rankism" structures even our most basic and simple
exchanges. The book that introduced this notion speaks about "somebodies" and "nobodies", suggesting a binary polarity (Fuller, 2004). As ever,
things are more complicated than this. There is a calibration along the line
between somebody and nobody, as anyone who spent time in a secondary
school classroom knows only too well.

It has always struck me that, from the school perspective, people in
a classroom can be crudely categorised thus: the ~five students that the
teacher recognises as academically gifted; the ~five students that are likely
to derail a lesson due to a lack of engagement with what we do to people
in schools; and a morass of ~20 students, who rarely seize the attention

of the educator. Hence, we have five somebodies and the same number of nobodies – and a large group that sit in a contested space between them, which might also lend itself to delicate real-time categorisation. For the students, this structuring is likely to be different: there may be five cool kids and then five kids who are relegated to the bottom of the pack for whatever social constructed reasons. And another group sat in the middle, with varying degrees of proximity to coolness and ostracism.

These structurations remind us that power does not automatically reside in the formal hierarchy, although it will be there. Instead, we need to recognise that the pulsing of power between people in a social context generates its own hierarchy. Hierarchies may co-exist on top of one another, making that terrain all the more difficult to navigate. And that power can arise out of an individual actively placed into a position – or power can move people into a position as somebody in an informal hierarchy. Sometimes the apex of a pyramid is where power is suggested to reside – but, equally, power can be detected in the base of the pyramid. And it is possible to see the pyramid as being completely consumed by power – the top-down hierarchical version and the less obvious flux of community constraint embroiling everyone.

This conceptualisation seems useful to me when considering how confident people feel to speak out; how likely they are to be heard; and the extent to which they will be actively encouraged to stay silent – or that their speech will be greeted with silence. This goes some way to explaining this person's experience, which may feel familiar to many of us:

> Contractors/Consultants rarely tell us anything we don't know but somehow their 'expertise' is listened to more than those who have worked in the organisation for many years.

These "professional services" voices are listened to for a number of reasons, all of which speak volumes about the generalised failure of senior leaders in corporate life to think for themselves through the complementary lenses of criticality and reflexivity (Cole & Higgins, 2021). Regardless of why these voices end up being privileged in business life, the fact remains that foregrounding them serves to silence voices within a senior leader's organisation, especially the voices of people immersed in the quotidian warp and weft of the business and hence best located to offer insight into what's good, what's not, and what could work better.

One colleague with whom I had a conversation about her experience of voice and silence in a professional context offered another dimension to this. She works in a specialist area and has developed an approach and complementary materials that reflect her experience in that domain, her rich knowledge of the field, and her capacity to bring a fresh view to the work. She described talking about her work with others – and these were exclusively men – only then to hear them talking with others as if they were their ideas and work. They had stolen her voice – and imposed a silence on her that seems to have rendered her invisible.

This tendency to amplify certain voices and thereby dial down the volume of others sits alongside the experience of people in respect to the language that might be used about and to them, which – to me – often sounds at the least hostile and at worst outwardly aggressive. These powerfully expressed experiences hit me every time I read them in terms of the unfairness and imbalance in the remarks, and their belittling and threatening effect.

> [A] tendency toward dismissive language 'time to put your big girl knickers on and get on with it' (direct quote said to some nursing colleagues) and at others cruel and demeaning behaviour.
> I was literally silenced by the most senior person advising me to "stop digging my own grave" when I challenged them.

I hear these observations with a heavy heart, mindful of the amount of corporate codswallop we're all compelled to endure these days about the value placed on people in the workplace and the mobilisation of concepts such as "compassionate leadership". As I listen carefully to these two people speaking about instances in their work lives where they have been spoken to in this way, I am reminded of stories that I have heard elsewhere recently of managers screaming at staff via Zoom and belittling them with what might best be described as bullying behaviours. It reminds us, perhaps, that, notwithstanding what corporate life looks like these days at a superficial level and the suggestions that it is all somehow more generous and humane, ultimately power and rankism undergird our organisations.

But, again, my thoughts turn to power as a nuanced idea, something that resides in the channels that spring up in any context where human beings come together. It's not exclusively about a "bad person" sitting at the top of the structure and behaving in a beastly fashion, because the hierarchy seems to give them permission so to do. It's not even about the culture in an organisation that arises from the way in which those at the apex of the structure behave to one another and to those below them, important though that is. In passing, I must make note of just how slippery a term "culture" is in a corporate context and that the idea of "culture change", as something that can be done to an organisation, is premised on a perverted redefinition of the term and a perspective that unwittingly owes more to totalitarianism than to humanism (Willmott, 1993).

Instead, power is a characteristic of our relations with one another. It pulses through those connections; sits behind the written word in the corporate documents that we produce; resides in the categorisations that we unthinkingly apply, and inhabits our language in a profound way. This then reminds me that our voices are instruments of power: not just in terms of what we say, but how we say it and where we choose to say things.

I play a lot of tennis these days. It offers me physical exercise, seems to help with my mental health, and gives me great joy in the moment. Because I am somewhat forgetful – perhaps because I am not so proficient a player as to find myself in "flow" that much of the time, so need to focus on the technical aspects of my game pretty constantly – I tend to keep the score by calling it out point by point. As I do this, I am compelled to acknowledge that, whilst what I am saying fits a standard pattern, the way in which I say it can be seen to be imbued with power. The tone and timbre that I apply to speaking aloud the scores "Love 40" against me and "40 Love" in my favour is invariably different – and reflects the power that is woven into the fact that I have nominated myself to keep score and say it aloud. At its most basic level, if I call out "Love 40" against me, I tend to announce it without enthusiasm and with the stress dropping on the 40: if it's "40 Love" in my favour, my voice is lighter and perhaps louder – and there is a heavy stress on the 40.

I am going to finish my personal reflections with two remarks that I heard very clearly on reading the thirty-five voices:

> I keep pointing out issues about resources. And whilst I felt they were initially heard; nothing has been done to address them. So when I try to speak about them now I feel they are ignored – or that I am becoming a broken record.
>
> Awful levels of racism that have gone unchallenged and many have been silenced.

The first underscores for me the gap that John and I sensed, as we looked at corporate leadership, between "listening" and "hearing", reminding me that some voices will indeed appear to be heard – but that, instead of then using what has been said as the start of a dialogue, leaders offer a sop to the speaker rather than engaging in conversation or doing anything in response to what they have heard. Eventually, that habit of "hearing but ignoring" leads to the speaker self-managing their behaviour, worrying about being seen as repetitive. Here we see power at work again at the most subtle of levels, with the speaker silencing themselves in light of the unhelpful reaction to their voice. We speak, the listener hears, they do not engage. This happens again and again. Eventually, we internalise the power used against us and silence ourselves.

In light of this, the second comment feels all the more important to acknowledge. People speak about their experiences (not at a generalised but at a specific and localised level); the listener wrings their hands and makes various positive noises, but there is no engagement with thinking about what sort of open dialogue might start to address what the voices have shared. It concerns me that there will have been some silencing, that voices have ended up as docile bodies, cowed by the power of others, a power that they have then incorporated into themselves so that they have self-silenced.

References

Cole, M. & Higgins, J., 2021. *Stuck in the middle – and feeling the pinch.* [Online] Available at: https://radicalod.org/2021/10/12/stuck-in-the-middle-and-feeling-the-pinch/ [Accessed 13 January 2021].

Colfer, C. J. P., 1983. On communication among "unequals". *International Journal of Intercultural Relations*, 7, pp. 263–283.

Fuller, R. W., 2004. *Somebodies and nobodies: Overcoming the abuse of rank.* Gabriola Island: New Society Publishers.

Goffman, E., 1981. Footing. In: E. Goffman, ed. *Forms of talk.* Philadelphia: University of Pennsylvania Press, pp. 124–159.

Gurung, L., 2020. Feminist standpoint theory: Conceptualization and utility. *Dhaulagiri Journal of Sociology and Anthropology*, 14, pp. 106–115.

Martin, M., 2018. *The uses of understanding in social science: Verstehen.* Abingdon: Routledge.

Nilep, C., 2006. "Code switching" in sociocultural linguistics. *Colorado Research in Linguistics*, 19(1), pp. 1–22.

Smith, D. E., 1974. Women's perspective as a radical critique of sociology. *Sociological Inquiry*, 44(1), pp. 7–13.

Wall, C. J. & Gannon-Leary, P., 1999. A sentence made by men: Muted group theory revisited. *The European Journal of Women's Studies*, 6(1), pp. 21–29.

Willmott, H., 1993. Strength is ignorance; Slavery is freedom: Managing culture in modern organizations. *Journal of Management Studies*, 30(4), pp. 515–552.

12

SOME NOTES ON METHOD AND PRACTICAL APPLICATION

Reactionary listening

In the previous section, we have described how we sought to hear what all of the people said who completed an online survey that we put out in order to encourage a wider conversation about voice and silence in the workplace. We were adamant that this should not be about rendering the things that people said as abstract and manipulable in terms of a piece of formal research; so much of that sort of activity subsumes attention to what is being said to a desire to codify human experience. Instead, our motivation for this direct work aimed to help us hear at a meaningful level what people felt motivated to say about their experiences.

It felt as though they were bearing witness – and it was our responsibility to properly attend to that. It was not a data "snatch and grab", as so many of these exercises can feel, where the "respondent" offers something up that is eagerly grabbed and aggregated by the researchers. This, for us, was a genuine exercise in listening and hearing – with each voice seen as different and not merely something that could be categorised and numerated.

DOI: 10.4324/9781003296683-15

We cannot know how you, as the reader, engaged with and heard the thirty-five voices that we shared in this chapter. How you made your way through that is an experience that is entirely yours, although opening it up in dialogue with others will allow you to interrogate it and to examine the extent to which your reactions in the moment feel open and ethical in hindsight. But each communicative exchange – whether expressed via voice or silence and notwithstanding whence it arises – is worthy of scrutiny. And our view is that a selection of prompt questions might assist in the wider purpose of sense-making and specifically in regard to the thirty-five stories told through the survey.

We invite you to focus in and reflect on everything you have just read. Try to quieten your inner voice, which may be eager to concur with or contest some of the things that these 35 people are keen for you to hear. This is a point where you might discover the opportunity to listen so as to understand. This stands in contrast with listening so as to open a space in which your voice might be heard. These questions might help you to make that change:

- How do you find yourself **reacting** to these candid observations on the part of another person? What words sprang forward both during and at the end of your reading?
- To what extent could **your reaction interfere with your capacity to hear** what they are saying and to find a way in which to engage with them in terms of their experience? Do you want to hear more or less from them?
- What **judgement** about this person is sitting in your chest at this moment?
- Could it be that you have two reactions, one that would be your **public** response and one that would be a **private** one? If so, how are they different?
- To what extent are your **politics** interfering with your human capacity to listen to and to hear what this person is saying?
- In all honesty with yourself, is there part of you that would like to **stop them saying what they have said** – and why might that be?
- How strong is the temptation to **read so as to refute**, rather than to read so as to understand and connect?

This is the way we tried to engage with everything that was shared with us, by understanding it as a phenomenological statement on the part of an individual – but, in the course of our engagement with what was being voiced, it required us to attend to our deep-seated, personal, acculturated and ideologised responses to each testimony and to bracket those off, so that they did not directly interfere with our active attempts to listen but, more importantly, to hear.

John and Mark had different reactions to the statement in the survey from the white middle-aged man who had concerns about his experience of inclusion in organisational life. John's immediate visceral reaction was to disregard it, simply make it disappear from the summary we were seeking to draft. It felt uncomfortable to him, so his reflex reaction was to silence it by ignoring it and conjuring it away.

Mark saw it as a statement that underscored how power resides in the network of capillaries that feed our complex social interrelations and binds us in all manner of ways. This may have been the respondent's only opportunity to express their thoughts and anxieties openly, since there is an orthodoxy in terms of thought and these remarks seem to contest it. In every other circumstance, they may want to give voice – but instead walk away in silence.

This chimes with a survey from the US mentioned elsewhere about how confident people were in terms of speaking out about their political opinions. It reports that 62% of Americans felt as though the political climate prevented them from saying things they believe because others might find them offensive. Importantly, this self-constraint extended across political boundaries, with majorities reporting this regardless of whether they were Democrats, Republicans, or Independents – although it also found that 58% of those who said they were staunchly progressive said that they felt that they could say what they believe (Ekins, 2020).

This is a reminder of the importance of *processing*, *reflexivity*, and *conversation*. Understanding the need to process things rather than simply to experience them and react is an essential discipline. Similarly, the importance of reflecting on things in a way that acknowledges that life cannot be isolated and examined as if we were able to stand outside of it and peruse it as a separate thing. In the context of the social, we are implicit and inseparable, impacting on the minute-by-minute circumstances that constitute our existence. Hence, when we think of the world, the following applies:

> It is continually "present" for me, and I myself am a member of it. Therefore, this world is not there for me as a mere *world of facts and affairs*, but, with the same immediacy, as a *world of values*, a *world of goods*, a *practical world*.   (Husserl, 1931/2012, p. 53)

We were only able to come to a richer understanding of the data by laying aside our armour and having an honest and respectful dialogue about it. Had John not found space, time and safety to describe his reaction to the comments discussed earlier, our thinking would have remained where it was. Our sharing of this insight is not anecdotal but is offered as an insight that readers may choose to incorporate into their lifeworld. But, for this to happen, the silence needed to be broken.

Positive attention

Each of the thirty-five voices had something to say. To say things out loud is to assume that someone will listen, if only to simply acknowledge the sound of your voice interrupting a silence. Listening works at a superficial level, while hearing gets into the text of the spoken and the written word and seeks to find its way around it so as to make sense of it, to then open up channels for an exchange of experience and ideas. We chose to give space to every voice and to listen reflexively to the processing in our heads that took place in response, clearing aside as many of our internal interruptions as we could so as to leave room for us to hear what it was that was being said.

This echoes the positive aspects of inquiry approaches that fall under the umbrella of participative research, including action research. This is not just a different way of doing formal research but offers everyone involved in it the opportunity to engage with the world differently. In light of this, the following offers a rich description of its theory and practice – and its underpinnings and principles:

> It is not so much a methodology as an orientation to inquiry that seeks to cre-ate participative communities of inquiry in which qualities of engagement, curiosity and question posing are brought to bear on significant practical issues. Action research challenges much received wisdom in both academia

and among social change and development practitioners, not least because it is a practice of participation, engaging those who might otherwise be subjects of research or recipients of interventions to a greater or less extent as inquiring co-researchers.   (Reason & Bradbury, 2008, p. 1)

It should be stressed that our work was not action research. However, we take the view that the statement about the way in which action research engages with and seeks to make sense of the world resonates strongly with the way that we approach our practice. Indeed, it might be better to think about our activity in this sphere as Cooperative Inquiry, which is defined as

...a way of working with other people who have similar concerns and interests to yourself, in order to: understand your world, make sense of your life and develop new and creative ways of looking at things; [and] learn how to act to change things you may want to change and find out how to do things better.   (Reason, 1999, p. 208)

For us, research is not something we do as if it were a means of stepping beyond the everyday in order to create an illusion of understanding the everyday. The view of the world as something that we can remove ourselves from, so as to study it, reflects a scientism that is unhelpful in terms of supporting understanding and creating conditions for change. We are acutely aware that "research" (for want of a better term) is intrinsic to human existence, insofar as we are all actively engaged in sense-making activity and the generation of provisional hypotheses and proposals in terms of how to be as we live from day to day. We aim to be alert to the world with respect to attending to the myriad ways in which those around us are experiencing it. This means that our presence and agency in social life is ceaselessly observing things around us, hearing those around us and processing what we hear. And this applies beyond being a researcher to thinking about one's presence in organisational life.

Hence, each conversation and passing exchange – if one is properly attending to what one's interlocutors are saying – is a constant source of material through which one can sustain an understanding of others and the world that we collectively construct. Hence, hearing others matters both so that they genuinely feel heard and know that another has witnessed that expression and also to keep ourselves open to myriad views and perspectives in our world.

Lastly, our means of engaging and thinking afresh about research reinforces the importance of not seeing that inquiry as a thing in itself, as is so often the case. In too many instances, research is seen as a destination rather than a stepping-off point for impact on the world; very often it asserts that the research undertaken points the direction to more research. There is another way to think about all of this:

> Where normal science sees the dominant myth as reason or science, it sees the world in terms of a puzzle, which through rigorous observation the parts can be identified, assembled, disassembled and reassembled, radical research proposes the deconstruction of myths and the creative reconfiguration of conceptions of the world to include what the puzzle had repressed in the interests of order.   (Schostak & Schostak, 2008, p. 271)

Such a view borrows from the somewhat obtuse realm of Derridean philosophy. But accepting that things in the world – especially all that falls under the broad heading of "text" – are implicitly susceptible to deconstruction reminds us that this notion can nudge us towards a deeply critical engagement with the ideas and practices that we see around us. Hence, our commitment to criticality and reflexivity (Cole & Higgins, 2021) – both in terms of our scholarship and practice and as something to promote as a key facet of leadership – which translates into a commitment to look askance at the commonplace and tease it with a range of challenges, which encompass the following:

1. Rethink the everyday as something alien and unknown to you
2. Do not take things at face value
3. Deny the power of authorship; once something is out in the world, it is no longer defined by its author's intentions
4. Expose the cultural biases that become apparent on close reading
5. Consider the language in use (style, complexity, character, emphases, jargon, etc.)
6. Bring to the surface the cultural underpinnings and consider possible alternative or subaltern perspectives that do not find space therein
7. Bring to the fore the inconsistencies, paradoxes, and contradictions
8. Examine the tensions between the spirit and the letter of the text

Our way of thinking about research is to democratise it and call out the power that is implicit in the relationship between the social science researcher and the subject (who, in the process, is rendered as an object for investigation rather than a human agent). To that end, we are committed to immersing ourselves as partners into a milieu where we collectively seek to make sense of the world and – crucially – to work in a dialogic and collaborative fashion so as to change it. This fractures the existing inflexible relationship between researcher and the "object" of their study, which unwittingly reproduces power relationships in our wider society. But it does not presuppose a vision of the future to which we wish condescendingly to guide people, a conceit writ large in the practice of supposedly progressive movements whose provenance resides in oppressive metanarratives, such as Marxism and its Leninist extension.

At the same time, we endeavour to encourage those with whom we work to apply their own criticality and reflexivity to the world and the things they find in it. Hence, one of our suggestions is for people to pick up an artefact from their corporate life (for example statements of strategy, policy, advertising, values, vision, protocols, processes, reports or plans) and read it using the eight critical orientations indicated above. We also underscore the importance of individuals coming together to make sense of their shared world and to allow new understanding, practice and ideas to arise out of the free-flowing dialogue in which they are involved. This exercise needs to be as clean as possible, so those involved need to be committed to spotting and interrogating their (often initially tacit) presuppositions and familiar routes in thinking.

In summary, we turn our backs on traditional research and embrace an orientation that is described thus:

> Ultimately, participatory research is about respecting and understanding the people with and for whom researchers work. It is about developing a realization that local people are knowledgeable and that they, together with researchers, can work towards analyses and solutions. It involves recognizing the rights of those whom research concerns, enabling people to set their own agendas for research and development and so giving them ownership over the process.
>
> (Cornwall & Jewkes, 1995, p. 1674)

We hope you see the potential for absorbing that commitment to participative research into the everyday conversational space in organisations – and to your personal presence in that environment. To embrace this approach is firstly to accept that such spaces are riven with power, whatever public statements exist around involvement, engagement and empowerment. Then it requires a principled commitment to work to hear what is being said, as opposed merely to listen in order to echo or refute what the voices in your corporate milieu are saying – or choosing not to say.

To support this and bridge into the final part of the book, where we offer guidance to people in organisations whatever their role or position as to how to move beyond listening to hearing, we offer this framework.

Listening and hearing, above and below the line

We take as our starting point the broad assumption that it is possible to think about two spaces in which conversation takes place in a corporate setting, which are shown above and below the solid line (Figure 12.1).

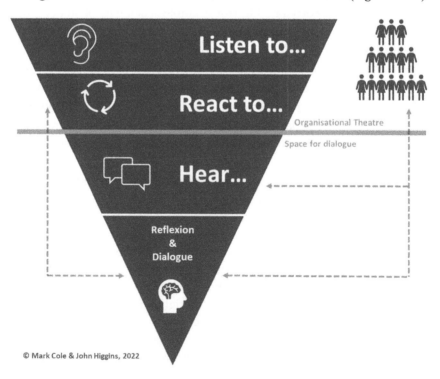

© Mark Cole & John Higgins, 2022

Figure 12.1 Moving from listening to hearing.

The realm in which the most superficial and performative conversational activity takes place sits above that line and is what we have called the *organisational theatre*. This is the most managed context of corporate life, where people interact in light of their roles and status and through a range of scripts, where each knows what they are meant to say and not say. Hence, in this framing we can see the leader and the follower as dramatic parts to be played, engaging in severely constrained forms of communication.

Below the line is a domain of possibility, in which people can connect as agents with one another in a *space for dialogue*. To us, this is somewhere rarely visited in corporate life other than perhaps at times of crisis when organisational constraints can – as many of us saw in the course of the pandemic crisis – fray and disintegrate. It requires the sort of attention to what is being said and by whom as we have tried to apply to the thirty-five voices. It also needs people to connect as fellow human to fellow human, rather than on a master-servant basis or on prescription, where some voices are encouraged and others are silenced.

Organisational theatre

We have become very used to the practices around human exchange that take place in this domain. It has a familiarity that to us should be breeding contempt and an active desire to find a very different way of communicating, but we are often simply too locked into this way of being with others. This domain is where we all actively manage what we say and whether we say it. This is where leaders pay lip service to speaking up whilst failing to hear what people might then say – or to even acknowledge that a silence in this space might be saying something significant. Indeed, those leaders may be offering a public invitation for people around them to speak whilst acting in ways that contradict the invitation. It is not so much a mixed message as a communicative tactic, which allows them to tick the leadership checklist in terms of openness and responsiveness while not having to pay attention to the legitimate concerns and insights of those with whom they work.

Such behaviours on the part of everyone in the organisational theatre define what can be said and what must stay hidden. It is not as crudely totalitarian as someone at the top simply proscribing speech, although this can also be a feature of organisational life. Instead, everyone is complicit in creating and reproducing a regime of voice and silence just by their presence and interactions in the organisational theatre. It grants permission for some things to be said but reminds speakers in that space that anything falling outside of that defined list of the sayable must remain silent.

In the organisational theatre, we see people listening to react. A leader, manager, influencer, or group in the organisational theatre are seemingly open to the voices of others but they listen in a way that privileges their habitual reaction to what is being said. The time between listening and reacting happens in a heartbeat, constricting the space and opportunity to actually hear what is being said. The listen-react nexus converts every utterance by another person into a caricature, a recasting of what has been said that says more about the listener's interpretation than it does about the speaker's intentions.

Space for dialogue

The traditional dramaturgy of the organisational theatre – defined in terms of its staging, the characters that are permitted to play a part in this staging, the lines people are allowed to say and the silences that must be kept – stands in sharp contrast to the improvisational domain of the space for dialogue. Below the line is a way of being that eschews artificiality and performativity in favour of seeking meaningful and candid relations between people as full human beings.

An important aspect of the space for dialogue is the way in which it allows each individual to connect with their experiences in the organisational theatre so as to make better sense of that realm. In the space for dialogue, the individual listens so as to hear what is being said as opposed to prompting a reaction. Instead of reacting, they embrace the notion of reflexivity, crafting space and time to process what is said. But that reflexivity goes beyond ensuring a meaningful engagement with the voices of others. It requires us to relate to people as fellow human beings rather than as mere speaking objects; it also insists that we identify the reactions we had in the organisational theatre and subject them to scrutiny.

In light of our individual commitment to criticality and reflexivity when we are below the line in this space for dialogue, there is an expectation that we will work with this newfound scrutiny to connect with those around us and engage in reflexive dialogue, listening to hear rather than react and speaking to connect and inquire rather than to privilege and/or silence voices around us.

And some concluding information from and about the survey

Researchers tend to place upfront in their deliberations all of the notionally factual material about how they did their work. In this section of the book, we have chosen to invert this and foreground what really matters in terms of the work that we are seeking to do, namely that we have listened to and heard what the people that responded to our survey had to say. Ideas about how research should be conducted (and, by implication, how leaders should relate to the speaking subjects all around them) can be felt as a layer of intermediation that prevents us from engaging human to human with what is being said.

Throughout this section, we have underscored the idea that someone seeking to hear what others are saying needs actively to privilege those voices. In that respect, Jean-Paul Sartre's reported observation that we should try and view the world through the eyes of the least favoured and those treated most unjustly offers a useful starting point, although its reductionism carries with it communistic as opposed to an existentialist air (Bakewell, 2016, p. 271). This should not mean that the listener needs to efface or erase themselves in that process, even if such a thing was ever possible in human relations. It does, however, serve as a powerful reminder in every circumstance to seek out voices that you perhaps would not ordinarily notice, let alone hear, in particular, those subaltern and oftentimes hidden voices to which we desperately need to attend.

Looking at the numeric responses to the survey

Asking people to give a numeric value to their experience is a well-established and accepted habit in carrying out surveys. It is also deeply problematic. The quantification of human experience can assume a variety of disguises. Most obviously, it shows up in the ubiquitous "pulse survey" or indeed the net promoter score. Equally, it manifests in the icebreaker at the start of a meeting, where on one occasion we saw participants instructed to rate themselves on a six-point Likert scale – each score point being illustrated by a piece of toast, from lightly browned through to charred to a cinder. This takes someone's corporate (and possibly personal) misery and substitutes it for a number.

Its positive intention is to try and find comparable patterns, find a way for a mass of experience to be assessed quickly using a consistent yardstick. And with that intention comes some important questions, namely:

- Who is setting the yardstick and so the nature of the understanding that will be created?
- What gets lost when consistency of response and speed of analysis are the governing features of survey design?
- Why are numeric expressions seen as "truer" than worded ones?

For those of us who see all social activities through the lens of truth-power, the creation of numeric yardsticks is not a neutral activity, it is most certainly not objective (and is often a classic example of the misuse of the scientific method) and is a political act that usually sustains a particular ideology around who has voice, authority and agency i.e. Whose truth has most weight?

When we started designing the survey, which has given us the personal narratives already explored, we did not expect such a rich set of expressive experience, although Mark was conscious of his experience of the value that lived in people's written-in responses. John in particular was thinking more in terms of playing the traditional survey game and the face validity that comes from having some quantitative data to appeal to the world as it is (playing the research game).

Hence our joint pleasure when we began to get beyond a few respondents, with 75 people completing much if not all of it – especially as they came from such a mix of sources i.e., various of John's co-operative inquiry groups and their networks as well as Mark's LinkedIn connections. As the responses came in, we also began to realise that people were using the free space to share strongly felt, personal experience – which we suspect had nowhere else to go.

Our analysis of the quantified data has therefore been reimagined by us as a secondary aspect of the survey, something worthy of attention, but not the figural and all-encompassing importance it is often given. We have also tried to find a way to set the data within a commentary, eschewing the fanciful belief that data such as this can ever speak for itself. We provide this material with a heartfelt request that you use each number as a cipher that will offer insight into experience – and bear in mind throughout that these numbers can often have the effect of taking the edge off the realities of human experience. And, of course, supplanting people with a collective numeral reduces the human subject and their experience to a symbol, which is a practice that is patently riven with power.

Responses to three overarching, context specific questions

We started the survey with three questions that were deliberately phrased to invite a personal, subjective response to the messy social realities that people would be answering from. They were:

- Over the past 18 months, how easy has it been for you to speak up in the workplace?
- In that same period, have you felt that people – potentially those at the senior level – have been listening to you and others in your organisation?
- Where senior people have been seen to listen, to what extent do you feel they were hearing what was said?

Respondents were able to respond with a sliding scale that ran from 0 to 10, with zero representing the negative end of things i.e., not being able to speak up and not being listened to and heard, while 10 was associated with the opposite, positive experience.

The first thing that stands out from the 75 respondents is that someone's answers fell into every category from 0 to 10 – in other words, some people had had a really good experience, and some had had a really negative one. Any generalisations we draw from the overall pattern mustn't lose sight of that unsurprising truth – that people's subjective, personal experience varies a lot. It echoes with a recent conversation John had with a rising star of a large US corporate, who said words to the effect that he'd had "a really good COVID!"

With all those provisos in place, these are the headline numbers for each question:

Over the past 18 months, how easy has it been for you to speak up in the workplace?

The average response was 5.95 and the most popular score was 7 – so edging on the positive side of being able to speak up. In terms of the spread:

- 38 scored a 7, 8, 9, or 10 i.e. reported a moderately or strongly positive experience

- 12 scored a 0, 1, 2, or 3 i.e. reported a moderately or strongly negative experience
- 25 scored a 4, 5, or 6 i.e. what can broadly summarised as a "meh" experience

In statistics speak, not far off a normal distribution, but skewed towards the positive. As a summary sentence you could say something like: "While more people have had a positive speak-up experience than negative, the overall picture is a mixed bag"

In that same period, have you felt that people — potentially those at senior level — have been listening to you and others in your organisation?

The average response was 4.88 and the most popular score was 6 — so weakly edging on the positive side of being able to speak up, at the upper end of "meh". In terms of the spread:

- 19 scored a 7, 8, 9, or 10 i.e. reported a moderately or strongly positive experience
- 30 scored a 0, 1, 2 ,or 3 i.e. reported a moderately or strongly negative experience
- 26 scored a 4, 5, or 6 i.e. what can broadly summarised as a "meh" experience

In statistics speak, not far off a normal distribution, but skewed towards the meh-negative. As a summary sentence you could say something like: "While more people have had a negative speak-up experience than positive, the overall picture is a mixed but slightly eggy bag"

Where senior people have been seen to listen, to what extent do you feel they were hearing what was said?

The average response was 4.77 and the most popular score was 5 — so edging on the negative side of being able to speak up. In terms of the spread:

- 18 scored a 7, 8, 9, or 10 i.e. reported a moderately or strongly positive experience
- 26 scored a 0, 1, 2, or 3 i.e. reported a moderately or strongly negative experience
- 31 scored a 4, 5, or 6 i.e. what can broadly summarised as a "meh" experience

In statistics speak, not far off a normal distribution, but skewed towards the meh-negative. As a summary sentence you could say something like: "While more people have had a negative speak-up experience than positive, the overall picture is a mixed negative meh"

And attempting a synthesis

In one sentence what is the story we can see from the above... many people have found it easy enough to speak up, but more than that are unsure that what is being said is being listened to or heard. Confirming the comment Brené Brown made in her podcast with John and Megan Reitz on 28 February 2022, that if you're serious about encouraging a speak-up culture then it's less about the voice for the voiceless and more about "ears for the earless" (https://brenebrown.com/podcast/leading-in-an-age-of-employee-activism/).

Responses to six more specific statements

There were six more specific statements we asked people to respond to about their experience of being silenced over the last 18 months in terms of the extent to which they agreed or disagreed – which garnered between 47 and 66 responses. What stood out is how much the numbers dipped on the last two questions, which has certainly got us thinking and building a mountain of supposition! The six statements were:

- I have felt silenced by people more senior to me in my organisation
- I have felt silenced by my peers
- I have silenced myself on occasions
- I have seen others silenced in my organisation
- I have compelled people around me to be silent
- I have encouraged people around me to be silent

In terms of the drop off of respondents to the last two questions, we wonder if these are experiences impossible for people to notice or too shameful to admit to – and so people prefer to jump over them. In John's recent work (2019) with a group working on "Speaking Up and Listening Up", he thought he was being the perfect, invitational facilitator when he went around people working in their small groups. It took a young woman he was facilitating with to point out that as a white, older man who'd only moments before stopped giving an expert lecture to the whole group, he was not something that this group of largely Black and Ethnic Minority women would feel relaxed around. He recalls his co-facilitator put it a bit more strongly than that: 'You're scaring the shit out of people'. She then took over, going to the people in their groups and was welcomed in, in an instant.

Where in the first section of the survey, people were invited to express an opinion about what they had seen, in this section, we asked people to rate their level of agreement with the six statements. The scoring was different than to the previous questions, with 0 being strongly disagreeing with the quite general statement (i.e. not feeling silenced or silencing) and 10 strongly agreeing (i.e. feeling most silenced or most silencing). As with the scores on the doors with the questions already analysed, the responses to each question fell into every number category between 0 and 10 – except for the last two questions where answers fell into every score except 9.

With all the provisos and caveats we've already raised, here then are the numbers associated with each statement.

I have felt silenced by people more senior to me in my organisation (62 respondents)

The average response was 5.9 and the most popular score was 8 – so edging on the negative side of feeling silenced by people senior to them. In terms of the spread:

- 15 scored a 0, 1, 2, or 3 i.e. reported a moderately or strongly positive experience
- 32 scored a 7, 8, 9, or 10 i.e. reported a moderately or strongly negative experience
- 15 scored a 4, 5, or 6 i.e. what can broadly summarised as a "meh" experience

In statistics speak, something akin to a Poisson distribution (i.e., skewed away from the normal with a much larger spread at one end), with a large number reporting a silencing by seniors' experience. As a summary sentence, you could say something like: "Many people have had a negative experience when it comes to feeling silenced by senior others in their workplaces"

I have felt silenced by my peers (61 responses)

The average response was 3.98 and the most popular score was 1 – so edging on the positive side of feeling silenced by their peers i.e. they don't feel silenced by them! In terms of the spread:

• 28 scored a 0, 1, 2, or 3 i.e. reported a moderately or strongly positive experience
• 11 scored a 7, 8, 9, or 10 i.e. reported a moderately or strongly negative experience
• 22 scored a 4, 5, or 6 i.e. what can broadly summarised as a "meh" experience

In statistics speak, something akin to a Poisson distribution (i.e. skewed away from the normal with a much larger spread at one end), with a large number reporting the experience of not being silenced by peers. As a summary sentence, you could say something like: "Many people have had a positive experience when it comes to their peers and haven't felt silenced by them in their workplaces"

I have silenced myself on occasions (66 responses)

The average response was 6.32 and the most popular score was 6 – so edging towards an experience of self-silencing. In terms of the spread:

• 10 scored a 0, 1, 2, or 3 i.e. reported not self-silencing, or only slightly or occasionally
• 33 scored a 7, 8, 9, or 10 i.e. reported self-silencing to a considerable degree
• 23 scored a 4, 5, or 6 i.e. what can broadly summarised as a "meh" experience

In statistics speak, something akin to a Poisson distribution (i.e. skewed away from the normal with a much larger spread at one end), with a large number reporting the experience of self-silencing. As a summary sentence, you could say something like: "Many people have self-silenced to a greater or lesser degree in their workplaces"

I have seen others silenced in my organisation (66 responses)

The average response was 6.59 and the most popular score was 8 – so edging towards an experience of seeing others silenced. In terms of the spread:

- 10 scored a 0, 1, 2, or 3 i.e. reported not seeing others silenced, or only slightly or occasionally
- 40 scored a 7, 8, 9, or 10 i.e. reported seeing others silenced to a considerable degree
- 16 scored a 4, 5, or 6 i.e. what can broadly summarised as a "meh" experience

In statistics speak, something akin to a Poisson distribution (i.e. skewed away from the normal with a much larger spread at one end), with a large number reporting the experience of seeing the silencing of others. As a summary sentence, you could say something like: "Many people have seen others silenced to a greater or lesser degree in their workplaces"

I have compelled people around me to be silent (55 responses)

The average response was 2.09 and the most popular score was 0 – so speaking pretty definitively to the sense that respondents did not feel they compelled silence in those around them. In terms of the spread:

- 42 scored a 0, 1, 2, or 3 i.e. reported not compelling those around them to be silent, or only slightly or occasionally
- 6 scored a 7, 8, 9, or 10 i.e. reported compelling others to be silenced to a considerable degree
- 7 scored a 4, 5, or 6 i.e. what can broadly summarised as a "meh" experience

As previously, we are seeing something akin to a Poisson distribution (i.e., skewed away from the normal with a much larger spread at one end), with a large number reporting the experience of not compelling others to be silent. As a summary sentence, you could say something like: "Many people do not compel others to be silent in their workplaces"

I have encouraged people around me to be silent (47 responses)

The average response was 2.32 and the most popular score was 0 – so speaking pretty definitively to the sense that respondents did not feel they encouraged silence in those around them. In terms of the spread:

- 36 scored a 0, 1, 2, or 3 i.e. reported not encouraging those around them to be silent, or only slightly or occasionally
- 4 scored a 7, 8, 9, or 10 i.e. reported encouraging others to be silenced to a considerable degree
- 7 scored a 4, 5, or 6 i.e. what can broadly summarised as a "meh" experience

In statistics speak, something akin to a Poisson distribution (i.e. skewed away from the normal with a much larger spread at one end), with a large number reporting the experience of not encouraging others to be silent. As a summary sentence you could say something like: "Many people do not encourage others to be silent in their workplaces"

And attempting a synthesis

In one sentence what is the story we can see from the above…

People see themselves and their peers as pretty blameless in silencing others; silencing comes about more as a matter of personal choice or because of the behaviours/presence of senior others.

The demographics – who were we speaking with?

The people who responded were skewed to being: white, heterosexual, able-bodied women over 40. In more detail the breakdown was as follows:

Organisational position (Performers, Manager of Performers, Manager of Managers) – 55 respondents

- **25** Performers – someone involved in the direct delivery of the work on which the business depends and has no direct supervisory responsibility

- **17** Managers of Performers – someone who has a supervisory responsibility, such as a team leader who may also contribute to the direct delivery of the work
- **13** Managers of Managers – someone who has supervisory responsibility for overseeing the work of Managers of Performers

Sex – 60 respondents

- 17 Male
- 40 Female
- 1   Non-binary/Third Gender
- 2   prefer not to say

Age – 60 respondents

- 1   16–25
- 1   26–30
- 8   31–40
- 20 41–50
- 22 51–60
- 7   61–70
- 1   Prefer not to say

Race – 60 respondents

- 7   Asian or Asian British
- 2   Mixed
- 4   Black or Black British
- 42 White
- 4   Other ethnic group
- 1   I do not wish to disclose my ethnic origin

Sexual orientation – 59 respondents

- 1   Gay woman/Lesbian
- 2   Gay man
- 1   Bisexual

- 50 Heterosexual
- 1   Other
- 4   I do not wish to disclose this information

Do you consider yourself disabled – 60 respondents

- 11 Yes
- 48 No
- 1   I do not wish to share this information

What could we learn from all of this – and from our experience of hearing others?

In this section, we have endeavoured to do three things: hear the responses of all those who completed our survey, so as to bear witness to their bearing witness. We have not tried to cluster the comments – as some researchers and a good many OD facilitators might be prompted to do – so as to commodify those comments, but instead have taken steps to hear each voice. Then we have listened to how we have reacted to what we have heard, introducing the crucial element of reflexivity we see as being foundational for anyone who aspires to work with others. Lastly, we have extended that reflexivity to the point where we are jointly applying a crucial level of criticality to what we're doing and how we're doing it. This keeps our practice under constant real-time review – and thereby allows us to adapt to our reflections in the course of the work.

It is our hope that this chapter has in some way showcased how it might be if we listen so as to hear, rather than listen in order to react. But, in the section that follows, we are going to be more explicit about our thinking in this respect. And, off the back of that, we intend to embrace the power that arises from having the authorial voice to offer prescriptions as to how people in the workplace might make sense of all of this in their context, offering direct guidance to those who aspire to leadership and those anointed as leaders, as to how they can be different and better in that role.

Before we launch into that section, we reinforce the key message that runs through this book – and the practice we advocate – that we all owe every voice a proper hearing, rather than a perfunctory listening.

References

Bakewell, S., 2016. *At the existentialist cafe: Freedom, being and apricot cocktails.* London: Chatto & Windus.

Cole, M. & Higgins, J., 2021. *Stuck in the middle – and feeling the pinch.* [Online] Available at: https://radicalod.org/2021/10/12/stuck-in-the-middle-and-feeling-the-pinch/ [Accessed 13 January 2021].

Cornwall, A. & Jewkes, R., 1995. What is participatory research?. *Social Science & Medicine,* 41(12), pp. 1667–1676.

Ekins, E., 2020. *Poll: 62% of Americans say they have political views they're afraid to share.* [Online] Available at: https://www.cato.org/survey-reports/poll-62-americans-say-they-have-political-views-theyre-afraid-share#introduction [Accessed 31 January 2021].

Husserl, E., 1931/2012. *Ideas: General introduction to pure phenomenology.* Abingdon: Routledge.

Reason, P., 1999. Integrating action and reflection through Co-operative Inquiry. *Management Learning,* 30(2), pp. 207–226.

Reason, P. & Bradbury, H., 2008. Introduction. In: P. Reason & H. Bradbury, eds. *The Sage handbook of action research: Participative inquiry and practice.* London: Sage, pp. 1–10.

Schostak, J. & Schostak, J., 2008. *Radical research: Designing, developing and writing research to make a difference.* Abingdon: Routledge.

Part IV

DIALOGUE RETETHERED

13

PUTTING DIALOGUE TO WORK

JOHN: What does dialogue mean to you?

JT: It's a feeling as much as anything else… it's nurturing, supportive… [there's] vulnerability in it and a sense of security, safety as well… clarity of mind. It makes sense when you juxtapose it with transactional or adversarial forms of conversation… there's nothing adversarial about it, mutually supportive

JOHN: The word spacious came to mind as you were talking then, talking slowly

JT: Yes. It felt spacious in that I could stop and think and pause. I didn't feel any pressure to be clever or anything like that. As dialogue slows down, that spaciousness opens up. They're not just pauses for me when I'm thinking, they're spaces where you may or may not step in. Those transactional or adversarial conversations there's so much interrupting, no time to consider what's going on

Notes from a conversation about dialogue on 6.2.22

DOI: 10.4324/9781003296683-17

Our position is plain: the interplay of voice and silence in organisational life is not straightforward. We can feel pressured to speak and compelled to keep our silence. These reactions arise out of all manner of circumstances, from the intercession of a leader through to the constraints that arise out of community. The key message is simply expressed yet fantastically complex in practice, namely that we are primed to listen to react, when there is an urgent need for all of us to listen so as to hear.

And that attention to hearing what is being said is not merely a courtesy: it is a foundation for allowing us to step into dialogue. We listen to hear what the other is saying, the better to engage with them, human to human, in rich and meaningful conversation. An old British Telecom advert used to carry the strapline, 'It's good to talk'; we believe it's not just "good" in some abstract sense but essential – politically, socially, organisationally, and personally.

Let's start with some conclusions about dialogue – covering what we see as the key headlines, what is involved in taking dialogue seriously, and most challengingly what will need to be let go of if dialogue is to take root within a specific group or organisation.

Some key headlines about dialogue:

- It is a philosophy first, a skill second
- It is incompatible with competitive individualism
- It is incompatible with goal-driven instrumentalism
- It privileges the quality of relationship over individual technical skills
- It assumes knowledge and insight are social, emergent phenomena
- Its ethics are as good or bad as the culture within which it is practised
- Dialogue on the terms of the established elite is not dialogue (it's a PR stunt and/or powerplay)
- Co-production and co-design are at the heart of any living dialogic practice

And if you want to take dialogue seriously and create an environment of satisfying mutuality, creativity and belonging then this is what needs to be privileged:

- Inter-personal relationships and bonds of affection and intimacy
- Collective responsibility for and ownership of knowledge and wisdom
- Collective accountability for creating and recreating context-specific dialogic practices

It is unlikely that dialogic practice will take root in contexts which are driven or defined by:

- Contracts
- Individual performance
- Disproportionate distribution of risks and rewards
- Judgement and evaluation
- Control over autonomy

In a conversation with Steve Hearsum, riffing about the shortcomings of the practice of organisation development and the way in which it props up a shaky system that is widely being seen as no longer tenable, Mark came to an awkward conclusion. Organisation development (OD) should be about putting dialogue at the centre of the relations that connect people in their organising. Instead, OD dances to the tune of those who commission its services, working to create artificial spaces where that conversation can seemingly be had – but ensuring, through being held at arm's length, that the culture and practice of the organisation remain unchanged.

Hence, we set up action learning sets, facilitated workshops, and praxis groups. They stand separate to the organisation. Meanwhile, in the organisation, we continue to see top-heavy Board meetings, Committees and Sub-Committees, Task & Finish Groups, Working Groups, and so on, places where dialogue will not find a natural home. Instead, membership of those meetings and contributions made there modulate voice and silence, riven as they are by power and hierarchy

A similar thing can be said about initiatives organisations set up to encourage a more inclusive workforce. Often these interventions are kept distant from the daily warp and weft of the organisation; they are programmes of support designed for groups of people who are "Othered", or seen as marginal, in corporate life. They are driven by a deficit model, presupposing that there are people coming up short in terms of things like progression and offering them the chance to change themselves so as to fit in better. At worst – as Mark and Steve discussed – there is a saviour complex underlying this type of work. What seems clear is that these activities are designed to change the people but leave the system untouched. They act to induct people into cultural spaces, when what is actually needed is for the people who find themselves positioned at the edge to be supported to move into and disrupt those spaces which have historically marginalised them. To change those spaces and hence the organisation from within.

Dialogue in context – where we are now

Dialogue has become a badly abused, universal answer. When its practice is seen as no more than a method or a model, rather than a philosophy of human relating, then it can do little more than be another experience soaked in individualism and instrumentality.

The philosophy of dialogue, rooted in the world views of people such as Martin Buber (Buber, 1937) and David Bohm (Bohm, 1996), require a letting go of the autarkic individualism we've written about elsewhere (Cole & Higgins, 2022), where every individual exists outside of the society of others and we are no more than things to be manipulated by each other to achieve our self-referencing goals. The dialogic turn, to borrow from Megan Reitz's work, 'is a call for a serious inquiry into the nature and quality of our relating' (Reitz, 2015, p. 2).

JOHN: What makes it possible to have a dialogic encounter?

JT: When we need to say something that hasn't been said before, this can't be done with anybody. The relationship is already there. I know there are some people in our business that I can engage with in dialogue, create with them… and some I can't. What's in the relationship? A safety in it, a physiological state. In adversarial conversations you might feel reluctant to say something, there are things you know you're not prepared to say, or you're so pumped full of adrenalin you can feel a little bit foggy, your tongue feels like a flip-flop. In dialogue none of that, like now, my breathings good, I can integrate my breathing and my speech, I can set the pace

Notes from a conversation about dialogue on 6.2.22

The legacy of untethered dialogue

John was recently walking with one of the finance world's "Masters of the Universe", as they were satirically christened in Tom Wolfe's 1987 novel, The Bonfire of theVanities. As John realised that his part in the encounter was to either listen to the certainties of a world lived solely through the lens of algorithmically driven investment, or to be the brief purveyor of "tosh" (to quote the Master of the Universe) by suggesting that the life may not be reducible to a quantifiable financial return, he was reminded of how little impact the dialogue movement has made on the thinking of the world's elites. Bill

Clinton is reported as saying that when he next came back, he'd like to come back as the Bond market, because that's where the real power lies.

News and social media continue to pour gasoline on any imagined or real dispute or points of difference. Everything is expressed categorically, as we have just done here. Advocacy, especially adversarial advocacy, continues to rule and inquiry is given little more than lip service. Consultations are rarely more than PR exercises or rubber stamps to fit with the world view of those who see themselves as both rulers and rule makers – and certainly not rule takers (rules, like taxes, are for the little people). In a recent research inquiry into the experience of members of a disability network in a large health organisation, John was unsurprised to hear that this group were never involved in co-design and co-production when it came to designing patient services – many (if not most) of whom were experiencing a range of existing and acquired disabilities. Instead, the management relied on the insights of able-bodied, under 35-year-olds from the world's most expensive management consultancies. Meanwhile, in a recent major report on the philanthropic industry, all the major donor decision-makers when it came to allocating funds to black projects were white. Go figure, as the young people might have said a few years ago (Manderson Evans et al., 2022).

Dialogue has become a method, a process to be gone through, which has taken what the current elite mindset sees as useful (engagement with the insights of many) and turned it into what it always turns insights into – another vehicle for sustaining ideological hegemony i.e. the privileging of the self-serving world order of managerial, financial and political elites.

This is what happens when dialogue is untethered from its philosophical roots and put to another service, which is predicated on a world view fundamentally at odds with the tenets of dialogue.

JOHN: How do you land dialogue in a performance driven context? How do you give dialogue the chance to breathe?

JT: Over two years I've had a number of goes [at work] and its failed miserably. Creating an environment in which two people will engage in dialogue is hard enough, never mind a group… and a group is important. If dialogue is limited to two people you might have some diversity [of thought] in your organisation but there's precious little inclusivity, so it's got to be bigger than that… People don't feel socially engaged at work because work is inherently threatening, people don't feel [physiologically] safe, so the idea that we'd ask people to come together and dialogue or collaborate or innovate or any of these things [where] their nervous system is getting their heart to pump too fast seems ludicrous… If you don't have safety, dialogue will never emerge

Notes from a conversation about dialogue on 6.2.22

The tenets of dialogue

Dialogue is a social process, something that cannot be owned or directed by any one individual. It exists in the world where inter-dependence is the starting point, not independence. And the goal is not to become independent of each other but to learn how to be inter-dependent well. It requires the letting go of many seemingly unchallengeable virtues such as particularly in capitalist culture being a "self-made man (sic)", often presented as a sensible achievement alongside "not suffering fools gladly". By critiquing these two taken-for-granted cardinal virtues, we can see more of the tenets of dialogue that are eclipsed by the habits of mind revealed by such beliefs.

Is it possible for someone to be self-made?

What is foregrounded in this observation are the here-and-now technical skills, social skills, and personal character of an individual. What gets put into the background, or disappeared completely, is the individual's history and their social context. As an observation it is a variation of Henry Ford's view that "history is bunk" and plays a not too subtle role in disappearing how an individual is wrapped up in patterns of power.

On the terms of the cliché, we are all free agents and exist on a level playing field where any advantage or disadvantage can be worked with through sheer force of will and personality. It fits with all the aspirational guff that any one person can be anything they want to be, devoid of race, gender, age, class, education, physiology, intellectual capacity, sexual orientation, mother tongue, geography, upbringing, psychology, parental trauma, violence, love, and accident. What is ideologically audible here is as follows:

An entrepreneur is something we are supposed to become. The call to act as an entrepreneur of one's own life produces a model for people to understand what they are and what they ought to be, and it tells them how to work on the self in order to become what they ought to be. In other words, the **entrepreneurial self** [emphasis added] is a form of *subjectification*.   (Brockling, 2016, p. viii)

As one begins to dig into the underpinning assumptions of what makes the "self-made" statement true, quite quickly one butts up against notions of free will, and the arguments for and against its presence and relative influence. And this might be one of the shaping barriers that gets in the way of engaging with a dialogic orientation − to step into a dialogic encounter requires you to abandon an attachment to sovereign self-authoring and instead experience how much of who you are and what you know to be wrapped up in the "we-ness" of the group. We are reminded of another throwaway remark we are both familiar with that expresses this point well, that 'talking with you makes me more intelligent' and which fits with the Joyce Fletcher school of relational psychology and the notion of growth-in-connection.

If an individual is strongly attached to the idea of self-directed, self-learning then they are not going to find it easy to suspend all the judgements that come with that when it comes to being inter-dependent with others. One of the deeply held beliefs of much popular psychology is that as an individual matures so they will achieve independence, despite all the evidence to the contrary i.e. how their ongoing life is saturated with social norms, connections and inter-dependencies. Dialogue depends upon the suspension of that attachment to self-authoring and requires people to step into the experience of knowing the world in new ways in the company of others, where what is new and different lives in the spaces between people and not within their independent being. Most challengingly for those who see themselves as "self-made", dialogic encounters are reminders of how much we are authored by and with others.

JT: Dialogue is about experiencing something alongside somebody else in a way that other conversational structures aren't... the mutual flow of information, flowing equally in all directions simultaneously, the exploration happens in the dialogic space between people, [where all] are equally involved

Notes from a conversation about dialogue on 6.2.22

What is the relational take on not suffering fools gladly?

Not suffering fools gladly can be seen as an approval for the acuity of someone's mind. As an invitation for people to show up only with their best face and work. It clearly positions the one not suffering fools to be in a superior, judgemental role in the relationship. This is very different from JT's work with a "Wisdom of Trauma" group where:

JT: [We] spend a lot of time building physiological safety [and] have a ritual at the start of each meeting, which has emerged, to re-establish the physiological safety. We have a set of ground rules which are an attempt to ensure we dialogue rather than anything else... [these are] don't judge or evaluate, don't critique, advise or comment... [remember] you're here to witness whatever truth [the others] choose to express and that's what we're doing for each other

Notes from a conversation about dialogue on 6.2.22

The most direct relational challenge to the value of not suffering fools gladly is to ask: What is it about you that makes people behave foolishly around you? In much of John and Megan's work around speaking truth to power, they find that this is an inadvertent side-effect of people being blind to the consequences of their relative power and authority. Those of higher rank either do not see themselves as having high rank or they do not see the rank and high-status labels that others put onto them. Consequently, they discount the effects of power difference on how people engage with them and they with others. This is explored in one of their early Harvard Business Review pieces that unpicks the consequences of using the phrase 'My door is always open', which while often meant well sends a series of contradictory messages i.e. My door is always open, but it is up to you to come onto my territory where I am most comfortable rather than me seeking you out at a time and in a place where you will be most at home (Reitz & Higgins, 2017).

Those who admire those who do not suffer fools are discounting what many may feel when they are in the presence of someone they experience as having considerable power and authority over them. While some may be of a background and personality to revel in the opportunities to perform in front of the Mummy or Daddy figure, there will be many more who find such encounters emotionally challenging and so are likely to find it hard to be at their sparkling best.

The relational turn would insist on the dynamics between the "fool" and the "judger of the fool" to be the focus of attention, rather than focus on the individual strengths and weaknesses of the individuals alone, as if the relational dynamic was incidental rather than figural.

Drawing out the tenets of Dialogue

JH: What makes it possible to have a mutually satisfying dialogic encounter? And when do you notice you've stepped into that flow?

JT: (Long pause) There are some times when we know what we have to do is creative. We know that to be creative together we need to step into dialogue, a different form of interaction. It might be that we recognise that we are going to do something in the world which has not been done before… and therefore we need to say something that hasn't been said before

Notes from a conversation about dialogue on 6.2.22

Tenet 1 – Step away from the tyranny of the self. Dialogue is not an individual game; it only exists as something that is supra-individual. The unit of analysis in dialogue is the relationship, not the individuals as separate entities. Dialogue is a group experience or it is nothing, it is an ensemble production rather than a star vehicle to borrow a metaphor from the world of the stage. This does not mean the individual disappears but their attention is outwardly focused on themselves in the group, rather than inwardly focused.

This will be an alien habit, especially to those who have been rewarded throughout their lives for being individually competitive, for making sure that they win. Some years ago, John was talking with a friend who ran an outward-bound centre, regularly visited by the corporate great and good. One of the exercises was for a group to be blindfolded and find a way to reach a flag planted some way off. To succeed this required a group to co-ordinate and share information – if nothing else to stop them walking into gorse bushes. On one occasion the group consisted of the crème de la crème of the Business School world, all freshly recruited into a prestigious Management Consultancy. Their approach? To all walk off blindly on their own. Success was something that could only be achieved individually.

Tenet 2 – Step out of the tyranny of judgement and evaluation. Dialogue is an experience which cannot be known ahead of time, whose outcomes are unpredictable and contributions vary in type and form. However much suspending judgement and evaluation are advocated, our world is saturated in grades and scores, with the assumption that these historic measures and criteria are fit for purpose for the future. The psychological explanation would be that in the face of the monstrous uncertainty of life, as human beings we retreat into the pseudo-certainty of measurement and the prescribed activity it justifies (as seen for instance in the work of Isabel Menzies Lyth and her seminal exploration of the dynamics of nursing practice).

We have referenced before (Cole & Higgins, 2022) the work of Alfie Kohn, where he argues that we have adopted a *rattopmorphic* model of human behaviour, where people are understood to be simple beasts who respond to a limited range of sense stimuli with predictable results. He also presents the findings from education in the US and how financially rewarding students for performance both undermines current performance and reduces willingness to step into new forms of learning (Kohn, 1993).

Judgement and evaluation kill creativity. Dialogue is a creative process or it is nothing, so dialogue cannot live with habits of judgement and evaluation – which will frustrate the hell out of the benchmarking industry which no doubt has already tried to create a "best practice", measurable pro-forma for leading-edge organisational dialogue.

Tenet 3 – Step out of the tyranny of performative knowing. Over-trained as so many people are, and especially those who occupy the highest ranks, in Advocacy and Adversarialism it is little surprise to find how much of our popular discourse is dominated by the performance of knowing – especially by those who would peddle false hope or ideological certainty. What anchors advocacy and adversarialism is the actual or believed existence of a fixed curriculum – a body of knowledge that can be agreed upon as definitive, a yardstick of rightness. Or when seen through the truth/power lens, a body of knowledge whose boundaries and content are policed and negotiated through the relevant currents of power.

Within the frame of performative knowing the point of conversation is to demonstrate how one stands with regard to established custom and practice, the pursuit of novelty is a fringe and often socially dangerous activity. Much conversation at work performs no useful function in terms of an organisation's primary task, instead it is a yardstick of power, demonstrating one's social standing and potency. This is why dialogue is such a problematic concept when it relies upon people stepping outside of the bounds of the established discourse, where it is exploring and creating insight which lies beyond the pale of the authorised world view. Dialogue does not reflect or respect established rank and the knowing that goes with that rank, which is why it is so little practised.

The performance of knowing is a very limited form of learning, tightly negotiated by those invested in the status quo. Dialogue is a direct challenge to the power of the status quo to manage how the world is known through the rituals of performative knowing.

Tenet 4 – Privileging knowing that is not known. Working outside of the established boundaries of knowledge and knowing is no easy task. In the Doctoral and Masters programme John worked closely with for many years, students had to create their own inquiry process that was fit for their unique purpose, rather than taking one off the shelf (King & Higgins, 2014). This made the programme considerably more demanding and complicated for both students and faculty, requiring fundamental questions about quality and rigour to be constantly engaged and re-engaged with. John has particular memories of working alongside a student seeking to weave in the Sufi tradition, which is largely expressive and unwritten, in such a way as to stay true to that tradition while respecting the rules of the written academic game.

To go alongside this academic approach to stepping into the not known, John and Mark have often compared their working relationship to one akin to two seven-year-olds playing in a sandpit. When they are on song they sometimes play individually, and sometimes together, joining in each other's game as and when it looks like that's where the fun is to be had. Quite what the game is and how it is played emerges in the moment and neither of them plans it ahead of time – which is what can be seen when kids are playing in a sandpit and choosing how to play together.

Dialogue, in short, is a sandpit where you play.

Tenet 5 – Privilege the subjective realities and truths of participants.

JT: That [Dialogic] space opens up when we co-regulate our nervous systems to a settled place of social engagement, then we feel good, we can be playful, we can be intimate… collaboration is deeply intimate. Most of the time we're not in that space… we feel mortified at the stupidity of what we just said… we can't give voice to an idea just to see how it sounds when we say it aloud to this group of people… [this is an essential] element of dialogue, when we say things out loud rather than having them float around in our head… we hear them through the ears of other people. We can try things out when we're in dialogue, to see how they feel and sound… sometimes we spit things out and really meant it when we said them, but now they just don't sound or feel right… so we move on to a new space

Notes from a conversation about dialogue on 6.2.22

In dialogic encounter we can experience ourselves singing a new song, sometimes liking it and sometimes realising that it's not what we want. And we can only discover this by taking the words that are spinning around our heads and putting them out there, to see how they live when they go out into the world. This requires those who are listening to take what we say at face value and play with it, to see where it goes, so we and they see what happens when an idea or insight is given licence to roam. Of course, there is no guarantee this will go anywhere, deliver value or insight, but that's not the point. The point is to be part of creating a group experience, in which our partial, temporary or enduring truths are let out of their cages and given the chance to mix with the truths of others and so making the novel possible.

JT: Dialogue is about experiencing something alongside somebody else…
    in a way other conversational structures don't

Notes from a conversation about dialogue on 6.2.22

Tenet 6 – Allowing people in groups to create their own way. As always there will be pressure to create a "best way", one which is "scalable" and "replicable", because that will deliver two things: firstly, a sense of control for those who want to engage with dialogue but are scared by its lack of predictable order, and secondly a way of making money by those who make their living peddling the latest gee-gaws in management "thinking".

Giving people choice and responsibility for their collective experience is not widely practised, or when it is, quickly gets corrupted back into familiar forms. A colleague of John's told him of how a firm decided to let its employees design their own workplace, which they did and the result was actually something cheaper than that originally envisaged by management and the "experts" in the field. Having made a step into giving people an experience of autonomy/agency, the management now reverted to type – rather than stay with the approach of allowing employees to design their own workplaces, they rolled out the cheaper model found by the pilot group. No follow up exists around what this did to people's sense of engagement or the quality of future dialogue.

When John and JT were talking in the conversation widely distributed through this chapter, they got to this point around autonomy, co-creation and safety:

JT: Dialogue requires a greater degree of autonomy than a transactional conversation... [there's] choice in dialogue, in every context people will negotiate and find their own way... what will make people safe is obviously different and it varies from moment to moment... we deliberately get diverse groups of people together and it's only just begun to dawn on us that such a diverse group has such a different experience of their existence and what safety means to them... what safety means to me and you [John] is different but similar, two white middle aged Brits... for a 25 year old woman of colour, we might well simply be unsafe to her because of our age and colour

What it takes to retether dialogue to its informing assumptions

We are so far away from having contexts where dialogue will thrive, it is tempting to offer that unhelpful advice to a lost traveller that if you were them you wouldn't start from here. How we got to where we are starts young, most schooling is performative in nature, fixated with assessment and grading. Most workplaces are cut from the same cloth. Dialogic experiences are rare and given little space to exist. They do not fit with a world where it is assumed that by examining the parts and paying attention solely to material features, then we will understand the whole as a living entity.

In John's research for the "The Change Doctors", he was driven mad by one of the contributors who just could not agree upon a final text for his chapter (King & Higgins, 2014). It took John some time to realise that his refusal to be pinned down was because by pinning something down you kill it – in a metaphor they drew up between them, a butterfly in a display case is not a butterfly.

Ever since the invention of clock time, we have become slaves to its rhythms. Everything happens to the hour and the minute, everything has a schedule – which is a great boon for co-ordination and measuring the return on capital employed but an absolute killer for human experience which has its own logic, where some hours pass in a flash and some minutes last forever.

Let's finish where we started, with some conclusions about dialogue – covering what we see as the key headlines, what is involved in taking dialogue seriously and most challengingly what will need to be let go of if dialogue is to actually take root within a specific group or organisation.

Some key headlines about dialogue:

- It is a philosophy first, a skill second
- It is incompatible with competitive individualism
- It is incompatible with goal driven instrumentalism
- It privileges quality of relationship over individual technical skills
- It assumes knowledge and insight are social, emergent phenomena
- Its ethics are as good or bad as the culture within which it is practised
- Dialogue on the terms of the established elite is not dialogue (it's a PR stunt and/or powerplay)
- Co-production and co-design are at the heart of any living dialogic practice

And if you want to take dialogue seriously and create an environment of satisfying mutuality, creativity and belonging then this is what needs to be privileged:

- Inter-personal relationships and bonds of affection and intimacy
- Collective responsibility for and ownership of knowledge and wisdom
- Collective accountability for creating and recreating context-specific dialogic practices

It is unlikely that dialogic practice will take root in contexts which are driven or defined by:

- Contracts
- Individual performance
- Disproportionate distribution of risks and rewards
- Judgement and evaluation
- Control over autonomy

And finally…

JOHN: What does dialogue mean to you?

JT: It's a feeling as much as anything else… it's nurturing, supportive… [there's] vulnerability in it and a sense of security, safety as well… clarity of mind. It makes sense when you juxtapose it with transactional or adversarial forms of conversation… there's nothing adversarial about it, mutually supportive

JOHN: The word spacious came to mind as you were talking then, talking slowly

JT: Yes. It felt spacious in that I could stop and think and pause. I didn't feel any pressure to be clever or anything like that. As dialogue slows down, that spaciousness opens up. They're not just pauses for me when I'm thinking, they're spaces where you may or may not step in. Those transactional or adversarial conversations there's so much interrupting, no time to consider what's going on

Notes from a conversation about dialogue on 6.2.22

What do we need to do so as to do things differently?

People often demand a "take away" of training courses and books of this sort. And, as when we pick up a pizza or a curry from our local restaurants, the "take away" that people crave from a course or some writing is desired in order that the reader is absolved from having to do anything in the way of thinking, in the same way as opting for a take-away mean means that we don't have to do any cooking. We often refer to this in our work as people in corporate life – in particular those who carry the title "leader" – having outsourced their thinking.

Voice in the dialogue

As we've suggested, we can be silenced by another, by others, and by ourselves. For dialogue to come to life, we need to resist this, as best we can – whilst, at the same time, the wider social milieu (the leaders or leaders that we are told we are following; the communities to which we are told we belong; the discourse that envelops us, with its expectations and stipulations as to what we are entitled to say) needs to be adjusted so as to slacken the restraints that attend it. We have argued in Part II and demonstrated in Part III that there are various ways in which silence overlays voice. That silence emerges out of the combination of a wider context and from within our very being as human agents. These two facets – context and personhood – interplay, each depending on the other to create and amplify that silence.

To get to dialogue in the way we have discussed, it requires each person to do two things, regardless of who they are and where they sit in the wider context. They need to move from listening to hearing so as to create

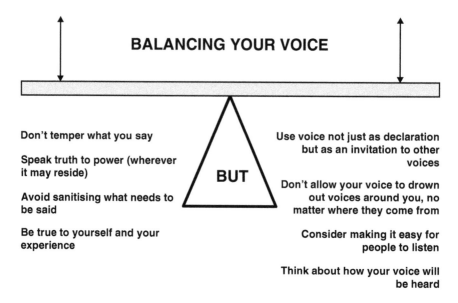

Figure 13.1 Balancing your voice.

the space for dialogue – and they need to think about how their voice will be heard by others, the extent to which the content and delivery of their speech invites engagement or enforces distance and resistance.

Our advice in light of this exists in the form of two sets of precepts that pivot around a BUT, as explained in this diagram (Figure 13.1):

Embracing a new way of being in the workplace

Beyond consideration of our voice, we need to give consideration to our presence as a human being in the workplace – and, of course, beyond. We hope the way we've approached the voices we heard through our conversations and via the survey has worked at two levels. On the one hand, we trust we've done justice to what was being said, to the way in which people took this opportunity to talk about their experiences. On the other, we hope that the way in which we approached this exercise – our "working out loud" in trying to rethink research – has offered an insight into how people might step out of the shadows of their own opinions, and interpretation of the world, and into a new space where they are paying close attention to voice and silence.

Throughout our work over the past two years, one phrase has come up again and again, namely that it is essential that someone *bears witness* when people find their voice to speak about their experience. This is particularly the case when one views this through the notion of "rankism", the ordering of the world into "somebodies and nobodies" (Fuller, 2004). The subaltern voice needs to be heard and witness needs to be borne to what is said by that voice. This is not to automatically assume that we have to accept what is being said; instead, it is to acknowledge that someone is speaking (who perhaps is not ordinarily heard) and their voice speaks about how they experience the world. Hearing this voice is to clear a space for dialogue, rather than simply accepting that it is speaking the truth. Our position, as the listener, is to listen to a truth – and open up the conversation that is essential to make sense of our collective experience of life.

In the course of our explorations around voice and silence – particularly in terms of our sense-making about how one can do research in this regard – Mark was serendipitously introduced to an old sociological concept that really resonated but about which he knew nothing. He was sitting on the sofa, tormenting himself by impressively knowledgeable young people on *University Challenge*, when a question came up about a German theorist called Wilhelm Dilthey and his notion of *verstehen*. Barely had the final credits run on the quiz than Mark was off and into the labyrinth of Google Scholar, looking for explanations of this work.

It turns out that Dilthey (1833–1911) was extremely mindful of the need to keep the natural and the social sciences methodologically separate, in contrast to others who thought that the latter could only be taken seriously if one approached them through the scientific method. This tension persists, both in science in general and more locally in our corporate settings. Scientism inhabits – and inhibits – all efforts to hear employee voice, because the default position in our companies and firms is to quantify people, render them manipulable as numbers, squeeze them through that process into broad categories. When you notionally add your voice to an employee survey, you are not speaking up, you are simply allowing people to aggregate you and define that grouping as a collective number. The voice is invited – but is nowhere near being heard. The staff survey allows managers to listen to react; these instruments need to be abandoned completely if you want to hear the rich and raw content of the voices of the people with whom you work.

Verstehen, in contrast, as developed by Dilthey and others, such as Max Weber, is an ethical orientation to engage in trying to understand people rather than to categorise them. Scientists will obviously contest it as a method: this sort of engagement with other human beings cannot be said to be "valid" or "reliable". But it is intimate and offers insight, it reminds us that understanding rather than classification and interpretation is vital if we are to connect as human beings. It is not our job to explain human behaviour but to work to understand it. To that end, it is argued that humanity '... can be studied by natural science, but only up to the point where human conditions are experienced' (Outhwaite, 1975, p. 26).

It was interesting to note how our improvised approach to engaging with the responses to the survey in Part III shared so much with the underpinnings of verstehen. In terms of thinking about human agents and developing an understanding of them, it is argued that: 'It is not a matter of establishing causal regularities in people's behaviour (...) but rather of experiencing their thoughts and emotions from the inside by "putting oneself in their shoes" and reliving their experience' (Outhwaite, 1975, p. 27).

As ever, there are those who want to take a complex practice and render it as a checklist or a step-by-step process to follow. This is the case with verstehen also, although we found one instance of this type of reductionism as potentially useful if undertaken with a recognition of the richness of working in this way. It offers a four-stage approach to trying to seek the sort of understanding to which verstehen refers:

- **IMAGINE** as deeply as you can what it is like to be the other person.
- Once you have a clear, affective picture of that person in your mind, then dwell on that image, breathe in that presence. **ABIDE** there for as long as that image has something to say.
- **DISCOVER** what it has to offer. What it is like to be this person? What is this image, this apprehension telling you about the other?
- **EXPRESS** what has been discovered. What was it like to be that person? How can the experience of being that other and one's reaction and responses to it be expressed?... Express as you see fit (Glass, 2005).

Our reflections on the experience of working together on Part III and exploring how we need to attend to speech as the voice of other human subjects, as opposed to data drawn from the objects of research, leads us to suggest how this might be made applicable if used by others elsewhere (Figure 13.2):

LISTEN TO BE PRESENT...

- **Keep your reactions on a leash**
- **See the person not the role, label or category**

Untie yourself from the tethers that bind you and your thinking. Refuse the collar and lead

HEAR TO UNDERSTAND...

- **Go with the words, silence and rhythm of the speaker**
- **Look to stay long and go deep with their account**

Cross the border so as to escape the boundaries that surround you. Step over into the space of another.

REFLECT ON YOUR LISTENING AND YOUR HEARING...

- **Notice what you've discounted and speechlessly rejected**
- **Notice what you've judged to be 'normal' or 'other'**

The crash test dummy has always been male, an assumption hiding in plain sight. What are your assumptions?

STEP INTO DIALOGUE WITH NOT-KNOWING...

- **Suspend big/anxious 'I Am' advocacy**
- **Suspend expectations of what a good outcome is**

Break habits of omniscient narcissism. Recognise the fact that uncertainty is not fixable – and embrace active inquiry instead

Figure 13.2 Adjusting your presence.

Above all else, open yourself to others, to their experiences – and their experience of you. Relate to people as one human to another rather than cleaving to the status that has been arbitrarily allocated to you by the artificial corporate structure that you inhabit. If you approach a conversation while considering yourself a leader, you are carrying power, presumption and prejudice into that exchange. If you define yourself in that space as the leader then the voices you hear from others will be those of followers, a categorisation that instantly degrades the person seeking to speak. This leads us to the meme that can be found on the internet featuring the cartoon character Foghorn Leghorn, which says: 'You see, people don't want to hear your opinion…they want to hear their opinion coming out of your mouth!'

This is the challenge for us all in terms of taking voice and silence seriously – and engaging with it in a way that works hard to set aside status, that invites in the subaltern voice and seeks to understand rather than explain or interpret all of the voices that are asking to be heard. We need to embrace the way in which power is experienced in voice and silence – and is realised and reinforced by that presence. Listen to hear, not to react; be aware of whence the silence comes and what it might mean. And, in the course of that hearing, bear witness to what is being said by the voices in terms of the experience being spoken about.

These are the foundations of the dialogue that our social, political and organisational lives so desperately need to embrace and enact.

References

Bohm, D., 1996. *On dialogue.* Abingdon: Routledge.

Brockling, U., 2016. *The entrepreneurial self: Fabricating a new type of subject.* London: Sage.

Buber, M., 1937. *I and Thou.* Edinburgh: T & T Clark.

Cole, M. & Higgins, J., 2022. *Leadership unravelled: The faulty thinking behind modern management.* Abingdon: Routledge.

Fuller, R. W., 2004. *Somebodies and nobodies: Overcoming the abuse of rank.* Gabriola Island: New Society Publishers.

Glass, J. E., 2005. Visceral verstehen. *Electronic Journal of Sociology,* pp. 1–15.

King, K. & Higgins, J., 2014. *The change doctors: Re-imagining organisational practice.* Faringdon, Oxon: Libri.

Kohn, A., 1993. *Punished by rewards: The trouble with gold stars, incentive plans, A's, praise, and other bribes.* New York: Houghton, Mifflin and Company.

Manderson Evans, E., Akinrele, C.-J. & Shah, A., 2022. *Racial justice and social transformation: How funders can act.* [Online] Available at: https://tenyearstime.com/wp-content/uploads/2022/02/Racial-Justice-and-Social-Transformation-2.pdf [Accessed 3 August 2022].

Outhwaite, W., 1975. *Understanding social life: The method called verstehen.* London: George Allen & Unwin.

Reitz, M., 2015. *Dialogue in organizations: Developing relational leadership.* Basingstoke: Palgrave Macmillan.

Reitz, M. & Higgins, J., 2017. *The problem with saying "My Door Is Always Open".* [Online] Available at: https://hbr.org/2017/03/the-problem-with-saying-my-door-is-always-open?autocomplete=true [Accessed 3 August 2022].

POSTSCRIPT – NOTES FROM AN AUTHORIAL PROCESS

We've learned a great deal from working together over the past 18 months or so, even though we have worked together for a few years now. We've spoken together on a weekly basis, developing our personal and shared thinking about voice and silence. In a world that seems obsessed with action for its own sake, we chose to allow ourselves time and space to connect. We've also ensured that our own dialogue was integral to our engagement with people who allowed us to bear witness to their experience. This practical experience has led us to some headline conclusions, which we feel are important to share.

You are not alone

There is a great emphasis placed on the idea of the sovereign individual in our culture. From the "captain of industry", anointed as an entrepreneur, to the frontline employee being reminded to take active responsibility for their own resilience, we see individualism fetishised. This partly reflects the dominance of what can usefully be called neo-liberalism, an ideology that unfortunately dominates our social, cultural and business conversation. This individualism is:

> ...based on a relational model of social personhood, in which respect is due to persons (generally male) who prosper by their own efforts within

> the webs of family, kin, and patron-client relations. Yet it can also raise the ruthless pursuit of self-interest to a kind of moral value in an unjust world. (Gledhill, 2007, p. 339)

This ideology moves beyond Classical Liberalism by allowing the market economy to shape and style an all-encompassing market society; to that end, neo-liberalism allows the market to intrude into even the most intimate elements of being human (Gledhill, 2007, p. 340). But it goes beyond this assertion of the supposedly self-made person, determinedly rising above the wider social networks in which they inevitably have a presence. This individualism is built on the:

> ...deconstruction of groupings (classes, firms, unions, parties, but also, in another way, churches or schools) that formed the basis for people's ability to enrol in collective perspectives, and pursue what was recognised as the common good. (Boltanski & Chiapello, 2007, p. 532)

Contemporary progressivism has unwittingly absorbed this fetishisation of the individual and the erosion of meaningful collective action in the wider socio-economic realm, as seems apparent in the current fixation on the cultural (or, to use a Marxian term, the superstructural) in respect to its exclusive focus on identity politics. The political Left's current perspective has morphed into a weird mixture of Enlightenment certainty – a crudely determinist assertion of being on the "right side of history" – and a misreading of poststructuralism, particularly in regard to the work of Derrida and Foucault.

If we fixate entirely on the individual – and, in particular, if the individual on which we focus is the "me" – the space for dialogue rapidly disappears. The "me" may listen but its primacy means it feels no obligation to hear. We place ourselves in something akin to a pre-Copernican social solar system, where others are deemed to revolve around us. Instead, we need to agree that we have no fixed orbit...and that our collective trajectories are boundlessly interconnected and intersect with the ebb and flow of the milieu in which we find ourselves.

Our suggestion – in light of the work we have done together and the things which we heard from others – is both complex and simple at the same time: **leaders in corporate settings who wish to move from merely listening to truly hearing those around them need to displace the individual – particularly the privileged "me" – so as to open up dialogic relations with all around them**.

The geometric shape that dominates the iconography of organisational life remains the pyramid. The ever-present "organisational chart" is invariably portrayed in this way, a base of performers and a leader at its apex. Instead of looking side on at this, so that this graphical representation of hierarchy reproduces an unhelpful corporate culture of somebodies and nobodies, we should reposition our point of view, so that we are taking a birds-eye view from above its peak, changing the "organogram" from a pyramid to a network through a slight change our perspective (Pritchard, 2020, p. 24). In so doing we disrupt the "normalcy" of hierarchy by actively challenging a symbol that subtly reproduces it.

Our view is that every corporate leader should be making this shift, abandoning the pyramid so as to embrace the network. No one should be fooled into thinking that this magically makes power disappear, simply by notionally flattening the structures. The "holacratic" or post-bureaucratic company is a fallacy which serves to bury power even deeper into the revised organisational structures. Instead, it prompts everyone involved to hold in mind how voice and silence are impacted by how we visualise and experience our organisations – and that, to commit to do things differently, one must begin with changes in oneself, rather than seeking to get others to change – which is, of course, the expectation that underpins every "transformation programme" in corporate life. And that precept applies in particular to those who see themselves as "leaders" in that context.

What do you mean by work?

As we worked together, the importance of what we were doing – particularly in terms of thinking about engaging with the voices in a different and far more open way – became very apparent. However, that didn't immediately alter the fact that our collaboration was inevitably slightly shadowed by ego.

On a number of occasions, we each produced something to which we felt personally wedded – but that allegiance said more about our individual voices and a demand to be heard than the overall project.

When, as part of the process, we sent a piece to the other for review and revision, there were a couple of occasions where we perhaps lost sight of the overall project and instead focused on an individualised defence of our voice. What was interesting was the dialogic opportunity we stepped into so as to challenge one another on this – but without it becoming an abrasive exchange. The idea of primary task – the work that an organisation has been developed to do – and the double task – the interrelations and cultural elements that undergird this and often remain unspoken and unacknowledged – arises from the Tavistock tradition and, in particular, from the work of Harold Bridger (Trist & Murray, 1990).

We were able to refocus our efforts by talking about "my work" and "the work". The former was where we felt overly invested at a personal level; the latter was the collaborative focus that foregrounded the project to move past listening in order that we could really hear. **Out of this experience flows another simple precept for leaders in corporate life: don't allow ego and status to leave you defensively protecting "my work" when your position demands that you focus on "the work".**

The professional is the personal

Our collaboration began in earnest just three or so years ago. Since then, we have had regular conversations – over the past two years, these became weekly calls – where we have free associated around the broad topics of organisational life and the practice of leadership. Out of those exchanges arose our first co-written book (Cole & Higgins, 2022) and the idea for this title. In the course of our deliberations, we have realised that how we think about and deliver what gets called "leadership development" omits three crucial elements that precede the curriculum and content of these sorts of courses.

The first two elements came to us as we inquired into the limitations that exist in the thinking needed by those who consider themselves to be managers and leaders in corporate life. For the sake of shorthand, we call these criticality and reflexivity, two practices we've defined in the following way:

CRITICALITY – the willingness to interrogate the obvious and the ordinary

- A commitment to…
  - ○ Take **nothing at face value**
  - ○ Look at everything around you as if you are **seeing it for the very first time**, so as to judge whether it makes sense to those fresh eyes.
  - ○ **Scrutinise** everything – notice what gets put in the foreground and what is kept in the background
  - ○ Explore your ordinary **familiar surroundings and routines** (your spaces and places, locations and relations, ways of thinking, accepted ideas, and so on) as if you were a tourist and so see the oddness of the ordinary!
  - ○ **Question everything**, no matter how acceptable or comforting it might feel. In the human world nothing is natural, everything is made and sustained by people for their own purposes
  - ○ Be as **suspicious of ideas or behaviours that feel normal to you** as those that seem very different to you.

REFLEXIVITY – seeing yourself enmeshed in the world you are seeking to know

- A way of looking at the world where…
  - ○ You consider yourself **as an integral and intimate part of that space and time** rather than seeing it as something that you can view at a distance, as if you were not actively involved in it.
  - ○ As in a team game, **you are not a spectator** – passively watching things unfold on the pitch or court in front of you – **but are actually a player**, someone who is part of the game and who watches the way in which the game develops as you interact with others – both teammates and opponents.
  - ○ Reflection is not merely taking up an experience and exploring it as if it was something separate to you and your life, but instead involves you **recognising your embedded presence** in that context and how you shape it through your acts.
  - ○ You are **active rather than passive when it comes to thinking about the ever-changing pattern of connections, relations and actions** that shape your context on a second-by-second basis.

 © Mark Cole & John Higgins 2021

In the course of our practice and through our subsequent conversations we have surfaced a third crucial element, namely that a leader needs to be working towards the development of their ethics. Indeed, there is perhaps a requirement for us all to attend to our needs for self-care, to find ways to develop as a person, and to surface and explore the personal values that we wish to guide us in our lives. *No one is worthy of the title "leader" if they are not involved in careful and practical consideration of their ethical self. Without that moral compass, it will be doubly difficult to move from merely listening to truly hearing the voices of those around you.*

Attending to the tensions

Alongside these essential requirements of anyone who might wish to step into leadership if and when the opportunity presents itself, our deliberations also lighted on two tendencies in organisational life which need to be tested in the practice of those who describe themselves as leaders. These seem to have become particularly noticeable over the course of the past two or so years, arising out of what a wide range of people with whom we worked during that period shared with us about their experiences, and so are worthy of some attention in corporate life.

Values gap

Since 2020, the pandemic has stress-tested the commitment of organisations to their espoused values. Elsewhere, we have highlighted how corporate values float free of the practicalities of the organisation, reflecting how they are often created some way away from the business of the business (Cole & Higgins, 2022, pp. 68–70). In a very small-scale survey that John undertook with people in an organisation late in 2021, he asked them to rate on a ten-point scale (with 1 being the lowest and 10 the highest) the extent to which the respondents felt that their organisation lived up to its values. Of the 40 or so responses, the average score came in at just under 6, which suggests – within the limits of this piece of work – a sense of what we have come to call a values gap, which may be experienced in a range of corporate settings.

This means leaders need to recognise that the values that get generated in a self-referencing corporate context invariably lack an authentic ethical grounding (Cole & Higgins, 2022, pp. 166–169). Their detachment from the experience of organisational life creates a gap that leaves people feeling, at best, played and, at worst, duped. They become vacuous chatter, an organisational noise that disregards the actual experience of being in that space, so there may be an espoused value of "respect" and a day-to-day managerial culture that means that the environment feels hostile – or perhaps even toxic. It certainly does not acknowledge the rich mosaic of complementary values that each and every person brings to the workplace with them.

The leader, then, instead of shutting themselves in their office to craft a set of boilerplate values, indistinguishable from those promoted by pretty much any other firm, needs to explore the ethical fabric of the organisation that they presume to lead. This means listening to the voices of those in the workplace and acknowledging the values that they bring to the work they do. It means a commitment not to homogenise the organisation, but to open up space for dialogue as to what adds value to the work that is done, as both an experience and an output. Such an engagement should help to narrow – and perhaps even bridge – the values gap, by ensuring an ongoing and genuine conversation about motivation and commitment with everyone in the workplace.

Leadership distance

Over recent months we have explored a number of experiences in big-corporate life and the ways in which those who occupy positions at the level of what is called "senior leadership" find themselves unhelpfully cut adrift from the practicalities of the companies that they are meant to serve. Atop hierarchical and bureaucratised edifices the uppermost managerial cadres find themselves separated from what it is that the business actually seeks to do. They occupy a rarefied space at the pinnacle of the company, which is a long way away from where the actual business of the business resides.

We see two reactions: one sees people at senior levels "working down", busying themselves with doing some of the lifting needed at the level below. Executive directors become preoccupied with operational matters hence those in the tier below are forced to drop a level in terms of activity. This prompts us to think again about what needs to be done and who needs to do what: if we segment organisations into performers, managers of performers, and managers of managers, this "working down" actively undermines the capacity of those closest to the real work to work autonomously or come together collectively to organise and deliver for the primary task. This "working down" therefore increases the supervisory burden when in practice the need is for less. In that way, we might reasonably need less people supervising that performance – and that might reasonably mean that the fewer managers would need less oversight (if, indeed, they ever actually needed it).

Meanwhile, the organisational chart, with its lines of accountability and responsibility, makes visible how mandated hierarchy displaces and replaces meaningful exchanges of voice across the vital relations that actually give shape to how things get done. This has a deeper socio-economic resonance that needs to be borne in mind:

> Ideas about hierarchy go back to the origins of mainstream business management. It was born as an applied social science which could be used to increase efficiency without necessarily sharing its benefits.
> (Casagrande & Rivera, 2020, p. 115)

Hence, business schools, professional services companies, and *soi-disant* thought leaders promote a way of thinking that naturalises hierarchy and bolsters the supposition that we are in need of people who are defined as Leaders, when there are other ways of coming together to organise (Casagrande & Rivera, 2020, p. 116).

The alternative reaction to working down is "looking up", where senior leaders fully turn their backs on the reality of the organisation that can be said to sit below them. Instead, they attend to activity that references the context in which they work but has little or no bearing on how it is done. This embraces the epiphenomenal, with senior leaders embroiled in overseeing the production of visions, missions, purpose, positions, strategies, and our old friend corporate values. Time was they would take on this responsibility directly; increasingly, we hear of these leaders getting this done by professional services companies, effectively outsourcing their thinking as well as what passes for the work of "looking up".

This means that these individuals are preoccupied with activity that is completely different to the actual business of the business – and the experiences of those most closely associated with that primary task. The more the people at the top focus on this "looking up" domain, the greater grows what we call the leadership distance between those at a senior level and those who are reasonably seen to be the lifeblood of the organisation. **The experience of leadership distance means that hearing the voices of those you are meant to be working in partnership with is all the more difficult; a lack of proximity denies potential channels for conversation – and a focus on activity that draws one's attention away from the business of the business closes down the potential space for a dialogue about shared experience. Leaders need to work to narrow that distance.**

Make space for dialogue – internal and external

In our weekly discussions, we ensured that we were in dialogue with one another. The artist Paul Klee spoke about drawing being about taking a line for a walk; for us, our conversations merely saw us taking an idea for a walk. There was no tightly defined structure to these exchanges, no set of rules to be diligently followed. We started where we began and finished where we ended up. Importantly, for this to work, it required us each to move beyond listening to react, which would merely see us on opposing sides of a conversation waiting for a space in which to lob our contribution at the other.

Our internal dialogues reminded us to clear a space in order to hear what the other was saying, instead of crowding it with things we wanted to say without referencing what had just passed between us.

This internal dialogue is important, as it is the thing that keeps us on our toes – and works against us lapsing into an unhearing verbal exchange. On occasion, each of us would perhaps veer away from the way in which we wanted our external dialogue to occur. But the internal dialogue constantly reminded us to tack back to where we wanted to be. Some deviations from the course were to be expected but attending to the potential for this – and redirecting oneself when one got a little lost – came out of allowing that internal dialogue to link into the external one and to drive it along.

The leader, then, needs to be in active conversation with everyone around them, listening to hear and then engaging in dialogue so as to hear even more and to take ideas for an unprescribed walk. But they will not be able to do this if they are not in dialogue with themselves. And this takes place in the moment, as part of the conversation that they are having with others, and just within themselves as they use their interior space to reflect on their experience – and their position and perspective within that experience.

The last word – ahead of a new first word

To be attentive to others is not a technique to be learned, something that a trainer can induce in you by taking you through a checklist of behaviours and practices. That is merely the grafting on of something superficial that will quickly fall away. Instead, the shift from listening to react to listening to hear – and all of the attendant deeply personal adjustments around things like power that are the sine qua non of this change – arises out of close attention to one's ethical self. And committing to hear is not something situational; there are no circumstances where there cannot be time for hearing what is being said and ensuring this acts as a key to open up dialogue.

But dialogue is not acquiescence. **To hear is to attend to what a voice is actually saying and to make sense of it and whence it comes. While it should be about displacing oneself, it is not about effacing oneself.** This means unseeing oneself is at the heart of the conversational universe – and to cede that position to someone that ordinarily does not occupy that position in your view of the natural order of things. But it is not about silencing oneself; it is about allowing a space for a chorus of voices to engage in this exchange. A recent article about writing history from an anarchist perspective offered some important insight into this:

> Writing responsibly toward one's research subjects does not necessarily mean bearing the burden of continuing their perspectives and projects, but taps a larger sense of responsibility as the ability to respond to them, to their thoughts, feelings and actions, to their struggles and their worlds.   (Ferguson, 2022, p. 16)

To be able to disagree with someone – to engage with them in an exchange of views – means that we have to listen to them and hear what they are saying in the first instance. To do otherwise is an *ad hominem* error. To use a footballing analogy, it would be playing the player rather than playing the ball – and it is the movement of the ball between players that creates the fluidity that marks a rich game.

References

Boltanski, L. & Chiapello, E., 2007. *The new spirit of capitalism*. London: Verso.

Casagrande, L. & Rivera, G., 2020. Leadership and authority. In: M. Parker, K. Stoborod & T. Swann, eds. *Anarchism, organization and management: Critical perspectives for students*. Abingdon: Routledge, pp. 111–122.

Cole, M. & Higgins, J., 2022. *Leadership unravelled: The faulty thinking behind modern management*. Abingdon: Routledge.

Ferguson, K., 2022. Writing anarchism with history from below. *Anarchist Studies,* 30(1), pp. 7–29.

Gledhill, J., 2007. Neoliberalism. In: D. Nugent & J. Vincent, eds. *A companion to the anthropology of politics*. Malden, MA: Blackwell, pp. 332–348.

Pritchard, G., 2020. Modelling power in anarchist perspective. *Anarchist Studies,* 28(1), pp. 9–32.

Trist, E. & Murray, H., 1990. *The Social Engagement of Social Science: A Tavistock Anthology – Volume 1: The Socio-Psychological Perspective*. Philadelphia: University of Pennsylvania Press.

INDEX

Note: **Bold** page numbers refer to Figures and page numbers followed by "n" refer to end notes.

Abrams, D. 101
absence of speech or sound, questioning silence as 5, 6, 41, 45, 58, 82, 125; *see also* meaning of silence; shades of silence; silence
action learning 197
activism 65, 66; political 105; workplace 19
Advisory, Conciliation and Arbitration Service (ACAS), UK 43
advocacy 199
Agamben, G. 119
Amburgy, P. M. 137
attention, positive 174–179
authorial process 215–224
autogestion 79
Auvinen, T. 13

Bataille, Georges 43, 114
Bell, S. 56
Benn, Tony 105, 121

Bible, silence in 56
BIRG (basking in reflected glory) 101
Black–Scholes model 12
Bohm, David 198
Boltanski, L. 216
boundaries 76, 100, 104, 110, 115, 120, 138, 163, 204; community 100, 105, 122, 123; defining 94, 108, 137; exclusionary silence 10–11, 12; group 101, 108, 123; and imposed silence 17; of knowledge 205; need for 14; political 173; territorial 72–73
Bourdieu, Pierre 101–102
Bradbury, H. 174–175
Bradlaugh, C. 132
Breitfelder, M. D. 131
Bridger, Harold 218
Brockling, U. 200
Brown, adrienne marie 84–85
Brown, Brené 185

Brown, S. D. 57
Buber, Martin 9, 198
Buddhism 56–57, 58
Butler, Judith 62
bystander effect 66

Cage, John 48–50, 58
"cancel culture" 84
Canetti, Elias 136
capital 81, 207
capitalism 91, 108; capitalist culture
    200, 208
Casagrande, L. 221
Challenger disaster, 1986 101
charisma 8, 22
Chiapello, E. 216
Chinese Communist Party 19
chosen silence 5, 14–17, 83–91, 125,
    148, 189
Christian Democratic Party, Germany
    64, 65
Christianity 88
Clune, Declan 25
code-switching 162
Cole, Mark 16, 19, 24, 27, 35–36, 40,
    64, 65, 81, 105, 107, 120–123, 197,
    205; and thirty-five voices free text
    survey 144–147, 157–169, 173
collective constraint, corporate
    context 125
collective rationalisation 101
Collins, P. 56
Colston 4 109, 110
commemoration, silence as 57
communication 53, 59, 78, 120, 162;
    compensatory conspicuous 116;
    constrained forms 179; internal
    9, 83; with management 150;
    organisational 38; performative
    nature 127; and silence 125;
    unethical 95n1; see also
    conversation; dialogue; language;
    speech; voice; words

communicative constitution of
    organisations (CCO) 93
community 99–118; boundaries
    100, 105, 122, 123; and Buddhism
    56; concept of 99, 104; context
    and the individual 102; defence
    99; divisive 131; importance of,
    and policing opinion 122; and
    membership need 99, 100, 103;
    political 104–105, 108–109; as
    transactional and not locational
    100; see also groups
compassionate leadership 167
competence-based employment
    interview 145
complicity 102
Conservative Party, UK 106, 122
Constituency Labour Party, General
    Management Committee
    (GMC) 106
conversation 11, 12, 15, 40, 78,
    84, 116, 173, 220; active 223;
    adversarial 195, 208; collective
    36, 204; community context
    103, 105; conversional roles 39;
    and dialogue 195, 196, 197, 198,
    200–203, 205, 206; honest 40;
    and meaning of silence 51, 53; and
    positive attention 175; public 133;
    purpose of 204; scholarly 121; and
    self-silencing 63, 64; and silence
    at work 71, 72, 74; superficial 52;
    transactional 207, 208; workplaces
    23, 164, 204, 213, 215; see also
    dialogue; speech; voice; words
cooperative inquiry 175, 182
"corporate ventriloquism" 160
COVID-19 pandemic 70, 73, 74, 77,
    130, 220; thirty-five voices free text
    survey 143, 149, 150, 156
criticality, and reflexivity 94, 139, 166,
    176, 177, 180, 218
crowds 24, 88, 116, 131, 136

culture 108, 113, 114; of Anglo-Saxon Global North 8; "cancel culture" 84; capitalist 200, 208; corporate, of somebodies and nobodies 217; cultural change 73, 168; demonisation of middle-aged white males 156, 161; and dialogue 196; entrepreneurial 8; individualism 215; limits of 114; of listening 154, 156; managerial 220; open 94; organisational 62, 160, 168, 197; of silence 148, 156; speak-up 13, 79, 185; terminology 168; and thirty-five voices free text survey 147, 154
curators 23, 146
Cynefin Framework 70

Day-Duro, Emma 19
"deaf ears," voices falling on 165
default at work, silence as 71–72
defence community 99
Deming, W E 8
democratic centralism 111
Derrida, Jacques 176, 216
dialogue 61, 111, 164, 169, 172, 209; adjusting one's presence **213**; and allowing groups to create their own way 206–207; and autonomy 207; being self-made 200–201; context of 198; and conversation 195, 196, 197, 198, 200–203, 205; and culture 196; experiencing something alongside others 206; external 223; and HR, policing function 132–133; internal 223; as a method 199; movement 198; not suffering fools gladly 201–202; open 169; opening up space for 8, 122, 126–127, 179, 180–185, 222–223; performative knowing 204–205; privileging knowing that is not known 205; privileging the

subjective realities and truths of participants 205–206; putting to work 195–214; retethering to informing assumptions 207–209; stepping away from the tyranny of the self 203; stepping out of tyranny of judgement and evaluation 203–204; tenets of 200–207; untethered, legacy of 198–200; voice in 209–210; see also conversation
Dickens, Charles 18
Diefenbach, T. 75
Dill, D. 62
Dilthey, Wilhelm 211
dominance 62, 64, 137; dominant and the subaltern 162, 163; future 133; of neo-liberalism 215; unchallenged/unquestioned 138; of voice 103
Dovey, K. 72–73
Dowling, D. 131
Doyle, A. 91
Durkheim, Émile 42

edgework 115
egoism 8–9, 138
elites 157, 162, 198, 199
Engels, Friedrich 37
Enlightenment 110, 216
entrepreneurial individual, revering of 8, 19, 200
ethics: ethical compass, awareness of 125; ethical grounding 220; ethical shortcomings 139; research practice 145–146; unethical communication 95n1; well-developed personal ethical orientation 138
exclusionary silence 5, 10–14; boundaries 10–11, 12; degenerative 12; generative 11–12, 13; in-groups and out-groups 10, 12; habits

13, 14; and power 12–13; and whistleblowing 14
executive–employee disconnect 73

facilitators 23
false consciousness 37
Ferguson, K. 224
Ferreras, I. 13
Fight Club (movie) 14
Fletcher, Joyce 201
Follet, Mary Parker 100
footing 162
Ford, Henry 200
formal education, and social expectations of silence 42–43
Foucault, Michel 36–37, 57, 58–59, 66, 104, 114–115, 216
4'33 (silent musical composition by John Cage): Buddhism, influence of 58; premiere at the Maverick Concert Hall, Woodstock 49; radical challenge to bourgeois notions of music 49; seen as open critique of acculturated practice of listening to music 49–50; web page 48
fragmented categorisation 104–105
free speech 89, 91, 139, 161; Free Speech Movement (FSM) 90
freedom of expression 138; see also free speech
Freud, S. 59

GDR see German Democratic Republic (GDR)
gender 62
General Management Committee (GMC), Constituency Labour Party 106
German Democratic Republic (GDR) 87, 88; see also Christian Democratic Party, Germany; Social Democratic Party, Germany

gig economy 80
Glaeser, A. 88
Gledhill, J. 215–216
Goldman, Emma 139
gossip 78–79
Grosse Pointe Blank (film) 27
groups: boundaries 101, 108, 123; dialogue 206–207; in-groups and out-groups 10, 12; out-group stereotypes 101; silence in group settings 24; subaltern 162–163; on trauma 202; "we-ness" of 201; see also community
groupthink 101
The Guardian 137–138

Hamati-Ataya, I. 37
Havel, V. 91
Healey, Denis 105–106
healthcare sector 70
hearing: actually, hearing another 52, 56, 57, 70, 71, 124, 127, 128, 148, 217, 219, 223; aids for 151; and deafness 151; to engage 164; and ignoring what is being said 169; learning from 191; and listening 144, 146, 169, 171, 174, 178–179; see also listening; listening to react; listening without hearing
Hearsum, Steve 197
heresies 132
hidden curriculum 42
hierarchies 40, 63, 77, 116; COVID-19 pandemic, impact on 149; formal or informal 166; graphical representation 217; hierarchical ladder 11; hierarchical pyramid 78; hierarchised social structures 137; leadership distance 92, 221, 222; maintaining 20; monolithic 10; normalcy of 217; organisational 76, 120, 136, 137; permissions given by those at the top 41, 168;

and power 13, 14, 30, 64, 135, 197;
    presumption of 135
Higgins, John 12, 14–16, 19–24, 27,
    28, 38, 52, 63, 64, 71, 78, 185, 197,
    202, 205; and thirty-five voices
    free text survey 145, 146, 155–157,
    164, 169, 173; and thirty-five voices
    text survey 144
Hirsch, J. 90
historical materialism 37
honesty 124–125
hooks, b. 69
Hostetter (Californian teacher)
    111–112
hubris 73
human presence, organisational
    73–74, 77
Human Resources (HR), policing
    role 131–133
Husserl, Edmund 174

ideology 11, 17, 25, 182; as form
    of false consciousness 37–38;
    leader–follower 38–39;
    managerialism 75, 93; neo-
    liberalism 215–216; socialist 37; as
    a totalising force 86
idioms 144
imposed silence 5, 17–20; external
    imposition 19; reasons for imposing
    20; self-told imposition 19
inclusionary silence 4–5, 7–10;
    barriers against 8; engagement
    and consultation 7–8; generative
    inclusion, silence of 8; and
    genuine connection 9; listening
    without judgement or prejudice 8
Independent Workers of Great
    Britain (IWGB) 80
individualism 8–9, 61, 104, 198,
    215–216
insight 139
instinct 59

invitational silence 5, 9, 20–22
isolation 64–67, 123, 152; fear of 66,
    67, 115, 116
I-Thou moment 9

J G Wells centre, South London 105
Jack, D. C. 62
Jackson, Phillip, *Life in Classrooms* 42
James, Steve 129, 130
Janis, I. L. 101
Johnson, Boris 139
Jones, Jim 88
judgement and evaluation 203–204

Kafka, Franz 115, 119
Kipling, Rudyard 28
Klee, Paul 221
knowledge viii, 12, 102, 167, 196,
    208; boundaries of 205; common
    129; creating x; denial of 44;
    everyday 50; performance of 204;
    professional 27; and subjectivity
    59–60

labor investors 13
Labour Party, UK 105; Constituency
    Labour Party 106
Lampmann, E. 44
language: absence of, silence seen as
    (*see* absence of speech or sound,
    questioning silence as); dismissive
    167; English as a second language
    144–145; pauses in 26; silence
    deriving from paucity at heart of
    51; silence giving rise to words 51
leadership 71, 79, 128, 138;
    compassionate 167; development
    139, 218; and insight 139; leader–
    follower ideology 38–39, 127;
    opening up space for dialogue
    8, 126–127; orthodox 12;
    performative 94; and privilege
    139; responsibility to be seen to

be listening 8, 69–70, 128, 154; role-oriented concept of 92; self-management 138; and structure 74–75; visibility 70–71; *see also* leadership distance

leadership distance 92, 221–222

Leninism 111, 177

Leymann, H. 95n1

liberalism 129, 137–138; classical 89, 216; neo-liberalism 46, 104, 109, 215, 216

Lichter, A. 87

limit-experience, concept of 115

LinkedIn 182

listening 8, 49, 83, 93–94, 131, 178–179; act of 124; culture of 154, 156; and disagreement 224; genuine 52, 56, 57, 70, 71, 94, 124, 127, 128, 148, 183, 184, 196, 217, 219, 223; and hearing 144, 146, 169, 171, 174, 178–179; opening up space for dialogue 8, 126–127, 179, 180–185, 222–223; perfunctory 191; to react (*see* listening to react); responsibility to be seen to be listening 8, 69–70, 128, 154; to understand 172; without hearing (*see* listening without hearing); *see also* music

listening to react 171–174; avoiding 158; denial of meaningful dialogue 164; and hearing to engage 164; interfering with capacity to hear 172; judgements 172; *versus* listening to hear 112–113, 191, 196, 214; by managers 211; in organisations 180; public and private responses 172; *see also* listening; listening without hearing

listening without hearing 46, 94, 169; at work 92–94, 124–125, 127; *see also* hearing; listening to react

Lynch, Mick 25

management 14, 19; agenda 23; charismatic 22; and feeling silenced 80; "kindly" 11; line managers, relationships with 154; "management eyes only" reports 12; management gurus 14; middle managers 156–157; orthodox thinking 11, 14, 25; science 77; tools and techniques 4; *see also* leadership

managerialism 75, 93

manipulative silence 5, 22–26; how silence manipulates 26; within inter-personal contexts 23

Marx, Karl 37

Marxism 177

meaning of silence 3, 48–54; as absence of sound (*see* absence of speech or sound, questioning silence as); active withdrawal of the word 51, 53, 58; deriving from paucity at the heart of language 51; giving rise to words 51; intimacy between speech and silence 50, 54; *see also* 4'33 (silent musical composition by John Cage)

meditative practices 56–57

method and practical application 171–192; positive attention 174–179; reactionary listening 171–174; surveys (*see* surveys); synthesis, attempting 185–189

mindfulness 22, 57, 58

miners' strike, UK 121–122

Mintzberg, Henry 9

"mobbing" 85, 95n1

moderators 23

Moore, R. 88

music: challenging bourgeois notions of 49; gaps between notes in 26; open critique of the

acculturated practice of listening
to 49; of people talking 36; *see also*
4'33 (silent musical composition
by John Cage)
muted group theory (MGT) 162

narcissism, promoting 8–9
National Health Service (NHS) 77,
107, 129, 130, 154; constitution 152;
inequality and racism 154; NHS
People Promise 152, 153
National Union of Miners, UK 121;
supporters' group 122–123
NDAs *see* non-disclosure agreements
(NDAs)
neo-liberalism 46, 104, 109, 215, 216
new public management 75
newspapers 137–138
Nguyen, C. T. 83
NHS *see* National Health Service
(NHS)
Noelle-Neumann, E. 64, 65
non-disclosure agreements (NDAs)
43–45

The Observer 137–138
Ofsted 113
O'Leary, T. 114
organisation development (OD) 191
organisational culture 168
organisational presence: human
73–74, 77; interrelationship
between 77–79; physical 72–73,
77, 99–100; structural 74–76, 77;
systemic 76–77
organisational theatre 179–180
organised religion, silence in 55–56
orthodox leadership 12
Otherness 63

parrhesia 66
participative inquiry 146
patriarchy 153, 160

pedagogy, traditional 42
People's Temple, California 88
performance 21, 138, 148, 221;
charismatic 8; data 18; and
dialogue 199; dramaturgical 92;
financial 12, 204; improving 57,
75; individual 197; of knowing
204; leadership 8; measures of 25;
superficial 83; targets 6
performativity 20, 22, 108, 127,
128, 179; communication 127;
leadership 92, 94; performative
knowing 204–205; schools 207
physical presence, organisational
72–73, 77, 99–100
Picard, M. 41
Platonic ideal form 18
pluralism 100
pluralistic ignorance 66–67
Poisson distribution 187, 188
politics: alternative forms 108–109;
and community 104–105,
108–109; identity 216; political
activism 105; political parties 64,
65, 105–106; speaking of political
opinions 173
Pollock, M. 82
positional authority 17
positive act, silence seen as 56
positive attention 174–179
post-industrial society 114
post-structuralism 86
poststructuralist relativism 162
power 37–38, 42, 173; being both
affected by and invested with
137; complexities of 89; felt in a
wide range of human-to-human
activity 136; and information 12;
and interconnectivity 135–136; in
psychotherapeutic relationship
36–37, 59; and rankism 167;
relational 3; and speech 54; and
subjectivity 58–59, 64; use and

abuse of 157; well-developed
personal ethical orientation 138
power and silence: and
exclusionary silence 12–13; in
psychotherapeutic relationship 37;
silence as an assertion of power
3, 37; silence chosen as an act
of powerlessness 17; and voice
135–140
privilege, sense of 139
processing 173
progressivism 84, 86–87, 89, 109,
137, 216
psychical terror 95n1
psychotherapeutic relationship,
power in 36–37, 59
public opinion 64, 65
punctuating silence 5, 26–29
Purser, R. E. 57

Quakerism 23, 24, 55; and
Buddhism 56

racial identity 82
racism 154
radicalism 86–87, 89
rail disputes 25
rankism 165, 167, 211
rationalism 11
reactionary listening 171–174
Reason, P. 174–175
reflexivity 173, 191; and criticality 94,
139, 166, 176, 177, 180, 218
Reitz, Megan 14, 15, 19, 23, 198, 202
Rejmer, M. 120
relational psychology school 201
repression 59
research practice 145–146
resistance 38, 59, 69, 76, 88, 125, 127,
210; vocal 79
resources 155, 156, 168
Riley, A. 40
Risser, J. 51

ritual, silence as 55–60; Buddhism
and silence 56–57; Quakerism 23,
24, 55, 56; questioning silence as
absence of sound 58; silence seen
as a positive act 56; two-minute
silence 57
Rivera, G. 221
Rosenberg, M. 111, 112
Russian revolution (1917) 111

Sartre, Jean-Paul 181
schools 165–166, 207
Schostak, J. and J. 176
Schröter, M. 112–113
secret societies 12
self: dialogue as self-made 200–201;
tyranny of, stepping away from 203
self-censorship 125
self-silencing 61–68; silence,
judgement and action 66–67;
spiral of silence 63–66
seven shades of silence 3–30;
implications for organisational
practice 5, 29; listed (see silence);
overview 4–6
Sherf, E. N. 126
shop stewards 121
signal-to-noise ratio 38
silence 6, 22, 24, 51, 53, 56, 125,
189; breaking of 15, 39, 174; as
commemoration 57; culture
of 148, 156; and leadership
(see leadership); meaning in (see
meaning of silence); and power
(see power); power and silence;
and reflection 27, 28; regimes
of 84, 103–104; as ritual (see
ritual, silence as); as a secret
password 91, 99–118; seven
shades (see seven shades of
silence); social expectations of
42–43; sound of 45, 46; spiral of
63–66, 67; as stillness 56; that

invites 5, 9, 20–22; that is chosen 5, 14–17, 83–91, 125, 148, 189; that is imposed 5, 17–20; that is intending to exclude 5, 10–14; that is looking to include 4–5, 7–10; that is manipulating 5, 22–26; that is punctuating 5, 26–29; in therapy 35–36; understanding 4; and voice 79, 82, 110, 124, 125, 128–133; at work (*see* workplaces); *see also* absence of speech or sound, questioning silence as
"Silence of the Impractical" 18
"Silence of the Intangible" 18
Silvo, Mario 90
Skinner, Dennis 121
Smith, Dorothy E 161
Social Democratic Party, Germany 65
social expectations of silence 42–43
Social Identity Theory 101
socialism 87–88; socialist ideology 37
"somebodies and nobodies" 10, 162, 165, 166, 168, 211, 217
sound of silence 45, 46
soundlessness, impossibility of 45, 48–49, 50, 54
speech 41, 52, 59, 85, 92, 103, 113, 123, 147, 166, 212; absence of, silence seen as (*see* absence of speech or sound, questioning silence as); act of 120; choosing not to speak 119–120; feeling able to speak up 126; free 89–91, 139, 161; intimacy with silence 50; and listening 83; management of 125; non-speech acts 37; pauses in 26; persuasive 119; and power 54; proscribing 179; refusal to speak when people expect it 57; respectable 114; silence as a constituent part 5, 26, 50, 51, 54; speak-up culture 13, 79, 185; uncontrolled 59; *see also* communication; dialogue;

language; speech and silence, interplay between; voice; words
speech and silence, interplay between 119, 120; intimacy between speech and silence 50, 54; social functions of voice and silence 128–133; *see also* voice
spiral of silence 63–66, 67
Spivak, G. C. 89
Srnicek, N. 108, 109
statistics 187
status quo 13, 18–20, 25, 27, 86, 158, 204, 205
stillness, silence seen as 56
structural presence, organisational 74–76, 77
structures 16, 54, 59, 77, 147, 167–168; artificial corporate 213; asylum 36; conversational 59, 201, 206; flattening 217; hierarchised social 137; and leadership 74–75; organisational 11, 41, 74, 76, 77, 93, 217; "rankism" 165; reporting 18; social epistemic 83; totalising 86; union 81
stuck thinking 18
subaltern 5, 10, 16, 84, 176, 181; and the dominant 162, 163; groups 162–163; voice 89, 127, 137, 138, 211, 213
subjectification 200
subjectivity 58–59, 64, 103
surveys viii; anonymous 6; pulse survey 181; staff 6; traditional 182; *see also* thirty-five voices free text survey
systemic presence, organisational 76–77

Tajfel, Henri 101
Takala, T. 13
Tatman, L. 53
Tavistock tradition 218

Thatcher, Margaret 105
thirty-five voices free text survey 143–170, 172, 181–189; concluding information from and about 181; and COVID-19 pandemic 143, 149, 150, 156; demographics 189–191; numeric responses to 181–183; outline of commentaries 147–155; overarching, context-specific questions, responses to 183–185; scores 183, 186, 187, 188, 189, 190–191; selection of excerpts from 165; setting of data 182; six specific statements, responses to 185–189; *see also* method and practical application; research practice; surveys
Thompson, J. B. 102
TINA ("there is no alternative") 76
Todnem By, R. 75
Tormey, S. 86
totalitarianism 85–86, 91, 124, 168
trade unions 19, 25, 80, 81, 120, 216; socialistic 121
transactional analysis (TA) 92
triangulation of data 159–160
two-minute silence 57

unanimity, illusion of 101
unions *see* trade unions
Unite The Union 81
United Kingdom: miners' strike 121–122; newspapers 137–138; politics 105–106; unions in 81; *see also* National Health Service (NHS)
unity, fostering 131–132

values gap 220
verstehen 211–212
Voegelin, S. 50–51
voice: amplification or dialling down of 167; balancing **210**; in dialogue 209–210; dominance of 103; leaders not wanting to hear 79; listening to all voices 131; not simply a leadership resource 128; "professional services" voices 166, 167; and silence 79, 82, 110, 124, 125, 128–133; subaltern 89, 127, 137, 138, 211, 213; withholding one's voice 82; *see also* communication; dialogue; speech; speech and silence, interplay between; thirty-five voices free text survey; words

Weber, Max 211
whistleblowing 14
Williams, A. 108, 109
Willmott, Hugh 91
Wittgenstein, Ludwig 48, 50, 51
Wolfe, Tom, *The Bonfire of the Vanities* 198
women 162, 189; Black and Ethnic Minorities 186; expectations of silence 62; and femininity 62; and feminism 138; as "good employees" 62–63; and romantic relationships 62; silencing themselves 62; social role 62
words: active withdrawal of 51, 53; silence giving voice to 51; *see also* communication; dialogue; language; speech; speech and silence, interplay between; voice
workplaces 29, 70, 79; attending to the tensions 219–222; conversation 23, 164, 213, 215; corporate context 119–134; creating a collective climate around voice and silence 124–126; default, silence as 71–72; divide between workplaces and wider society 19; embracing a new way of being in 210–214; feeling silenced 79–82; "good employee"

62–63; hierarchies 76, 120, 136, 137; inclusive workforce, encouraging 197; leadership distance 221–222; lessons for 119–134; and meaning of work 217–218; modelling exemplary behaviour, to encourage proper attention 129–131; normalisations of 24–25; organisational chart/ pyramid 217, 221; organisational culture 62, 160, 168, 197; organisational presence (*see* organisational presence); the professional and the personal 218–219; seeming to be listened to but not heard at 92–94; silence at work 54, 69–98; unity, fostering 131–132; workplace activism 19; *see also* leadership; work, silence at; workplaces
workshops 197
Wragge-Morley, A. 49

zealotry 102
Zen Buddhism 58
Zoom meetings 23

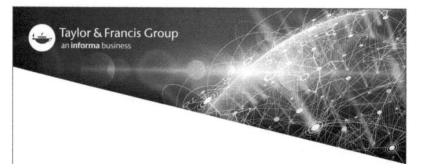

Ingram Content Group UK Ltd.
Milton Keynes UK
UKHW022020120423
420086UK00021B/159